Praise for *Be*

"In his memoir, Pelullo recounts the repeated sexual molestations he suffered as a child and how he and his parents kept the acts a secret for more than forty years.

"Pelullo has written a frank, often painful account of his molestation perpetrated at the hands of two older boys in his neighborhood. (One of his rapists was the son of one of his mother's best friends.) When Pelullo's parents discovered the truth, they took him to their family doctor, who advised them not to discuss it and hopefully Pelullo would forget the experience. As an adult, the author became a leader in his industry and the leader of his family, the man to help his siblings, nieces and nephews. But Pelullo's rape made him incapable of intimacy, and he grew into a cold, detached, nervous man. He couldn't give up control, couldn't see the connection between love and intimacy; he saw only sex, a release, a calming influence, and he sought out women he sensed were as emotionally damaged as he. Thinking the love of a good woman from a fine family would save him, Pelullo married an attractive woman from his neighborhood, and they adopted two sons. For many years, Pelullo kept his secret, hiding the truth and cringing at human warmth and touch. When his sons were older, an e-mail left on Pelullo's computer screen was found by one of his boys, and the incident forced Pelullo to face his demons, leave his home and family and begin a long journey of recovery. He could no longer be his extended family's leader, fixing their problems; he learned he had to take care of himself first. After seeing several psychologists, reading many books, joining a group for men and women in the grip of sex addiction, making a new connection with his spiritual side and facing the responsibility for his mistakes, Pelullo eventually remarried his wife and founded the Let Go…Let Peace Come In Foundation, an online community where survivors of child molestation can tell their stories and continue the healing process. Pelullo's story is well-told, written with smooth transitions that keep the narrative flowing. As a successful businessman lacking a college education, the author might be expected to produce a choppy, disorganized work at worst, or, at best, a dull, workmanlike story that covers all the bases but doesn't engage the reader. However, Pelullo does an admirable job of bringing the reader into his painfully honest story, offering a beacon to other victims of sexual abuse and addiction. An impressive, candid effort from a first-time author."

—**Kirkus Reviews**

"Armed with determination and a budding academic partnership with the Johns Hopkins Bloomberg School of Public Health, Mr. Pelullo's ready to help adult survivors on their journeys to heal with *Betrayal and the Beast* as their roadmap."

—**Marilyn Van Derbur, former Miss America;
author of *Miss America by Day***

"With unusual depth and clarity, *Betrayal and the Beast* provides hope and comfort to survivors of great childhood trauma. What's more, it offers inspiration and new insights to professionals."

—**Dee Ann Miller, mental health nurse-writer;
www.takecourage.org**

"Although there are countless victims and survivors of child sexual abuse, not enough people know what to do to help them cope with the devastating physical, sexual, emotional, and spiritual effects of the violence perpetrated against them. This results in their having to suffer, alone and unsupported, through years of fear, shame, guilt, lack of intimacy and trust, and, in many cases, self-destructive behavior. Pelullo's graphic and moving portrayal of his decades-long journey toward healing and recovery offers important lessons for parents, spouses, doctors, teachers, and other adults who come in contact with survivors of this horrendous violence. His painfully honest story will also bring hope to those survivors who have lived in fear of not finding support or achieving recovery and help them start their own journeys toward healing."

—**Adelita M. Medina, executive director, National Latino Alliance
for the Elimination of Domestic Violence (Alianza)**

"*Betrayal and the Beast* by Peter S. Pelullo is gripping, gutsy, and generous in explaining what so many cannot fathom: how sexual violation, particularly at a very young age, has deleterious effects on the victims and their subsequent relationships and behavior, perhaps for a lifetime. Pete shows it is not too late—it is possible to recover and create relationships that are honest, mutually supportive, and filled with love."

—**Deborah D. Tucker, executive director,
National Center on Domestic and Sexual Violence**

"Memoirs can also be painful while being cathartic. *Betrayal and the Beast* by Peter S. Pelullo is subtitled 'a true story of one man's journey through childhood sexual abuse, sexual addition, and recovery'. Pelullo focuses on his corporate life in the music industry where he gained recognition for recording acts like the Rolling Stones, Foreigner, and Stevie Wonder. He was active as well in the telecom industry, the Internet, and the financial world, but despite success in these fields, he could not overcome the scars of the sexual abuse he suffered at the hands of two older neighborhood kids in the 1950s. This book points out, as Pelullo notes, it is estimated that one in three girls and one in four boys experience sexual abuse before the age of eighteen. In his case, it led to a hidden life of sexual promiscuity and pain he sought to dull with prescription drugs, alcohol, and work. He had no one he considered a close friend. This book tells of his journey to recovery, which he shares to give other victims like himself hope they, too, can recover."

—**Alan Caruba,** *Bookviews*;
founding member, National Book Critics Circle

BETRAYAL AND THE BEAST

BETRAYAL AND THE BEAST

Peter S. Pelullo

Only Serenity LLC

Betrayal and the Beast
Copyright © 2012 Peter S. Pelullo
Published by Only Serenity LLC

All rights reserved. No part of this book may be reproduced (except for inclusion in reviews), disseminated or utilized in any form or by any means, electronic or mechanical, including photocopying, recording, or in any information storage and retrieval system, or the Internet/World Wide Web without written permission from the author or publisher.

For more information please contact:
Only Serenity LLC
630 West Germantown Pike
Suite 180
Plymouth Meeting, PA 19462
610-825-8805
www.betrayalandthebeast.com
info@betrayalandthebeast.com

Book design by:
Arbor Books, Inc.
www.arborbooks.com

Printed in the United States of America

Betrayal and the Beast
Peter S. Pelullo

1. Title 2. Author 3. Memoir

Library of Congress Control Number: 2011929527

ISBN 13: 978-0-61548625-3

In loving memory of my mother-in-law, Rafaella Bordo, an extraordinary woman of grace filled with compassion, love, and support. She blessed me with the wisdom of her virtues and elevated my soul during my darkest hours.

Table of Contents

Foreword xiii
Preface xvii
Acknowledgments xix
Prologue xxiii

The Beginning
Chapter 1   The Making of *The Beast* 3
Chapter 2   John—Fuel to the Fire 11
Chapter 3   Doctor's Orders 21
Chapter 4   Running Away 31

Success With Internal Failure
Chapter 5   Rein in the Environment 49
Chapter 6   Money Mogul 55

Love
Chapter 7   Jane 69
Chapter 8   Cerberus—Two Lives 79
Chapter 9   Paul and Luke 91
Chapter 10 Hello, Money and Gail—Goodbye, Dad ... 105

The Terminus of the Veil
Chapter 11 Discovery 111
Chapter 12 Descending Into Hell 117

Recovery
Chapter 13 Therapy 127
Chapter 14 Path to Healing 141
Chapter 15 Understanding *The Beast* 151
Chapter 16 Journey 163

Facing Myself
Chapter 17   I Get a Little Help From My Friends.................... 175
Chapter 18   I Die Daily..187
Chapter 19   Groups... 205

Schism
Chapter 20   What About Jane?...215
Chapter 21   Mirrors...221

Hope
Chapter 22   Divorce..235
Chapter 23   Marriage—The Whole Is Greater
             Than the Sum of Its Parts..................................... 243

Epilogue
The Let Go…Let Peace Come In Foundation............................253

Appendices
Appendix I.. 305
Appendix II 315
Appendix III...323

Foreword

Secretary of State Hillary Clinton wrote a book called *It Takes a Village*. I'm hopeful that this book, the foundation I created eighteen months into my recovery, as well as the relationship the foundation has with the Johns Hopkins University Bloomberg School of Public Health, will deliver a message to every society throughout the globe that it takes the world to learn and understand how to help heal and assist an adult, who, as a child, was sexually violated, through the nightmare of their perpetration. Understanding a child's loss of innocence and childhood is just the beginning. There is an equal if not greater need to understand how these sexual attacks, in the majority of us, crafted and depicted our adult development and characteristics of fear, shame, guilt, lack of intimacy or trust, and, in many cases, addictions as we entered adulthood.

The overwhelming majority of us were sexually violated by people we trusted or loved. Some of us were told we were "special" by our perpetrators; some of us were told "this is what God wants you to do"; some of us were told this is just a "game"; some were threatened that if we told they would hurt our families; and others were even told we deserved it and brought it on ourselves. As we entered adulthood, the realizations of the betrayal and degradation were devastating to our psyches and lives. On the outside many of us functioned in everyday life. On the inside most of us lived with anger and dissociation, and acted out with self-destructive behavior. Quite a few of us took an unrealistic position to try to control every aspect of our lives, friendships and relationships. From the *moment* we experienced these violations our lives were changed forever. There is simply no way a child can develop normally into a mature and healthy adult without the proper help and support and extensive therapeutic care to understand how the abuse devastated our lives. Growing older doesn't make the effects any less, and in fact the problems only intensify without the proper intervention.

While you may find my story of being a sexually abused child growing into adulthood with resulting addictions and maladies at times difficult to read, I have learned, during four years of recovery, that my story is far from unique. Hundreds of millions of men and women like me are living with the havoc that was perpetrated on them as children. Like many survivors of childhood sexual abuse, I always knew something was wrong with me, but I could never connect all of my life's unstable issues to the sexual attacks I suffered at age seven. A major reason for this discovery is that while childhood sexual abuse could be the greatest affliction since the beginning of time, no one wants to talk about it, especially victims like me. This silence and its resulting effects on an adult's physical and emotional development might be the best-kept secret ever.

Since I started my journey to learn how to live again, many survivors have come forward publicly with their own stories. This includes Queen Latifah, Tom Arnold, Tyler Perry, Ashley Judd, Sugar Ray Leonard, Shania Twain, Don Lemmon, as well as Senator Scott Brown of Massachusetts. You only have to read some of the comments that were made after the senator's disclosure—"typical Republican," "trying to get sympathy votes," "forty years after the fact he's just trying to get publicity and sympathy," "it's about public status"—to understand why survivors are hesitant as well as fearful to reveal their childhood sexual abuse. I have never met Senator Brown, nor do I know his politics, but I do know it took a great deal of courage for him to come forward. I immediately understood the pain he suffered as a ten-year-old and how those events affected and altered his life. His disclosure will undoubtedly help other adult survivors to start their journeys to health and peace, and he should be commended for his courage to speak about the unspeakable.

To all the survivors throughout the world, you have the God-given right to enjoy life and all that it offers; please take the first step toward gaining back your life by telling your story. Do it for yourself, for your family, for your friends, and for the whole human race. In every one of us who has been sexually violated is a story of a child from whom all of what life is about was stolen. Together we can find the happiness and health we so richly deserve. Together we can educate, change, and wake up the world to the effects sexual abuse caused in our lives and what it will do to children who experience this trauma in the future.

By telling our stories and showing the staggering number of survivors who have come before them, we will let the children of tomorrow know they are not alone in their suffering, and hopefully they will start their personal journeys to healing sooner than we understood we needed to begin ours.

Preface

It was the fifth day following the total and complete collapse of my life. For forty-eight years I had managed to bury the pain and trauma I had suffered as a child. The world I had been so meticulous in controlling and manipulating was now crashing down around me. All the steps I had taken and all the defenses I had created to keep the world at bay were suddenly at risk—and the therapist sitting across from me was suggesting I document it all, from the beginning of that horrible nightmare at age seven to the now-daunting journey of recovery ahead of me at age fifty-five.

I sat in a daze as the therapist suggested that writing a journal may help me as I tried to heal from "one of the most severe, life-altering events a human being can live through." I remember hearing the words and shaking my head at him but never responding. I couldn't speak. The statement was just another shockwave added to the unnerving emotional events of the previous four days. While I incoherently nodded, I was saying to myself, *Write a journal? God! This man doesn't have a clue.* I would never write a word about what happened to me in 1959. Save for a peripheral mention to my wife in 1986, I had never even *spoken* a word about those sordid sexual attacks since they happened at age seven. He must not have understood that writing a journal or documenting my childhood nightmare would never happen.

Four months later, following twice-a-week psychotherapy sessions, I began to scribble the first few words of what would become a full, detailed manuscript. Somehow I took the first tentative, painful steps of documenting the details of the sexual attacks that had destroyed my entire life. Slowly, my feelings about the abuse and my understanding and recognition of the devastating effects it had on me—sexually, physically, mentally, emotionally, and spiritually—came pouring out.

In the years after that first therapy session, writing this book became a major step in my recovery, my journey back from the most unfathomable betrayal a child could experience or imagine, and my ongoing battle with *The Beast* that still lies within me.

Acknowledgments

My deepest gratitude is reserved for my two sons, Paul and Luke: you never left my side as I started the journey that would transform me from being a victim of childhood sexual abuse to being a survivor and a functioning member of the human race.

To my wife, Jane: You are my best friend and the love of my life. While it took you a little over three years to understand what caused my dissociated and unconscious behavior, I am eternally grateful that you entered the recovery process with me which would ultimately bring our family from implosion and ruination to reunification. Not only was this work excruciating and tedious for you as a spouse of a survivor but it also brought you to look at your own personal journey of life—a difficult process but a rewarding one.

To my mother, who eventually understood my need to withdraw from our family system and ultimately gave me her full support and love to carry through the process of my recovery.

To my eighty-one-year-old godmother, Aunt Josephine: When I so desperately needed someone from the generation before me to help me understand what, if anything, was known about my sexual abuse and attacks…you helped me, supported me, and loved me by spending countless hours listening and helping me through my healing process.

To my godchildren, Peter, Joseph, and Greta: your interaction, kind words, and notes during my journey were extremely supportive and loving.

To my nephews, Peter and Sal, who picked up our extended family flag when I could carry it no longer.

To Paul, Jeff, and Annie, whom I met in recovery: you became my support…my lifeline…and my salvation to learn how to live again.

To Dr. DiCesare, Dr. Richard Gartner, Dr. John O'Connor, Dr. Meg Miller, and psychologist Allie Miller (no relation to Meg), the five professionals who, over four years, took the time, patience, and care to bring me out of the depths of an abyss that no human being should ever know or be driven to: may your higher power continue to give you the strength and time to continue your personal journeys and to bring many more adults back to life, as you did for me.

To Michele, for her support and patience in helping me write the manuscript that was the foundation for this book.

To Kerry Zukus, Natalie Fisher, and Tom Vandegrift go my sincere thanks for their help and support in turning the manuscript I first wrote into this book.

To my niece Stefanie Godfrey, for her input concerning proofreading the book.

To Alfredo Villa, my friend and partner from Lugano, Switzerland, who gave me the support, understanding, and love I needed during my many business trips and extended time spent in Europe, specifically during the first two years of my journey.

To the founding members of the board of directors, who followed me in starting the Let Go…Let Peace Come In Foundation (www.letgoletpeacecomein.org.): Annie, Margie, Lonni, Mike, Loren, Paul, Larry, and Jeff, you believed we could make a difference.

To Michael Forte, successful international musician, publisher, producer and friend of thirty-five years who co-created the title track of the foundation's song *Let Go, Let Peace Come In* on YouTube and iTunes.

To Marla Green DiDio for your tireless passion and work in supporting both both me and the foundations outreach concerning it's partnership with the world renown Johns Hopkins Bloomberg School of Public Health.

To my legal and accounting firms that continue to complete all the necessary work required for the foundation I founded pro bono: Bernard Eizen, Herb Fineburg, Gary McCarthy, Ted Greenburg, Eve Thomas, James Fredericks, CPA, you are more than professionals—you are my friends.

To Martha McGeary Snider, a true friend and dedicated philanthropist who will be an integral part of formulating and spreading the foundation's mission throughout the globe.

To Alon Goldreich, my colleague and friend from Switzerland. Alon speaks eight languages fluently and has an ability as an IT specialist that is second to none. He was completely responsible for the construction of the foundation's international Web site as well as the World Alliance Web site that I would form with foundations from India, Australia, Africa and the United Kingdom (www.wapsac.org).

To Peter Saunders of the United Kingdom, Anuja Gupta and Ashwini Ailawadi of India, Nikki Wells of Australia, Joseline Fugar of Africa who together have traveled thousands of miles and spent countless hours doing so to meet in the United States to start the world's first global alliance, World Alliance for People Sexually Abused as Children (WAPSAC).

To Gretchen Paules, whose heroic efforts and hard work have been the voice and human connection to the thousands from throughout the world who have visited our foundation's Web site.

To Ernie, Bob, Virgil, Mike, Jake, Johnny, and Howard, my

friends of twenty-five-plus years before I entered recovery, who kept in constant contact and were not afraid to speak to me or learn about my healing process.

To my friends Peggy and Jo Webber, who could have easily cast me aside since our friendship was only a few months old when my life completely unraveled. Instead, they gave me the hope and confidence that I could heal and, more importantly, wanted me to heal.

To the many members of my men's groups and SIA meetings. To my Saturday SIA group, without whose friendship and courage to share their vulnerability I never could have shared mine: Andy, Mark, Matty, Daryl, Louis, Josh, Dave, Sandy, Evita, Margaret, Ron, Dianne, Mike R., Rachel, Jason, Dan, and Scott.

To Billy, who gave me his twenty-four-hour chip that he had carried for years. It wasn't the chip he gave me; it was his strength and courage that I will carry for the rest of my life.

To Vince DePasquale, who founded the Starting Point, whose thoughtful and caring love put me and countless others like me on our way to recovery over the last thirty years.

Prologue

It was 11:00 p.m. when I received the e-mail from "Gail." I was at home alone. My younger son, Luke, had called to say he'd be sleeping over at his friend's house. My older son, Paul, was away at college, and my wife, Jane, was skiing with her sister in Utah.

Gail's goodbye message included detailed and explicit descriptions of my dozens of affairs over the past several decades as well as my present affair with her. The e-mail elaborated on Gail's thoughts regarding my emotional instability. She strongly suggested I seek professional help to identify how I could live two such separate and conflicting lives. An excerpt from the e-mail read, "You are like a moving target, always running and constantly trying to save everyone but yourself." In her opinion I needed serious and intense therapy. In the forty-eight-plus years I'd been living as a dissociative and dysfunctional human being, she was the first person to uncover a piece of who I really was. However, I intended to ignore her advice and to continue on with the patterns of behavior to which I had grown accustomed. Little did I know how deeply rooted my problems really were.

Gail had become more than just another sexual encounter. We had something in common, something more than the office work we did together and more than the times we spent together in bed. Our shared interest was *me*—psychoanalyzing *me*. Gail was a recovering alcoholic who came from generations of people with alcohol dependency. Through her own recovery process she clearly identified the warning signs of addictive behavior and codependency in my life—she just didn't know the true cause of them.

Gail could plainly see that I was not just a man who simply liked to have sex with women. She knew what it was like to be in bed with me; she saw the anxiety, and she felt me withdraw without emotional intimacy as I would slowly work my way to the door. I can't remember any other woman noticing or speaking to me about these traits.

But Gail knew. She knew the signs. Just as I subconsciously looked for certain attributes in women in order to zero in on the ones who were at my emotional level, Gail's sixth sense about addiction was pinging like a busy pinball machine when she was with me and as she got to know me in every way.

This e-mail was Gail's last attempt to reason with me, to tell me that I was a sick man and that what I was doing was neither normal nor healthy. I was on a path to implosion, and there was no telling exactly what form it would take, but she knew it was coming soon. Little did she know that she was about to bring it on unintentionally.

Gail cared about me, and I don't believe this was simply a case of a woman scorned, looking to lash out in anger. She was so cognizant of my emotional damage that she confessed she'd have been out of her mind to fall in love with me and try to build a relationship at that point in my life. While I told myself I was fine—making money and coming home to a picture-postcard, American-dream family—Gail thought I was emotionally broken.

Jane, my wife of twenty-six years, never knew of my affairs. Not only was I able to bury the sexual trauma I had suffered as a child for so long, I was also able to hide years of sexual liaisons as well. Just as I had seized control of my financial destiny and established undisputed status as leader of my family (and my extended family), I controlled and manipulated the women I slept with. They knew my name. They easily could have found me, my home, and Jane if they really wanted to. They all knew I was married. But I had developed a sixth sense from the sexual-abuse trauma that linked me to those who were my emotional equals. I instinctively knew who was most vulnerable. I knew who would keep a secret and not ruin my marriage or, should I say, assist *me* in ruining my marriage.

Besides having a seemingly foolproof selection process in my indiscretions, I wore a cloak of dedication, loyalty, and stability. I appeared normal. Jane once said, "If I went into a room with a hundred men and you asked me to point out the one who I felt was completely faithful to his wife, I would have pointed to you." I guess it's true what they say about sexually abused children like me: we grow into the best adult actors.

Some people, when they know they are doing something wrong, develop a kind of death wish. You hear police talk about certain criminals this way as well. It's when they secretly wish they'd get caught in order to stop compulsively abnormal behavior. I was not one of those people—I would not and could not give up my imagined self-control. I desperately did not want to get caught. I needed to maintain my perfect home with Jane and the boys because the family setting gave me a feeling of normalcy and sanity.

Unbeknownst to me, Luke decided not to sleep out that evening and came home around 11:30 p.m. At the time I was in the living room speaking with Gail on the phone and trying to maintain damage control as I had done consistently over the years.

Luke walked in the back door, which lead to the kitchen, where we kept our family computer. Hearing the back door open I re-entered the kitchen and saw Luke standing by the computer desk.

Could it have been possible that he read the e-mail and overheard parts of my conversation with Gail? He mentioned nothing. He kissed me on the cheek.

"Good night," he said, and he went to bed.

I checked the monitor and was shocked by my own recklessness. I *had* left the e-mail open on the screen when I had gone into the other room. This wasn't like me, and no, it wasn't part of a death wish. It was nothing more than pure carelessness and imperfection—and I did not condone imperfection, especially in me. When I would allow myself to consider the years of unfaithful behavior—imperfect behavior—in my marriage, it would set me off on a wave of disconnection and dissociation and into my dysfunctional behavior.

The next day, when I saw Luke, he was on edge. I knew immediately that something was amiss. Still he said nothing. The day after, more of the same—more silence. On the third day, when I asked him what was wrong, he broke down and said, "You're my idol, Dad. How could you have affairs with other women? What's going on with you and Mom?"

"When a story is told...it's not forgotten."

The Beginning

Chapter 1

The Making of *The Beast*

I was born on February 7, 1952, in Philadelphia. The country was rebuilding itself following one of the most devastating wars in history, World War II. My father and my namesake, Peter, and his two brothers had served their country. My father and his second-oldest brother served in the army, and his eldest brother in the navy. Fortunately all three returned home.

My father had taken up arms and had defended his country in overseas war zones, and the experience left an indelible mark on him. He often recounted the horrific scenes of death and destruction he had experienced, but nothing impacted him more than the atrocities he witnessed firsthand when he entered one of the Nazi death camps. My father found it difficult to tear those horrendous memories out of his mind, and he lived with them until the end of his life.

By the time she was fifteen, my mother, Louise, had already noticed the strapping (six-foot-three, 190-pound), handsome neighbor prior to his being drafted. Although both families were traditional Italian, that is where the similarities began and ended.

My father's family was blue-collar; my paternal grandfather worked at Stetson Hats during the week and rented bicycles on the weekends. They were hardworking, straight-talking, and not overtly emotional people. My father's parents, two brothers, and his sister were extremely virtuous and loving people. You knew they loved you deeply, but they weren't going to give you that gushy, kissing type of demonstrative love.

It was quite a different story with my mother's family. My mother's father was an entrepreneur—what one might have considered more upper-middle class than my father's family. My mother's mother—my grandmother—would cover you in kisses the minute you walked through the door. My mother had six brothers and sisters, all as warm and as affectionate toward me as my grandmother.

It may be one of the world's oldest clichés, but opposites do attract. My parents began a three-year courtship after my father's return from the war in 1945. He was twenty-one and she was seventeen. They married three years later, in 1948, and began a fifty-six-year union that ended with my father's death on December 28, 2004.

A beautiful bride on the arm of a handsome groom, my mother was absolutely stunning. This is not just my opinion formed from seeing the wedding pictures but the sentiment of countless friends and family. My mother was an elegant woman. My father was tall, thin, well-built, and striking. More importantly, he had to be the hardest-working man I have ever known. He taught me the work ethic I embrace to this day.

My mother and father's marriage gave life to six children, including me. I was the second in line to an older brother, with two younger sisters and two younger brothers—your typical Catholic-Italian family in twentieth-century, postwar America.

After my father returned from the fighting in Europe, he worked as a finish carpenter and went to college at night to learn architectural drafting. These skills enabled him to become a general contractor, which was the stepping-stone for my dad to become the first person in his family to go into business for himself. While he worked long, hard days and saved his money dutifully, we lived in an apartment building that belonged to my father's parents.

My mother and father eventually saved enough money to purchase their first home in June 1952. I was four months old. Although they purchased a row home, the neighborhood was considered middle class, as it was in the finest Italian section of the city. There were a few Irish and German households as well. This was the classic American melting pot, where most families were only first- or second-generation immigrants, and a second language was spoken in almost every home, particularly if it was a home consisting of children, parents, and maybe a grandparent or two from the old country.

The earliest age I can remember is five years old. I recall it so vividly because there was a strange occurrence during my first year in school. My parents enrolled me in a kindergarten program at a well-known Catholic school. In 1957, most Catholic-school teachers were nuns, unlike today.

Kindergarten was not a good experience for me. I missed my mother so terribly that I cried every day before leaving for school and for the better part of each morning after arriving.

Nuns led a unique and rather strange existence in my mind, being married to God and all. Many were tender, caring, and peaceful, while others could be as tough as General Patton. Many did not have the temperament to handle young children. Instead of coddling me when I cried and felt general anguish caused by being separated from my mother, they viewed my behavior as a major problem to be resolved by discipline.

The kindergarten class, with over fifty children, had perhaps the only nun in the school who was truly nurturing. Sister "Mary" would kneel down in front of me and wipe my tears and try to comfort me with a toy or a story with a happy ending. While I believe that Sister Mary had the temperament to help me and that logic dictated I eventually would have adjusted to the separation, Mother Superior would have nothing of my daily antics.

Following the second week of my constant carrying on, Mother Superior summoned my parents and me to her office.

She sat the three of us in front of her desk and gave me a stern dressing down. She had the perfect solution for my problems with leaving my mother. Since the first-grade class had about half as many students, and the teacher, Sister "Agnes," happened to be quite the disciplinarian, I would be advanced a grade in order for her to address my behavioral issues.

When my mother asked, "Isn't he too young to be put in first grade?" Mother Superior said, "I'm placing him there so Sister Agnes can discipline him. You should be prepared that he won't really learn anything and expect that he'll spend two years in the first grade. The first year will teach him that this is going to be a routine, leaving you and his home in the morning. By the second year he'll be prepared to learn." After some consideration, my parents agreed to her terms.

There I sat, a five-year-old in a classroom with six- and seven-year-olds because Mother Superior thought I needed to be disciplined. But my parents were astounded by how quickly I became engrossed in what was being taught. I remember overhearing them talking between themselves of my accomplishments and being in a state of surprise—so much so that my mother told this story for many years, especially since not only did I complete all the first-grade work, but I graduated near the top of the class.

Our family and neighbors were like the *Ozzie and Harriet* show from the 1950s: the perfect American family with the white-picket fence, the dad as the breadwinner, the mom as the homemaker, and the neighbors as part of the extended family. Years later it could have been compared to *The Brady Bunch*, or, for the next generation, *The Cosby Show*.

My dad was the epitome of a man's man. He worked excruciatingly hard and long days for his family, never complaining. Each weekday he'd be gone by 6:30 a.m., before we woke up, and my mom would get my older brother, Lenny, and me to school before the bell rang. She would send us off with solid breakfasts in our stomachs and brown-bag lunches that she prepared fresh every morning. After tending to Lenny and me, she would come home and take care of my eighteen-month-old brother, Arthur.

After school, Lenny and I quickly changed into our play clothes and ran out into the street with the other neighborhood boys to play stickball, wall ball, or dodge ball. Since it was a very close-knit neighborhood, we were allowed to play on either side of Porter Street and in most of the homes that made up our community of friends. While we were out playing, Mom would prepare a sit-down dinner that was ready when Dad came home.

Mom thought a consistent daily schedule was important, although she was far from obsessed about it. She was always happy and warm; looking back, I can see that she lived her life for her children and her husband.

Occasionally Dad worked late, sometimes until 8:00 or 9:00 p.m., and dinner would be only Mom, my two brothers, and me. But the majority of the time she would wait for Dad so we could all sit down as a family.

After dinner, Dad was exhausted from his contracting work and would fall asleep on the couch reading the daily newspaper. After putting my baby brother to bed, and with the house quieted down, Mom sat down with my older brother and me at the kitchen table, going over our homework until our bedtime.

They were caring parents. Like most of their generation and the one before, they were building a family system I'm sure they thought was going to be a thriving one. At the time, this young couple had their hands full with three boys, ages seven, five, and eighteen months. With well-defined parental roles and Mom's organizational skills, we kids grew up in what I thought at the time was a nurturing environment, with the love and support of two very devoted people.

The only thing I remember wanting more of was time with my dad. As I grew older, however, I realized that this just wasn't possible. My dad was either consumed by work projects or was too tired at the end of the day for any personal interaction. This was true for Saturdays as well, since that was a full working day for Dad.

Most Sundays we attended church, and dinner was usually at one of our grandparents' homes. After the big meal, all the cousins escaped into the backyard to play hide and seek or dodge ball while the adults sat around the dining room table talking, drinking coffee and espresso into the evening.

Shortly after my fifth birthday, Mom was pregnant with her fourth. After three boys, everyone in the family was hoping for a girl. Their wish was granted on April 22, 1957, when my mom gave birth to Angela, a healthy girl named in honor of my father's mother. After almost nine years of marriage, my mom and dad were living the good Catholic life, with four children and working to fulfill their American dream, working hard so their children could have easier lives than they had.

Over the next two years I flourished in school and socially throughout the neighborhood; in fact, my academic achievements were even better in the second grade.

There were a little over twenty brick row homes on our block, all meticulously cared for. They were filled with children, from newborn babies to young adults. Everyone was on a first-name basis, parents and children alike.

By the time I was seven, my parents had developed deep, sincere, and rooted friendships in our neighborhood. In fact, I can remember my mother referring to other mothers on the block like they were her own sisters. "Bob's mother, Joann, is just like your Aunt Regina," she would say. There was so much friendship and trust that hardly anyone knocked on doors or rang doorbells for entry. Most of the homes had screen doors, and you could look right in and yell a greeting. It was not unusual for neighbors to pop in unexpectedly for a cup of coffee and catch-up chat.

Of course, this unquestionable trust was extended to all the children of the neighborhood as well, both young and old. Again, this was the *Ozzie and Harriet* 1950s, and we lived in a postwar, ethnic neighborhood, everyone trying to pull themselves up by the bootstraps, every family in the same boat. It's even possible that some of them may have *come* to this country in the same boat! The common enemies were poverty and, for some, the oppressive situations that had caused them to immigrate to this country in the first place—lack of freedom, ethnic and religious persecution, and despotic leaders such as Hitler, Mussolini, and Stalin. Together, we felt a kinship that made us all, every family in our neighborhood, like blood relatives. Where else could a kid feel safer?

Chapter 2
John—Fuel to the Fire

Things were going well for me; my life was full of happiness and friends. There must have been at least thirty children on our block alone and dozens more spread out over a five- to six-block area that made up our neighborhood. As it was in other neighborhoods throughout the city and elsewhere, even though normally you played with kids around your own age, you still knew who the leaders of the neighborhood were, especially on the block on which you lived. These were the older guys who were tough and cool, those whom most of the younger kids looked up to and admired. As a seven-year-old, I would say to myself, "One day that's going to be me!"

Shortly after my seventh birthday, in the spring of 1959, I was alone, bouncing a ball off the side of my house. It was a great city-neighborhood game called "wall ball" where all the equipment you needed was a rubber ball and a wall. You could play it alone or with as many friends as were available. John, a teenager whom I perceived to be one of those cool guys in our neighborhood, approached me and asked if we could play together. After a few games of wall ball with John, we started to build up a sweat, and he asked me if I wanted to come to his house for a drink.

There I found myself, one of the smallest boys on the block, sitting at the kitchen table of one of the big, cool teenagers who rarely made time for any kid my age. Sure, sometimes some of the older kids might spend time with the younger kids, teaching them how to hit a ball over an outfielder's head or allowing us to sit as a captive audience as they regaled us with stories of their conquests on the athletic field. But to be singled out and invited to his house for a drink! John must have seen some enormous potential in me, I thought. My mind started to race with excitement as I imagined he had noticed something special about me.

John and I continued to meet and play together for the next couple of weeks. As I look back and remember our interactions, John was masterful. He wouldn't interact with me more than usual in front of my parents or adult neighbors. He would wait for times when I was with my peer group, away from my home and adult supervision, and then he would systematically separate me from the group for a game or a talk. A couple of my playmates would tease me, secretly envying my new relationship with John.

What my friends and I didn't know, what took me decades to learn, was that there is a name for this sort of attention. I was being "groomed" by John.

It didn't take long for John to take things to the next logical step for him. One day, after playing wall ball, John offered me a drink, which I thought nothing of since he had done this two or three times in the previous weeks. This time, while standing near his kitchen table, John sat in a chair next to me. I was a small boy for my age. With John sitting down and me standing, we met eye to eye. John put his hands on my shoulders and began slowly rubbing them, moving his hands down my back. At first it felt sort of macho, much like football players smacking each other on the butt after a touchdown. For this reason I did not immediately recoil. In my mind I was being treated as John's equal, for we had just played a vigorous game together. He was treating me like one of his real friends.

All of a sudden his hand was inside my pants, touching my penis. Now I was startled; I immediately pulled back as if jolted by an electrical shock, but John was clever and insisted that I let him explain.

What he was going to do to me was going to be "our secret." John told me, "This is what the older guys do," and I could always hang out with him if he could "trust me." Each of these catchphrases seemed designed to elicit precisely the response he wanted. As he continued talking, he was slowly pulling down my shorts. He acted kind and calm, although his voice contained a jagged quiver to it. My seven-year-old mind couldn't make sense of what was happening. John represented so many things. For one, he was older, and age was to be respected. For another, he represented something to aspire to—to be a cool older kid.

Within seconds he was behind me. Placing my hands on the table, he penetrated me. Since I was small in stature, he had a difficult time of it. Quite obviously, it was even worse for me, although the physical violation was to be the least of my injuries that day.

The pain was unbearable, but I was too scared to scream out loud. Whenever I began to cry out from the pain, John would try to calm me down immediately, whispering in my ear from behind, "It's okay, it's okay; I'm right here." As my anxiety inevitably grew, John would remind me that "big guys could take it" and "crying is for babies."

I was no match for him physically, but to John it seemed like more than just a physical victory. He seemed intent on my enjoying it—that I not just succumb but totally buy into and understand the ways of the world as they pertained to him and this act he was sharing with me.

In John's twisted mind, this was a seduction more than a rape. John seemed more intent on selling his act than stealing my free will, although the results were the same and the threat was implied. But a rose by any other name…

My only response was to go into a state of shock, to enter

a state of mind where I really wasn't there. The next thing, all within a couple of minutes, he had me lying on his bed, where it made it easier for him to violate and abuse me. Now he really had control and power over me. His entire body weight smashed down on me, and he no longer needed my weak legs to support the both of us. Resistance was futile—our strength differential seemed to increase exponentially from the moment he was on top of me. He was like an 800-pound gorilla and I was nothing but a rag doll. My face was buried in a pillow, where any cries or screams would never have been heard even if I could have mustered up the strength and the wherewithal to conjure them from the bottom of my soul.

No matter how much John whispered enticements in my ear, there was still something deeply embedded in my being that said that this was not right. It hurt, and it was just *wrong, wrong, wrong, wrong, wrong*. John did not love me. Where were the people who *did* love me?

As he was becoming more excited, he was losing control, and I could sense that he was forgetting I was even there, which frightened me beyond any kind of fear I had ever felt. I didn't know what he wanted. I didn't have words for what he was doing to me. His actions separated my mind from my body. All the while, never once did he threaten me or hit me. As he was becoming more aggressive and excited, he stopped trying to calm me. By the time he finished, everything I knew of myself and my carefree, playful world was gone—*forever.*

When he got off of me and let me get up, I was frightened and very confused. John assured me that I had passed my "initiation" and that now I could hang out with the cool older guys and do things like this, the kinds of things that cool older guys did together when the little kids and the parents weren't around, sort of like smoking.

Despite this sell, he still insisted I swear to secrecy, promising all the while that I was going to be one of his best friends. Me, a little seven-year-old, best friends with a guy in his teens! Right—as if that made any sense. But I was seven. What was my frame of reference?

Part of me felt like telling my parents, while another part thought better of it. In my child's mind I was blaming myself, knowing that what had happened between John and me was not just *his* fault but must have been mine as well. Despite all of his assurances, I felt it was wrong, much like I knew smoking at such a young age was wrong. At that point in my young and tender life, smoking was the only frame of reference I had for what my parents taught me was wrong. I can't recall if my parents had spoken to me about inappropriate touching. I know for sure I was told to stay away from strangers. But none of us was ever taught to fear the neighborhood kids, especially not the sons of our parents' friends. There had been absolutely no parental preparation or warning for John's vile acts. This was an era when families simply did not have such discussions with their children.

And so, as John had asked, I kept his secret—our secret. But John was like the thief who found an easy way into a bank. He was going to just keep going to that bank vault over and over again until he got caught, which is why most career criminals eventually end up behind bars. John, with his seductive, persuasive ways, was able to continue to coerce me to come over to his house to play ball. To this day I don't really understand how and why he was able to convince me to do so.

With each episode, despite John's cajoling efforts, my anxiety grew rather than dissipated. I didn't truly understand what was going on. I don't recall anything we spoke about, or if we even spoke at all. I just remember the ball hitting the wall over and over. There was no sound. No excitement. I just waited for the inevitable. I was simply responding to his attention. But physically and emotionally it was breaking me down and making me feel numb and lifeless. It hurt and it made me feel manipulated and taken advantage of. John could physically dominate me, and no matter how much he tried to convince me that this was something for us to partake in and enjoy mutually, in the end it was all about John, and I was simply a receptacle for him—someone without feeling or value.

My anxiety turned to fear. I was becoming more withdrawn and nervous. I was biting my nails, finding it increasingly hard to sit still, and finding it extremely difficult to fall asleep at bedtime. My mind was preoccupied with wondering what was going to happen next.

I became more distant with my friends. With John it became only about his self-gratification. Yet I had no idea what to do about it. As logical as it seems in retrospect, going to my parents did not seem to be a viable option. The truth was that the longer this went on and the more time that passed since the first attack, the more horrible I felt about what was happening to me and the more I struggled to understand what John was doing to me. Therefore, I feared that my parents would not side with me or would rain down a world of trouble upon John, which would ultimately lead to my getting in trouble.

John was still acting as a seducer, not a bully. The candy John offered was the attention he paid me—maybe even protection and social status—within a very cloistered neighborhood where everyone seemed to know the social pecking order and everyone else's business. If that were really true, why didn't they know what John was doing to me, and why weren't they doing anything about it?

As the abuse continued, John expanded his perversion to performing multiple exploits on me, both orally and anally. I was terrified. I got to a point where I didn't want to go to John's house anymore, which I think he was sensing. He stopped asking me to play wall ball. We stopped talking about baseball. He stopped the grooming process, and his only concern became getting me inside and shutting the door behind me. As he sensed I was growing fearful and as I began to refuse his advances, John started threatening that he wouldn't play with me and I wouldn't be able to hang around with the cool older kids.

Shortly after my growing refusals, one of the other cool teenagers, Jimmy, a little older and stronger built than John, stopped at my home, as he did often. That particular day, I heard him in the kitchen, talking to my mother, as I was playing in the basement with one of my toys. I heard him ask, "Louise, where are the boys?" She answered that my younger brother was upstairs napping and that my older brother was across the street at "Bobby's," and she was going to pick him up and have a cup of coffee with Bobby's mother. Jimmy responded that he'd go downstairs to look after me until she returned and to make sure that I was all right while she went across the street for a chat and to pick up my brother.

This was not a strange or unusual scenario in our neighborhood, particularly since Jimmy's mother and my mom were the closest of friends. What would my mother think other than that Jimmy was going to look after me until her return? We were all like extended family; Jimmy was simply being a nice kid, acting sort of like a babysitter.

I heard the front screen door shut as my mother, with my baby sister in tow, went to retrieve my brother. Before I knew it, Jimmy was downstairs. Within a few seconds, he was standing in front of me with his pants off, exuding all the excitement of a madman. I became extremely frightened and felt like a trapped animal. My heart was racing; my entire body was trembling with fear. I kept saying to myself, *Do whatever he wants and he won't hurt you.* I thought I'd never feel a fear worse than when John first attacked me, but as Jimmy came closer and closer to me, backing me into the subcellar, my seven-year-old brain began processing this as a life-or-death moment. Today, I liken this sensation to what a baby gazelle feels when a 400-pound tiger is about to pounce on it for the kill.

Whereas John had been breaking me down episode after episode, what Jimmy did to me that day was the vilest act I had ever before or since experienced, sending nauseous quivers throughout my entire body. He positioned me in every way possible to attain his self-gratification, like I was nothing more than a puppet. At times, he became angry that I was not performing to his liking and sternly told me what I was doing wrong. He then repeatedly used me until he received what he wanted and how he wanted it in order to be satisfied.

John took my childhood. Jimmy took my mind, my heart, and my soul.

Together they caused the ruination of my life, destroying my ability to trust and experience intimacy and setting me on a course of multiple addictions including anorexia, prescription drugs, alcohol, and, most of all, sex. By the time I reached my early twenties, workaholism became another affliction developed from their wreckage. Together they murdered my entire emotional and physical well-being.

If John had played the seducer, Jimmy was my assassin. By each boy I had been raped, but if there could ever possibly be a differentiation, John's approach had been at least to plant the seed in my child's brain that this was something I had wanted and had at least partially agreed to. With Jimmy it was rape with a capital R. I can only imagine that these are the ways of the predator.

John and Jimmy may have had two different styles, but they were both cut from the same cloth. Our neighborhood was made up of a diverse group of children—young, older, overweight, skinny, big and athletic, and puny and bookish. So what made John and Jimmy target me? Why was I the focus of their distorted, sexual violations?

I've grappled with this question my entire life. It's a simple, common plea: why me? I wish there was something I could have done about it, some way in which I could have reinvented myself so I would not have fallen victim to John and Jimmy.

Maybe if my older brother Lenny had been older and stronger, these trusted sons of our neighbors would have thought twice before sexually abusing me. Maybe life simply isn't fair. Maybe it was nothing more than being in the wrong place at the wrong time. Maybe a lot of things. The truth is, as little children, we are who we are. We have a *right* to be who we are.

One thing was certain: John and Jimmy were predators—pedophiles! They were animals that stalked around, sniffing for victims, checking the air for fear and the opportunity to do what they felt they had to do in order to give themselves some sort of perverse satisfaction and power over a child.

Looking back at the attacks, particularly Jimmy's premeditated, risky approach, led me to think, years later, that maybe John and Jimmy conspired to put the fear of God in me, having Jimmy do the deed. I was seven at the time and felt as though one just passed me to the other as if I had no value other than a fulfiller of their desires. I felt like I was in a world of trouble.

Though John and Jimmy killed my childhood—destroying me spiritually, emotionally, physically, mentally, and sexually—there is nothing I wish to change about the seven-year-old boy I was prior to the day John raped me. I was a good boy, a nice boy, a fine boy. *I* was not the problem. But no children who have gone through what I went through feel that way. Shortly after it happens, they begin to feel differently about themselves. Following these life-altering sexual attacks, they begin to break down and shatter in ways they may never fully grasp or recover from their entire lives. The world around them becomes a very foreign and dangerous place. For me, it took a lifetime to understand it all, and I'm still learning.

Chapter 3

Doctor's Orders

What was I going to do? What *could* I do? I was scared to death to tell my parents, especially about Jimmy's attack. His mother was so close to mine; from my perspective they were completely inseparable. I can remember many occasions when Jimmy's mother and my mom sat at our kitchen table and talked about their kids, having coffee, laughing, and hugging each other when they said goodbye. It was very confusing for me to see my mom and the mother of my worst nightmare sharing such happiness and love. How could my mom be friends with this woman?

In addition to not wanting to break up my mom's close relationship with Jimmy's mother, I feared retribution. This was the late 1950s, and corporal punishment was the rule of the land for children who didn't show respect or who caused problems. While I felt what John and Jimmy were doing to me might have been wrong, I was hesitant to say or do anything about it. I was afraid that I had brought this nightmare on myself in some way and would be punished if I disclosed the details of their attacks.

I was a child seemingly caught in the grips of two ferocious lions—John using guile and cunning to get me back to his house somehow again and again, Jimmy using brute force and fear to gain entry into my home to terrorize me. Jimmy was so bold as to order me to open the side door to our basement so he could slip into my house undetected and violate me, at times with my mother just upstairs. He instilled such terror in me that I somehow imagined a horror worse than the sexual savagery he had already dished out if I didn't follow his commands.

One night, around 10:00 p.m., some six hours after Jimmy had once again violated me in our basement, my parents came upstairs and woke me. The light immediately startled me. They both sat on my bed and asked me to talk to them for a moment. I immediately knew something had to be terribly wrong for them to disturb me at such an hour on a school night.

They began talking slowly and in low tones. This was not the usual case if Dad was going to hit me. Gradually they came out and asked, "Has John ever done things to you that shouldn't be done? Touched you where you shouldn't be touched?" I immediately turned to check my father's face. That cringing expression I'd come to know right before he was going to hit me wasn't there. In fact, I saw almost a blank stare. When I finally did say yes, all I can remember is that my mother held me in her arms. My father, a hulk of a man, put his arm across my mother and me, and I thought I even saw a tear in his eye—something I never saw again until the day his father died.

My mother was *definitely* crying. All I could think about was that I wasn't going to get hit for what John and Jimmy had done to me—or, worse yet, what they had made me do to them. In my child's mind, this was the most important thing of all at that moment. Children live only for the moment—the future and the big picture are foreign concepts. I would have let my father beat me for a year straight if I thought that would've cured what turned out to be a war within myself—a forty-eight-year psychological and clinical nightmare.

My parents were frantic when they learned that John had done these perverted acts to me. They were so distraught, they never asked if anyone *else* had touched me in that way. They didn't ask and I didn't tell; we were all in uncharted waters. Surely if they knew about John, they had to know about Jimmy too. But if they *didn't* know, I was too afraid to say his name.

Again, ours was an insular neighborhood. I knew Jimmy and his family, as did my parents. From what I thought, Jimmy and his father were dangerous men. Jimmy's father worked at the Navy Yard, and I remember seeing a gun on his hip at times. While today I understand it was probably part of his uniform, as a child, combining that with what Jimmy was doing to me, I concluded that I should be fearful. Since this was clear to me even as a seven-year-old, I am sure it was also obvious to my parents. I was also fearful that my mother would be upset with me if I said anything wrong about the son of one of her closest friends. In addition to this, I realize now that Jimmy was purposefully terrorizing me in order to keep me quiet. That was his way. John's, on the other hand, was to play the friend. For years I often wondered how lucky Jimmy probably felt that I never told anyone about his hideous violations of me.

By late spring 1959, when my parents came into my bedroom that night, the sexual abuse had lasted a little over three months, with the majority of it inflicted by John. Although fewer in number, the attacks by Jimmy in my own home were more abusive, violent, and despicable. It would be *decades* before I'd learn in recovery that John and Jimmy's vile sexual molestations left an imprint in my brain of manipulative betrayal, cruel dominance, utter fear, and a distortion of sexuality that no human being, let alone a seven-year-old child, should ever be made to feel or experience.

As an adult now in recovery every day, I ask God's help and support in my daily meditations and prayers that the memories—of the gag reflex caused by Jimmy, of wiping semen and blood from John off my seven-year old body—and the resulting pattern of distorted behaviors caused by their attacks will leave my mind forever. As a child I didn't realize how horrific a situation I was living in and didn't even think to pray for it to stop. I had never seen the one substance, and the blood just scared me to death. It wasn't until almost five years later that I could identify and understand where semen came from.

By my teens, my sexual behavior was completely out of control. Forty-eight years later I was told in recovery that my perpetrators had created *The Beast* of sexual addiction inside me from their brutal sexual violations. The compulsive, unconscious, and self-destructive behavior that would produce unbelievable havoc and turmoil in my life had now been unleashed.

In the 1950s, there wasn't much information out there—no Internet at the fingertips—to provide guidance for two young parents dealing with a sexually abused child. So, the very next day, my mom and dad took me to see our pediatrician. Back then, a family doctor was truly a family doctor, making house calls and no appointments necessary. Still, it's laughable today to think that this was the way to go. What was a pediatrician going to do? I didn't go to school that day. I didn't understand why I was being taken to the doctor. No one was talking to me about why I was there. My mother and I went together into the examining room, where I took off my clothes and waited. When the doctor came in, he instructed me to lie on my stomach on the examining table. I knew something was different; the doctor always previously examined me on my back. I said nothing. He said nothing. He then left the room and I heard him declare to my parents that I wasn't anatomically damaged. He examined me physically—which was all he was trained to do.

My psyche? He knew nothing on that topic, nor did he ask me anything or discuss any part of the attacks with me. Unfortunately, it was my mind that had been scarred—deeply buried in a land of darkness, isolation, shame, fear, and undeserved guilt.

Today, if a parent takes a child to a doctor as a result of sexual abuse, the first thing that medical professional is required to do is contact the proper authorities. But again, it was a different era. Doctors were like priests; they kept secrets. My parents, had they been truly motivated to do so, could have gone to the police themselves. Why didn't they? I have no idea. I don't believe they could answer the question any better themselves. Fear. Shame. Guilt. All of the negative obstacles that plagued me must have also plagued them. Their son had been raped. What did this say about them? Were they bad parents? I don't think they were. But if they told the police or some other authority about it, would that other party agree? Or would they question why they had been so trusting as to leave me unattended so that such a thing could happen?

Only recently, at age fifty-five, more than four and a half decades after the attacks, after I entered recovery, was I able to reveal to my mother the savage sexual abuse that Jimmy had wreaked upon me. She was *shocked* that the son of one of her closest friends had inflicted such horror and pain on me. She was stunned and at a complete loss as to what to say. My mother did share with me that she and my dad had gone to John's house and confronted his parents. She told me John's parents said they knew something was wrong with their son and they were going to take *him* to a doctor. Medical doctors would somehow cure everything! What did they think would happen? A doctor would somehow produce some miracle pill that would cure John of pedophilia? If so, maybe the same doctor would also have a magical pill that could somehow give me back the life John and Jimmy had stolen from me.

Instead of my getting some sort of medication—I'm being facetious here—to make all my demons go away, the doctor's only advice to my parents was this: "Don't talk about it. Don't keep asking him about it. Don't bring it up. He's young. If nothing else like this happens again and if he's given time to heal, he'll eventually grow to forget about it."

Wrong. Dead wrong.

I could be bitter; I *am* bitter sometimes. I was a child surrounded by ignorance. Was it malicious ignorance? No, it probably wasn't. But I look around and see that even today, fifty years later, so many people—parents, teachers, doctors, religious leaders, friends—cloak themselves in denial and make some of the very same ignorant assumptions and decisions about childhood sexual abuse.

Avoiding the topic was *not* going to make me all better. I should have been in intensive therapy. My entire *family* should have been in therapy. Whether things like this existed or not, I doubt my parents would have ventured into this arena. Like many parents of that age (and even some today), they simply were not mentally or emotionally equipped to address the trauma and devastation that sexual abuse inflicts on a child.

I don't know if my parents ever quite looked at me the same after the sexual abuse was discovered. Although they never said that they blamed me in the least, I never got the full satisfaction of hearing that from either of them. Even without professionals, we should have been talking things out—things like sex and love and feelings; things like right and wrong and what to do once I had been damaged in such a way.

Unfortunately, none of these conversations ever occurred. The doctor had said not to talk about it—and doctors were God, right? One thing you learned in a Catholic home in the United States in the' 50s: never argue or disagree with priests or doctors—God spoke to them directly, and they were always right.

In today's world, I believe John would be considered a sex offender who would be treated as an adult in the court system. Once released, under Megan's Law he'd be instructed to notify local law enforcement and register himself as a sex offender for the rest of his life. He would have to re-register every *few* years. And why? Only recently have there been efforts to try to rehabilitate sex offenders; therefore most continue to reoffend throughout their lives. Without acknowledgment and research there is little hope for successful treatment. Sentencing a pedophile to prison for a certain amount of time does not miraculously knock the sex offender out of the perpetrator. Without proper treatment, a sex offender released from prison will likely reenter the community unchanged and be more apt to continue to commit sexual offenses.

As for Jimmy, while I never—out of pure, unadulterated fear—told anyone about his vile, pathological sexual abuse, and although my parents never asked about him, the word must have gotten back to him about John getting caught because Jimmy never sexually abused me again. It was quite apparent to me that news of John's perverted attacks was being spread throughout the neighborhood. Why else would my parents have woken me up that night to ask me about him? I had never gone to them to expose his attacks. Obviously some other child had said something to someone, or maybe John had been caught in the act somehow, somewhere.

While I was extremely relieved that John and Jimmy's abuse would never happen again, I could tell many things from my parents' reactions: my father's not hitting me, my mother's crying, and my being taken to the family doctor. Their reactions confirmed for me that what these trusted neighborhood sons subjected me to was *not* what all the older guys did. I learned from my parents that it was something bad and something terribly wrong. It was far, far worse than underage smoking. I certainly knew that it felt that way as John and Jimmy were abusing me, but seeing my parents' reactions to it confirmed my thoughts from the first attack.

I also wondered if I was the only one who was victimized. Years later, I learned that other children had also been violated.

John and Jimmy were pedophile predators. Children were their prey. Had they just attacked any child? Highly doubtful. More than likely, they used the same street savvy that most criminals use. A good cat burglar can quickly spot the house that's easiest to break into. The mugger goes after the little old lady walking alone rather than the gang of big, tough guys who will kick his ass.

Maybe being naïve, impressionable, and needy, I looked like the type of kid against whom they could perpetrate their crimes. And yes, make no mistake about it—John and Jimmy were into little children. That was their perversion. Just like the mugger and the burglar, they seemed to have a sixth sense about who they could have power and control over to do this and potentially get away with their deception.

I somehow doubt it was only about being a particular type of kid. In the kind of game they were running, John and Jimmy used their status to manipulate young children like me in the neighborhood. John, the groomer, probably tried his act with any number of younger boys just like a guy in a singles bar trying out lines on women. It was a numbers game: if he approached enough kids, eventually a few might buy into his con, and with practice, his con just kept getting more and more effective.

Then there was Jimmy the bully. Bullies are everywhere—always have been and always will be. Maybe some children had been double-teamed by John and Jimmy, as I thought I had been, or maybe Jimmy had gone after some simply on his own, menacing the children he violated to keep them from speaking up. Either way, theirs was a sick, perverted jungle culture that operated in an all-American, friendly neighborhood. Guys like John and Jimmy took an idyllic social structure and ruined it by destroying little boys like me. There must be a special place in hell for people who devastate children in such a way.

Shortly after these horrific events, maybe within a couple of months, I became much more withdrawn. Even as a child I noticed these emotional shifts in myself. I would do anything to keep peace in the family. I couldn't stand any arguing or bickering in our house. Common, everyday things I had once been able to deal with now tore at me and made me want to quash them, like one might try to turn down a radio being played too loudly. Tension—normal, everyday family tension—somehow gave me sensory flashbacks to Jimmy screaming at me to do this and that, dammit! The extreme anxiety was almost crippling. I also noticed that this angst turned into a deeply rooted stress, which, decades later, would be diagnosed as a severe anxiety disorder coupled with a deep river of depression as a result of the sexual attacks. I went from being a carefree boy who took for granted that life was fair, happy, and full of games shared with my friends in the street to an eight-year-old who had become withdrawn, sad, and wrought with anxiety.

I remember a number of times when I isolated myself in my bedroom, playing a record, *The Battle of New Orleans*, over and over and imagining being down on the Mississippi, far away from the city. The song brought me out of myself, out of Philadelphia, to someplace else. My mother noticed this solitary behavior and would say something about how God wouldn't like that I was doing nothing with my time and that I should be outside playing or doing something more productive. But I felt the outside wasn't a safe place for me anymore.

As I grew older, I developed a heightened sensitivity to any human being in distress from emotional or physical abuse, whether bullying, teasing, or isolation. This would cause me to become extremely protective of that person. If someone were vulnerable and another person had the power to inflict pain on that person, my personal abuse and trauma would race to the front of my brain—sense memory. As a result, I would react by trying to help the person being tormented in any way I could. In some way this was as close as I could get to saving myself, which I couldn't do at age seven.

This might be construed as a good trait in me—a kind and gentle trait. Unfortunately it had its roots not in peace and love but in a severe and unresolved post-traumatic reaction. Sure, it may have made me more sensitive to conflict and to stand up for the oppressed and those in pain, but I would eventually discover that it had its negative sides as well. I had a gash deep inside my soul that wouldn't heal. For all of my adult life, the emotional injury caused by the depraved sexual acts committed on me permeated everything I did and ruled my interactions with everyone who came into my life. Emotionally, part of me was destined to remain seven years old until that seven-year-old could find his peace and restore his value as a human being.

Chapter 4

Running Away

As I remember, things in our home changed considerably over those next few years. Shortly after the abuse was uncovered, my parents moved my older brother and me to a private Catholic academy—a step up from the parochial school we had been attending. We would be dropped off in the morning by my parents, and they would go on to work. By this time my mom was helping my father operate his business. After school they would pick us up and drop us off at my paternal grandmother's home, where we waited to be collected by our parents at the end of the workday.

The next major change in our family's evolution was moving to the suburbs. Although it was not instantaneous, I can remember my parents talking about moving shortly after my abuse was discovered. Cause and effect? Probably. If so, I pledge my love to my parents for trying to figure out on their own what steps they might take to help me given their limited knowledge of childhood sexual abuse and its treatment. Unfortunately, in trying to help a child recover from such a trauma, this geographical move was but a drop in the ocean.

It was difficult for such a young couple with a growing family to afford the substantially increased private-school tuition for two boys. In the fall after my abuse ended, my mother gave birth to her fifth child, Mary Louise, on October 12, 1959. I can remember there was such joy in our home with my sister's birth. Although my sister's life was just beginning, now at just age seven, unbeknownst to me, a *significant* part of mine had already ended. All the attributes and emotions she would have the opportunity to embrace—trust, safety, intimacy, honesty, and sanity—had already been deceitfully and savagely ripped from my defenseless body and underdeveloped mind. These characteristics were replaced with any skill sets I could conjure to just survive life for the next forty-eight years.

Concerning my movements now, my parents knew exactly where I was and with whom I was every part of every day—a worthy effort, but in my case an example of closing the barn door after the horses had already gotten out. Unfortunately, what they failed to understand was that none of these alterations addressed the real problem going on inside of me. It was like buying a new set of clothes for a burn victim—he may have looked a little jauntier, but his flesh was still savagely burned underneath. I suppose they thought that, along with the misguided advice from the pediatrician not to discuss the abuse with me again, getting away from the scene of the crime would do me good. Perhaps it did ever so slightly, as I never again encountered John or Jimmy.

Within a few months after the abuse stopped, I started sexually acting out. Just shy of eight years old, I began recapitulating the acts done to me by John and Jimmy with a nine-year-old girl from the neighborhood. "Donna" and I would slip into the crawlspace underneath any neighborhood house where we could go undetected. With our clothes still on, we would rub our bodies together, recreating the abuse and overstimulation I had been sentenced to by my perpetrators. As an adult, I often wondered whether she could have been one of the children who had also been abused. If she were, it would only make sense for us to recreate the experience or do something with each other—two confused kids, afflicted by sexual abuse and not knowing how to deal with it. If she weren't, I'd say that she was *my* first victim resulting from *my* sexual abuse and trauma.

What a frustratingly complex situation for such young children to be in! We didn't even understand our own bodies or how to interact truly socially, let alone deal with the sexual urges inside us.

I had been doing rather well at the academy, although my grades—and my attention span—were far from what they had been before the sexual abuse. Still, what seemed to keep me from not sinking altogether was the strictness and structure of the academy. They expected a lot from their students, and they gave a lot in return. Kids rarely slipped between the cracks. It was a fine place.

Once we actually made the move, a short while later—I assumed for economic and geographic reasons—I was pulled out of the academy and placed in a new parochial school. But once I was pulled out of the structure of the private academy and placed with nuns again, I completely crashed and burned. Prior to the abuse, my grade point average had placed me at the top of my class in first and second grade. I was an active but very respectful and usually quiet child. Following the abuse, my average started to slip toward the lower end of the class and my behavior changed dramatically.

By the time I was eleven I was acting out socially and in any way I could sexually. I knew something was wrong with me, but I didn't understand what it was or why I was behaving the way I was. By age twelve I was having sexual experiences with and pursuing girls who were usually a year or two older than me. In recovery, I learned I usually identified someone at or below my emotional level and I had developed my own sixth sense about which girl was as sexually curious, malleable, and needy as I was. I would make eye contact, and if she held my gaze I knew she was the one. In other words, I had now become a predator of a different ilk—a pre-teen lothario who could look out upon a group of girls and tell which one would succumb to my charms even though neither of us was emotionally ready.

These acts would be repeated with the same type of woman for the next forty-eight years. All of my emotional growth stopped in 1959, and I lived in an emotional fantasy world that wouldn't change until the day I could finally deal with the sexual abuse I'd suffered.

At age twelve I was calling girls on the phone to arrange "dates," but they weren't really dates; I simply wanted to make out, grope, explore, and perhaps even go all the way if I could convince a girl to do so.

Was I like Jimmy the bully? No, not at all. If anything, I was more like John the seducer, who taught me how to lure and convince others to trust me, as I did him. But the fear of hearing "no" never got in the way of my trying to see how far I could take things, and I was successful far more often than not. Again, it was all a case of picking out the right girl and working my manipulation on her as John had done with me. This was just another piece of the lasting wreckage John had wrought on me.

At the time, none of my friends were having sex or anything even close to it. If they so much as touched a girl they would brag about it for days as if it had been the coolest and most amazing thing anyone had ever done. I, on the other hand, was having exploits that were way out of bounds for a twelve-year-old, yet I remained silent. For as much as sex was a conquest and a release, it was also for me a private affair. It was as if I could still hear John whispering words to that effect in my ear: "This is our secret. This is what the big guys do."

I listened to my buddies boast about accidentally on purpose brushing past a sweatered breast. Feigning interest, I sat upon the sort of sexual exploits that would've blown their minds. For me, it wasn't about bragging rights or getting a big rep as a lady's man. Perhaps the girls would tell their friends about our sexual escapades, and that would lead me to other girls and other sexual encounters. But no one would hear it from my lips. I "chased the dragon," as heroin users say, and once I caught it I felt embarrassed and ashamed. Sex was nothing to be proud of. It somehow felt good while it was happening, but when it was over I felt dirty and totally disenfranchised, much like I felt when John and Jimmy violated me. But only a short while after that, I buried those negative feelings because it was time for me to chase the dragon once more.

During those preteen and early teenage years it seemed like I was getting into trouble daily—not just the sexual adventures but simply getting into mischief and going from being a good kid to a less-than-good kid in general. Every day after school was an adventure. I would almost never go right home; a good Irish-Catholic friend and I could get in more trouble than two stray dogs. Even then, I often wondered if my parents noticed or put together how out of control I was. But this was the early 1960s, and so I imagine they just thought that I was going through puberty and decided that punishment was the answer.

Back in those days, in our area and culture, corporal punishment was the norm. Sure, some parents were downright sadistic about it, but not my father or mother. Still, it was not at all uncommon to have your backside slapped with a belt or an open hand, and hollering was certainly a part of it. The yelling always reminded me of Jimmy's depraved voice reprimanding me for failing to do *what* he wanted and *how* he wanted it done. These were not modern, politically correct New Agers who thought the answer to everything was to sit down, light some incense, put on some ambient music, and talk it out. You did something wrong, you got screamed at, you got hit, and you were sent to your room. It was that way in my house; it was that way in most of the homes of the children I grew up with. It was how our parents back then showed that they cared enough to try to make sure we didn't grow up to be delinquents.

Something that happened in seventh grade has remained with me through today. At the end of class, all the boys and girls would go to the back of the room to retrieve our coats from the closet. One afternoon, my friend and I got a little goofy and started to push the girls to move faster, and one thing led to another. I fell on top of "Joann" in the closet. There was time enough only to steal a kiss and to grope her. Unfortunately it was just enough time for Sister Theresa to get an eyeful of what I had done.

When he got the call later that night, my father went out of his mind with anger. I could see he was fit to be tied. I was prepared to be strapped again for my behavior and was becoming almost immune to it by this time. Unbeknownst to me, he had a better idea for punishment. While I could see he was really upset at dinner, he calmly said he was going to take me to school the next day and speak to Sister Theresa about the incident.

Dad didn't say much on the ride to school, but I could see he was really angry that this excursion was going to make him late for work. After parking his pickup, it took only minutes before we were in front of Sister Theresa and my classmates. Dad and I walked into the room just as all the children were sitting down. It became very quiet when all the kids saw me, my father, and Sister Theresa standing in front of the class.

Sister Theresa told the children to sit down and then turned to my father. She said, "Good morning. How can I help you, Mr. Pelullo?" He placed me on his right side and said that he had heard that I had caused some trouble in class the previous day. Immediately, although I almost couldn't believe it, I knew what was coming next. In fact, even though Sister Theresa was a tough cookie, she cringed at my father's next move.

Looking back, I think my Dad couldn't figure out why my

behavior was so out of control and inconsistent. I believe that what he did next came from pure frustration and with no knowledge of how broken and injured I was and had been for over five years.

Dad announced, "I'm here to assure you, Sister, that Peter won't be giving you trouble or acting out in your class anymore." At that very second, he slapped my face hard to the right and then to the left. I was only twelve, but I was determined not to cry even though I didn't know what hurt more, the slapping or the humiliation of being so embarrassed in front of my classmates. In today's society this incident would be considered cruel and abusive. However, this was forty-five years ago, and there was only one combined rule: family and church.

As I stood there, again shamed, trying to be strong, my father told Sister that if I gave her any more trouble he'd be back again to deal out more of the same. As crazy as it may sound, she actually thanked him and asked me to take a seat. This stunning reprimand did give me pause for...oh, about two days. It made me think harder about how not to get caught the next time.

Also, I became even *more* popular by demonstrating that I could take two shots like that in front of the entire class. With the boys, this made me some sort of tough guy. Dad didn't know it, but that humiliation made more than a few twelve- and thirteen-year-old girls feel sorry for me and want to make me feel better.

As the years passed, it seemed as if my father hit me harder and more frequently after the abuse. I think that in his mind he did this as a way to ensure that I'd become a heterosexual and not a homosexual. Growing up hearing the words *queer* and *faggot* used in my home made this a realistic leap for me to make. It's a myth that if you are a boy and are raped by a male you will automatically become gay. In fact, once targeted, children of all sexual tendencies can be caught in the web of a sexual predator.

Over the remainder of the year, Sister Theresa would remind

me that if I didn't stop acting out, all she had to do was call my dad for a repeat performance. Even so, I wouldn't let her control me. I took my risks and was well on my way to developing the manipulative skills and emotional defenses that would serve me through age fifty-five. *The Beast* was growing and becoming more cunning every day.

I would identify and befriend boys and girls who were risk takers in and out of school. My best friend in eighth grade was beheaded in an accident after taking his brother's motorcycle for a joy ride. It wasn't that they were all so bad, as in criminally bad; it was just that they walked a thin and dangerous line and, much to my surprise, so did I.

I was not always this way; there is no questioning the fact that, as a person, I had changed. Yes, all kids grow up and change as a regular course of development, but my changes were far more drastic and sudden. It seems, in retrospect, that the same unspoken internal compulsions driving my need for sexual release were also altering other aspects of my life and personality. I misbehaved in school because I seemed to get a thrill out of trying to get away with it. Whereas sitting in a classroom and paying attention to the teacher's lesson once was a joy for me, now I squiggled and squirmed and wanted greater stimulation.

My attitudes toward my goals changed as well. Where once I had wanted parental approval from bringing home straight As from school, now I had more interest in getting a rise out of my friends or exciting a girl with my bravado. I lost my ability to learn. I couldn't concentrate, read, or stay focused for more than fifteen minutes at a time. My mind would drift, sometimes to a make-believe future in which I would be a good student and a good person again.

Even if I knew to stop well before getting into some real reform-school level of trouble, it was not always about how far I could go but more that I always had to *be* going period. Playing it straight and just being a good kid and a good student bored me. It was like I was hopped up on something. The similarities between what I was going through and my perception of a drug addict's need for a fix frightens me when I look back upon it.

I couldn't wait to get out of Catholic school. I had only one more year and then I would go to public high school and be away from the nuns for good.

In the beginning of my freshman year of high school I was only thirteen. I didn't turn fourteen until February, which made me one of the youngest children in the class. Also, for the first time, after eight years, I wasn't in parochial school or a private, Catholic environment.

The public high school I attended was predominately Jewish. While this was a new culture for me, it didn't matter as I loved being away from the nuns and their controlling personalities. Besides, I was one of the few who walked comfortably and socially through dynamically different groups. This chameleon-like behavior helped me assimilate with the crowd yet keep everyone at a safe distance. I knew everyone, but no one would ever know the true me.

My friendships were superficial, and I remained in control of myself in regard to them. I know that sounds callous, but I survived being sexually molested by cutting myself off emotionally and kept relationships risk-free by not investing myself in them. It wasn't that I didn't want to hang out with people—far from it. It was that my emotions had no depth. If a friend died, I wouldn't have been emotional over the loss. This was how I operated with my friends as well as the girls I was carrying on with, and this apathy toward others made me believe that I was truly callous, that I had become like Jimmy.

Although I didn't feel connected to any particular friends in my life, I did feel love for my older brother and the way in which he watched over and protected me. A superior athlete, he always made sure I was included in pickup games, and he worked with and tutored me extensively to make our high school wrestling team. My brother was a phenomenal wrestler, and though I didn't enjoy the sport, I followed him on to the wrestling team. Not only was he an outstanding athlete in football and all-state in wrestling, he was tough as nails. In his senior year he was named king of the pinners.

He started wrestling in ninth grade, but I didn't begin until tenth. It was fun, though; it was a sport we could do together. By the time he was a senior and I was a junior, he was already well-known throughout the state. My objective was to make varsity so I could go out on the mat with him when varsity was called out. I achieved this by losing 40 pounds from my six-foot frame and wrestling at 120 pounds while my brother, who was two inches shorter than me, wrestled at 165 pounds. Our builds were so different we must have looked more like a comedy team than blood brothers.

Other than putting myself on a diet of nothing more than fruit, vegetables, and water every day for most of the entire season, it was a fun year. On the outside, it appeared that I was losing weight to compete. On the inside (I would learn many years later in recovery), the drastic weight loss represented my hunger for control and my thirst for acceptance despite the price.

My brother had a perfect record in our dual meets, with all wins and no losses, while in my first year I had gone five and four. On another team that would have been considered pretty good for a first-year starter, but on our highly ranked team it was merely tolerable. My brother was extremely exciting to watch as he won match after match. It was clear I wasn't as talented an athlete and I would likely never match the feats of my brother on the mat.

That was evidently Dad's attitude as well; he attended only about half of my matches my senior year. How did that make me feel? Disappointed, obviously. I had never really gotten the impression that my father thought I was a good athlete. When he was in the stands and my brother was wrestling, a lot of the other fathers would pat him on the back and tell him how proud he had a right to be. What father wouldn't want a reception such as that?

Being an athlete had its advantages, however, considering the cheerleaders and the girls who came to the matches. The only other wrestler of my brother's caliber was a boy in my class who became ranked as highly as my brother. In fact, during our senior year he went a step further to the state finals at Penn State, which was the ultimate honor and achievement. Although this boy was an A student and a strong athlete (the complete opposite of myself), I could immediately sense that he was off in some way and a little out of sorts. I found out later when we became best friends that he had a troubled past as well. Despite this revelation, I never desired to speak about my sexual abuse attacks with him or anyone else.

As I entered my senior year, I was only sixteen and yet had already had many female sexual encounters, starting when I was almost eight. There's no doubt in my mind that I was the first kid in my class to lose my virginity—in the traditional sense, not as a result of the rapes. Yet I never really had a girlfriend since I really didn't feel the need. To me, it would only complicate my thoughts about girls. Girls were there for acting out. Though I did treat them nicely, some may have left feeling miffed that I would not become a steady boyfriend, but none ever accused me of using her or of forcing myself upon her. It was always just about sexual exploitation for me.

I learned in recovery that sexual behaviors are often dictated and recapitulated by the patterns of the abuse experienced by the child. My need to hunt and capture girls was derived from my being hunted and captured by John. I was replaying his tactics, and my hunting became an integral part of how I replayed the abuse over and over.

During my high school years I navigated my way through every group in my grade. The Christians drank beer and whisky, the hippies smoked pot, the athletes did everything and anything, and I spoke as freely and as often to the brainiacs as I would the jocks. As a senior athlete, I became intertwined with the sophomore and junior classes as well—more specifically, the girls of those classes.

My wrestling buddy "Kevin" and I were misbehaving daily with liquor and girls or just hanging out and looking for trouble. My behavior was way out of control. Despite his penchant for getting into trouble, he fit the classic mold of what all parents wanted their boys to grow up to be. He was smart and hard-working, got good grades, was a star athlete, and, despite his devilishness, was a really good and respectful kid whom all the adults genuinely admired.

After graduation we didn't see much of each other. He went on to a highly regarded and academically prestigious university on a wrestling scholarship while I went to prep school in order to pass English so I could get my high school diploma.

Kevin eventually dropped out of college and became a large-scale pot dealer. Some years later I heard that his boat, his ID, and his clothes but not his body were found by the Coast Guard. Counting my eighth-grade classmate who was killed on his brother's motorcycle, this was the second friend I had lost. Neither loss left a lasting impression. As much as I considered them friends, I really had no emotional attachment to either of them.

One girl in the junior class was cute, attractively built, and, I could see, interested in me. In the beginning of the friendship she definitely took a backseat to all of my other activities, such as my sexual dalliances with a variety of girls as well as my constant hanging out with Kevin.

This was until one day when "Betsy" asked me for a ride home. It took about twenty minutes to get to her house, so I actually was forced to spend time having a conversation. This was something I usually limited because I just couldn't let anyone get close to me—I couldn't let anyone see *The Beast* inside me, to which I was blind and wouldn't learn about for almost another forty years.

As we chatted, I found her to be funny and easy to converse with, and I wondered what it would be like to have a real girlfriend, not just a sex partner. I wasn't too sure about this because it might have stymied my other sexual activities with girls, or at least those at our school. I had a need that required constant filling, and Betsy didn't seem to fit my mold in that department. My first impression was that she wasn't going to be like the other girls; looking back, I can see that it was probably because she was more emotionally mature than I was.

As I got to know Betsy better, I thought I might give this boyfriend-girlfriend thing a chance, and it became an immediate challenge. Her dad wasn't crazy about me because I wasn't Jewish. I didn't mind, though; I liked him. He was a straight shooter, a no-nonsense man, much like my own father. Besides, her mother thought I was nice, so I knew I could break through with him via mother and daughter. This eventually happened, because she and I went on to date each other with the implicit permission of her father.

From the onset of our relationship, I could tell something was stirring inside me. It was the first time in my life I realized how my brain struggled to understand how sex and caring for someone went together. I immediately started treating her differently from all the other girls I had been with. Betsy would come to my home for dinner often, and her family had me over many times. In her home, I learned a significant amount about Jewish culture, especially acquiring a taste for lox, whitefish, cream cheese, and bagels.

Sex wasn't on my agenda with Betsy. When we were together she was the aggressor, initiating physical contact. This was new territory for me; I really didn't know how to let my guard down and express any feelings with a girl. The only feelings I had expressed before with girls were sexual.

Betsy was sincere, expressed loving emotion, and naturally wanted the same from me. Over the next six months we would kiss, hold each other, get very physically close to one another, and do some light petting, but I couldn't bring myself to go all the way with her. I felt awkward in this emotional arena. She wanted to bring together love and sex—two experiences I couldn't imagine or feel could be one.

I was starting to care for her and began taking care of her, which was what I understood to be love at the time. Because I was having feelings for her I needed to separate out the thought of having sex with her. Sex was not an activity I could have with someone I cared about. The relationship went on for eighteen months but could not halt ten years of ingrained behavior. My sexual encounters with other girls continued. I believed that this did not affect my relationship with Betsy at all. Just as I had promised John that this was our secret years earlier, the sexual encounters I had aside from Betsy were my secret.

The following year, Betsy began attending a local college as a freshman, and we would often double date with some of her new friends. One afternoon I received a call from one of the fellows I met on one of those double dates. He sounded stoned, but he gave me explicit details about how he had had sex with Betsy numerous times. This filled me with anxiety and rage. After all, we were seriously dating, and *I* hadn't slept with her. How could she be sleeping with someone else? I hung up the phone and immediately drove to her house. I wanted every detail of what happened, what he did to her, and what she did to him. Betsy resisted at first, but eventually she broke down and confessed to everything they did together.

The betrayal revived feelings I had had in 1959, like I was being molested and raped all over again despite my own betrayal of her. That was the first time I had a glimmer—however faint—of giving my heart to someone else, and it brought me pure devastation.

Most guys would have walked away, calling her names, but I was not an emotionally balanced person. This was about exploitation, something all too familiar to me. After I got all the excruciating details (where, when, and how many times), she became a different person in my eyes. Within a week I began having sex with her, recapitulating everything that had happened to me during my sexual abuse. From where she was sitting, I had somehow forgiven her. This was far from reality. Her betrayal had touched the core issue of being sexually abused as a child.

Realistically, the only thing that I understood at that moment was that I had suddenly found just another girl to have sex with in order to stop the feeling of insurmountable pain and anxiety that had taken over my brain and nervous system. This went on for a couple months until I felt there was nothing special left and that it was time to move on. Once she moved from being someone with whom I had a relationship to someone with whom I was just having sex, she just fell into the same category as all the other girls before her.

Following this fiasco, I did not look for companionship, as most young men my age were doing. This was the first time in my life I thought to myself that maybe I would never get married.

The point was, except when I was having novelty sex, I appeared to have no passion at all for anything. Yes, I was working hard and I was ambitious, but I managed to do that with an emotional restraint that probably worked in my favor in the business world. Some people might say successful business executives show little emotion whether they make or lose a million dollars. For me, the abuse bred an emotional apathy that had its place in the business arena.

I truly wonder whether I *did* care if I lived or died, whether

I succeeded or failed. I was a machine, a hard-working machine fueled by an extreme anxiety disorder that did eventually create success for me in the business world, but I wouldn't suggest that anyone try to achieve that kind of success by going through childhood trauma such as mine. I would've traded all the money I later made in life if that would have healed the wounds so deeply cut into my brain, heart, and soul.

Success
With Internal Failure

Chapter 5
Rein in the Environment

After I broke things off with Betsy, I heard from my mother that she would stop by our house every now and then to ask what I was doing with my life, but I had no interest whatsoever. She was now just like any other nameless, faceless woman I'd had sex with—out of sight, out of mind, which was exactly where I kept any inkling of pain and betrayal that reminded me of the sexual abuse.

Several years later I ran into her in a club attached to a hotel. As soon as I saw her sitting at the bar, my feelings of betrayal returned and I became extremely nervous, almost unglued.

Only one thing would cure me.

After a few drinks we were in bed. When I finished, I felt like I had just been injected with a dose of calming medication. That was what sex had become for me, an opiate, and I later learned that was exactly what was happening inside of me—endorphins rushing to my brain in order to calm and soothe me. Sex was like heroin, another form of opium, or a painkiller. Some people are born with genetic propensities toward addiction, and fate or experience dictates what their addictive poisons might be. For some people like me who were brutally sexually molested, addiction can be caused by the severe trauma that, again, can pick its own opiate. For me it was sex.

I never heard from Betsy again. Looking back, I think maybe she thought that our sexual encounter might have led to something new. For me, it was just another time I needed to regain control of myself and calm my nerves.

By the time I was sixteen, acting out sexually was my only lifeline to feeling alive and sane; I seemed to have little genuine feeling for anyone except for my siblings, especially my younger ones. I would look after them as much as my mother needed me to. I was extremely protective of my younger brother, who had a slight learning disability and attended a specialized school for a few years. He did graduate from my high school and went to college, where he played football. Today he is a very successful businessman. But in those tender years, if anyone would make fun of or pick on him, I came to his rescue. I was afraid he couldn't protect himself. I can remember several times when I became enraged when someone picked on or laughed at him. I was going to make sure that nothing that happened to me would ever happen to him.

There was another significant family event in my senior year of high school that had a huge impact on my life. My mother gave birth to her sixth child, a boy. Although he was healthy and my mother was not seriously ill after the birth, she was nearing forty and needed at least three to four weeks' bed rest. My two sisters were too young to take care of the baby, so that left my older brother or me.

Lenny had just transferred home from a college out west, but taking care of a newborn just wasn't something my older brother, the superior athlete, would have felt comfortable doing. This child, consequently, became my main focus. My mother needed me, and that was all I needed to know; all I cared about was making her life easier. Helping my mother to that extent gave me a real sense of self-value. On her first day home she showed me how to make his formula and change his diapers, and by the second day he was in my complete care.

For the next couple of weeks I would feed and change him

before school, come home for lunch (a senior privilege) to take care of him, and return by 2:30 p.m., when school was over, to stay with him the rest of the day.

These were acts of duty and family responsibility, and I did them without any thought about shirking them. It made me feel good to help out and to be a part of something wholesome and good, which is what a family is or should be about.

As much as I loved and cared for my siblings, I later learned in therapy that I was probably looking to recover the innocence and trust that had been taken from me. Maybe I was trying to get that back by taking care of my littlest brother, still in diapers. And maybe I was flashing back in a positive way when I protected my younger brother—protecting one who was weak against evil forces that were strong. These emotions remained within me, but so much else was gone, having been stolen away by a thief in the night.

Once my mother recovered, I picked up my familiar habits—dating multiple girls at the same time, acting out familiar behaviors. Having a keg of beer in one of my buddy's cars was an everyday event. With a license and with access to a car, I was able to secure alcohol, pick up girls from school, or, even better, go downtown to the clubs. I lost all interest in my education.

My life was a mess. I felt I was in some form of crisis, but I couldn't understand about what or why. One thing I could keep in my control was making money. I could sell anything. I sold encyclopedias for a year when I was nineteen and made more money on commissions than most of the twenty-year vets at the company. I knew, however, that I couldn't sell encyclopedias for the rest of my life; there wasn't enough money in it. I was meeting some interesting women through the leads I received from the company, and I could instinctively tell if a woman had a weak spot and where it was. The right combination of opportunity and instinct—coupled with a triggering, unnerving event that raised my stress and apprehension before I had even knocked on the door—was a lethal mixture and would ignite my cycle of anxiety and sexual compulsion.

I'd taken up tennis around age seventeen and played every minute I could. I loved the sport. I loved it so much that I drove 3,000 miles to sunny California on my twenty-first birthday so I could play every day, with the thought that I would stay for around six weeks or so. I ended up on the doorstep of my mother's first cousin Gloria and said, "Hi, I'm your cousin Pete from Philadelphia." She and her husband Sidney took me in as if I were family; well, actually I *was* family, but I really hadn't known them before knocking on their front door. I ended up staying for almost seven months!

She was and still is one of the most loving people I have ever met. I was twenty-one and she was thirty-six. It was like having the big sister I'd never had, since by the time I was eighteen I felt I was a caregiver to my younger siblings. Here, instead, was my older cousin taking care of *me*. It was wonderful because she showed and gave me a sibling type of love I had yet to experience. In looking over my first twenty-one years, I would say it was undoubtedly the happiest time of my life since the attacks fourteen years earlier.

Of course she had girlfriends, and while I was active in giving a few of them tennis lessons, I also had sexual relations with a couple of them. Since they were older women and not of my age—most of them were in their early to mid-thirties—they were much more mature and skilled in their lovemaking than I was or than any of the girls I had dated up to that time. They really knew what they were doing. Most of the sexual liaisons I'd had previously were with young girls who could not loll around afterward in the afterglow; they had to return to their parents' homes. Not so for an older woman with her own place.

But when they would touch me in a tender way, I would turn

away, becoming nervous and very agitated. This was another sign that something was terribly wrong.

I remember an encounter one particular evening with a thirty-five-year-old woman that left me extremely troubled. After an hour of sex, she laid her head on my chest and began softly stroking my chest and the back of my neck. I jumped out of bed as if she had struck me with a hammer. Sex to me didn't include tenderness, caring, or emotional touching. Her tender contact reminded me only of how John had touched me.

No matter where I was living—Philadelphia or California—I started to realize I couldn't give myself emotionally to a woman, nor could I understand why. I was incapable of falling in love or truly connecting with someone through any act of love or intimacy. It didn't matter if they were eighteen or thirty-five. It didn't matter how old I was. While other guys had experienced puppy love or even very committed relationships full of true love, none of that was happening for me. What was wrong with me? Why would I turn away if a woman was tender? I would just shrug it off and think I wasn't ready for a serious relationship. At that point I started to wonder: for sex to be good, did it have to be bad? What I didn't understand until I entered recovery was that every time I had sex, I was somehow trying to master what had happened to me at age seven, to relive it and rewrite it so as to change the ending somehow.

Upon my return to Philadelphia, I was just turning twenty-two, and I accepted a job as a teaching tennis pro at a local country club. In 1974 I was making up to $900 a week teaching tennis to a primarily female clientele. It was a respectable amount of money, and of course the environment presented the opportunity for sexual encounters with numerous women when my anxiety overwhelmed me and my cycle or trance would be set in motion.

At that time my dad needed a hand with his business, so I went to work during the day with him and taught tennis at night.

Some days I'd work eighteen to nineteen hours. My financial future was in *my control*, something that no one could take from me. So I worked two jobs for a little over a year and saved up a significant amount of money.

But my dissociation and disconnection continued to grow and sabotage any chance I had for a real relationship with a woman. After a few dates with someone I'd feel no emotional attachment and move on. In recovery I learned that having the ability to pull someone into my bed and be in control without being emotionally invested momentarily satisfied my endless craving for power. But once the luring was easily had, the cycle would end and begin again with another uncertain possibility.

My life took a dramatic change the year I turned twenty-three. I met a man in the music business who began taking tennis lessons from me. Unfortunately, he couldn't play tennis worth a lick, but he was an extremely talented musician. One day he took me to a recording studio to show me what his real talents were. I came home and told my mother that I knew what I was going to do with my life. I was going into the music business.

Chapter 6
Money Mogul

I learned every facet of the music business. I did more research concerning the industry during the next six months than I had done homework or schoolwork during my twelve years of formal education. After a significant amount of work and thought, I concluded the recording studio business was the best course of action because you were paid by the hour, and ninety percent of the business was secured by purchase orders from the major record companies. The going rate in Philadelphia at the time to rent a studio was $140 per hour. If I could build three studios and work twenty billing hours a day per studio, I could potentially generate $8,000 of gross billing a day. In 1975, this looked extremely financially attractive to a twenty-three-year-old. I felt as though having my own business and working for myself would give me *ultimate* control over relationships and anyone entering into my life.

Growing up in a blue-collar family and working in the construction business, in which you could touch, feel, and see what you did, made the music business a foreign concept for my father. Fortunately, he came around (with a big push from my mom) and used his construction skills to help me build the studios. It took almost nine months and every penny I had saved from my collective jobs as well as a loan from a small bank that needed business so badly, I actually looked like a good risk to them. With those funds and my savings, my father and I built the studio from the ground up.

I built a single-purpose building—unique at that time in the recording industry. Most studios were in office buildings with doctors, accountants, and other businesses. In my operation I had the entire building to myself, and that allowed me to have the greatest soundproofing and sound reinforcement that anyone had ever built before in Philadelphia. More than thirty-four years later the facility still stands and operates.

Because I didn't have to share the space with anyone else, I could do whatever I wanted with the structure. Ever since those dark days I have worked to place myself always in complete control of every situation I was in to the best of my ability. When I had been sexually attacked, I didn't have a scintilla of control. I felt nothing; I was hollow inside. I had no feelings and definitely no free will. Never again would I be made to feel like that.

Essentially we built a building within a building. Each studio was separated by cinderblock walls, and we poured over a hundred tons of sand between the cinderblocks. To soundproof the control rooms, we used five-inch-thick steel doors that we manufactured ourselves. The structure had floating floors that weren't connected to the inside walls, and floating ceilings that were suspended from the roof with steel springs—anything to prevent reverberation from outside noises or interferences.

We were also one of the first recording studios to have significant separation via individually crafted, enclosed sound booths for pianos, vocals, and drums. Other studios tended to use only portable sound baffles—temporary walls that went up only about five or six feet. Half of our flooring was parquet wood for more of a live sound, while the other half had carpeting for a softer, mellow sound. It was really the first recording operation in Philadelphia that had been built to address specifically every detail concerning sound waves and reverberation.

In 1968, a gentleman named Joe Tarsia founded Sigma Sound Studios. It was the second studio in the country to offer twenty-four-track recording and the first in the country to use console automation. Joe had an extensive background in audio engineering, while I was coming into the music business from nowhere with nothing.

I knew that whatever I did, I was going to be competing with Sigma Sound, one of the top studios in the world at that time, and it happened to be in Philly also. If I'd been in Moose Jaw, Saskatchewan, maybe I could have simply slapped something together and made money from being the only game in town, but not if I was to thrive in Philadelphia. If I had a second-rate operation, Sigma would circumvent my growth (like they did to most other startups in Philly), and I'd have to rely on second-rate clients paying lower hourly rates.

People talk about "the sound of Philadelphia," which was not simply a sound but the title of one of the most popular instrumental hits of all time, signaling the start of the entire disco era. Included in the sound of Philadelphia was a thirty-member house band complete with horns and strings named MFSB, which stood for mother, father, sister, and brother. Writers and producers such as Gamble and Huff, Thom Bell, and McFadden and Whitehead broke artists such as The Trammps, Hall and Oates, The O'Jays, Patti LaBelle, Billy Paul, The Delfonics, The Spinners, and The Stylistics—the list goes on and on.

Two major independent record labels were also born in this city of music—Philadelphia International and Salsoul. Philadelphia was not second rate when it came to the music scene. During the '70s, the city was hotter than New York, Detroit, Memphis, or Nashville. And I was crazy enough to think I could compete in this burgeoning business and carve out a piece of its history.

I opened for business on March 10, 1977. I had just turned twenty-five that February, had five people working for me, and was in debt over $500,000. At my young age the only credit I could qualify for to secure the recording equipment I needed was from leasing companies. Therefore, I was paying eighteen percent interest when banks were giving loans at six percent to secured borrowers. The working hours I had put in prior to this were nothing close to the hours I was now working every day. I installed a shower and a cot in the studio so I could stay there day and night to operate and build the business.

Since I wanted three full-sized studios, I needed to take on some business partners, but I would maintain my inner control system by being the majority shareholder. I partnered with "Vladimir," a Russian musician who had defected to the United States after a performance in Japan. Vladimir was a consummate master violinist. He went on to further mine the disco trove by forming and recording with USA European Connection, which produced a number-one hit in 1978 with an album called *Come Into My Heart*. This album was showcased on a *60 Minutes* segment as the number-one record in the country, during its airing of the phenomenon of disco music in America. Vladimir's heart was definitely more into playing, writing, and producing music than being a studio owner. I exchanged my share of the royalties on those records for his equity ownership of the studios—a deal that made us both content and prosperous.

I was so aware of Sigma's presence that my partner and I named the studio Alpha International. Sigma may have been established long before we were, but we were the first letter in the Greek alphabet, and they were the eighteenth. This was the result of my need to compete for sales and recognition.

My first break came very quickly when one of the sound consultants told me how he'd been hanging out with the Rolling Stones and that they were looking to do some vocal overdubs for their live album *Love You Live*, recorded in France. This was how a lot of the music business worked. People glommed on to other people, everyone eager to befriend a star, and in the process sometimes a business opportunity presented itself. This fellow didn't have a studio of his own, but he spread the buzz in the recording studio community about Alpha International's sound quality, and pretty soon I was talking to The Rolling Stones.

I had been open all of six weeks and suddenly I found myself on the telephone with Keith Richards—quite a rush. I babbled something about "no hard drugs on the premises." He said, "Then no publicity until after we leave." We agreed.

After the Stones' departure, their recording sessions at Alpha International were written up first in the local *Philadelphia Inquirer* and then in the national music press. I was lining my walls with pictures of Mick and me and Keith and me. The Rolling Stones' work at the studio gave a meteoric rise and national recognition to the studio throughout the recording industry. It was also quite a coup, considering that all the major acts coming into Philadelphia, particularly any big, international rock acts, ended up at Sigma Sound, my competitor and a worldwide leader in the industry.

My next big break came when a fifteen-year-old girl working as a cleaning woman at Sigma Sound was overheard singing in the bathroom—humming while she worked, so to speak. T. Life, one of the guitarists who recorded a significant amount of sessions there, heard her and was extremely impressed. He tried to talk Joe at Sigma into giving her a chance to record "on the come"—in other words, to waive or lower his price in hopes that her session might lead to something bigger down the line, but Joe was steadfast in his price. Because of Joe's domestic and international success he really didn't need to do anything for nothing. I suppose he'd become jaded by that time as studio owners were always hearing tales like this. If we didn't stand somewhat firm, musicians would try to talk us out of ever making a nickel.

I was perhaps only a little less jaded than Joe; I wouldn't waive my fees entirely. I remember my going rate at the time was about $140 per hour, and I gave T. Life the studio for $110, which he jumped at. This young teenager by the name of Evelyn "Champagne" King recorded "Shame," which became the biggest-selling record ever for RCA at that time, eclipsing even Elvis Presley's single-best recording…and the rest was history.

Evelyn's record sales were the reason I expanded from being solely a studio owner to moving into the record industry and creating my own record label. Her first royalty check for the multimillion-dollar selling "Shame" was for over six figures, and I received $32,000 from RCA Records as payment for her studio time.

The success of having The Rolling Stones from the rock world and Evelyn King from the R&B world utilizing our facilities gave Alpha International Studios instant visibility for a broad band of recording artists and a variety of genres both domestically and internationally.

Seeing how much money there was to be made on the record company side, I formed Philly World Records, which would go on to sign Harold Melvin and the Blue Notes, Cashmere, Eugene Wilde, and numerous other dance-oriented artists.

In 1981, I met a member of the Saudi royal family who was fascinated by the music business. Within six weeks I negotiated a $3 million equity investment (a significant amount at that time) from this gentleman, and I was off to the races. In 1983, we had the number-one record in the country on the R&B charts with "Gotta Get You Home Tonight" by Eugene Wilde—in the process bumping off Michael Jackson, whose song was crossing over to the top of the pop charts, as did all of his hits. I quickly understood the power of a radio program director, and within a year I was on a first-name basis with over seventy-five percent of these men and women throughout the United States.

My record label was handled by the independent distribution network, the way approximately fifteen percent of labels were distributed then. I hired my own promotion and marketing staff, and we worked with every radio program director and music director from coast to coast on a one-on-one basis. I was out on the road at every convention, pressing the flesh, making contacts, and looking to control every aspect of every record Philly World released.

Eventually, Atlantic Records signed up our label for a pressing and distribution deal. The success of this business relationship led to MCA Records' offer of a seven-figure contract to leave Atlantic Records and New York and move to Los Angeles. In this new business arrangement, MCA would handle all of the marketing and promotion costs I was carrying at Atlantic Records. Following this success, I formed a publishing company and hired a roomful of songwriters, collecting those royalties along the way as well—all despite never having picked up an instrument in my life.

I was driven. Failure was not an option. For the first five years of my multifaceted music operation I worked hard but played hard as well. My older and younger brothers married during those five years, so most of my family questioned why I wasn't married or hadn't even attached to anyone seriously. But to me, by that time, marriage was never a consideration.

All the men around me thought I was the ultimate playboy, while in reality I was being driven by a compulsive anxiety disorder in which I found sex to be something dirty, something I needed but never wanted to talk about. For all my activity within the music business I had never gone to a concert! I hated crowds. They gave me panic attacks. The same went for crowded nightclubs. Those were the places where most music business executives frequented, but they were impossible for me to navigate.

But none of this put even the slightest crimp in my encounters with women. I didn't have to hang out in clubs, trying to scream over loud music in order to talk to girls. I met them at the studio, at radio stations, or in the corporate arena. I liked it better that way—it gave me more control and a feeling of safety. Female singers and musicians were always at the studio. During those years I went out with and slept with dozens of women: lawyers, bankers, doctors, waitresses, corporate professionals, receptionists, secretaries, record company executives, and promotional people. Talented, attractive women constantly surrounded me, and I took full advantage of it, especially when my unacknowledged angst would shift me from a point of uneasiness to the brink of insanity.

Internally I always created an excuse—no matter how slight—to stop seeing any one woman. It may have been the way she dressed, talked, held her silverware, did her hair—the smallest thing would give me an excuse to make my exit. The bottom line was that even if a woman submitted to my manipulation, there was no future in the relationship because it reminded me of being conned by John. The woman was now damaged goods, just like I was from the many sexual attacks I had suffered. I always wanted to believe it was that I just hadn't found the right woman yet. But it was me who was not right inside.

I'd date three or four women at a time and by the fifth or sixth date tell them, "Look, my business is starting to slip. I can't let that happen, so we'll have to slow down." Inevitably it would be over in a week or so. I could not and did not want commitment. This awareness always brought on the "there is something terribly wrong with me" feeling again.

There I was, twenty-one years after my molestation and sexual abuse and still in a quandary about being in a relationship or just *trusting* a woman. I was becoming increasingly conscious that I didn't know how to be in a relationship. No matter what, I just couldn't fall in love or allow myself to let go with a woman, and so I was unable to let anyone get close to me in an intimate way. To do that I'd have to let my defenses down. That, however, would leave me extremely vulnerable, just like when I was a child, with no control.

I thought about the abusive sexual attacks almost daily but never connected it to my personal life or my sexual acting out. As I've now learned in recovery, it is not unusual to suppress and even deny the conscious connection between fear of intimacy and sexual abuse.

Even my friendships—or lack thereof—seemed affected. I never cultivated friendships outside of my business world because I was unable to get personal with anyone. Making friends through my business was safe because I could control the depth of the conversations and what I would have to reveal about myself. I had about five or six men in my life whom I considered friends, but I learned in recovery that they were merely good acquaintances.

And women…I could never be friends with a woman. Women were in my world for only one thing—and it wasn't something I was proud of.

I was always afraid of anyone knowing me, the real me, the *me* who had been sexually abused, damaged, and raped, the me who truly felt he had no value. I would bet the ranch that all the men I knew thought of me as an independent man who conquered many obstacles in the business world, feats most in my circle thought difficult to accomplish. How could I ever share my worst nightmare with them? I knew I never could speak a word about the atrocities that had occurred in 1959. I felt ashamed about what had happened to me and thought it had made me very weak as a man.

In 1980, disco music was driving the national charts. It seemed like every other national hit was coming from my studio. By that time, at age twenty-eight, I had developed a well-rehearsed exit strategy to use on women, which was useful since they were getting older and were much more emotionally developed than I was.

That same year I pursued a much-younger woman, a girl of just eighteen. Today, in recovery, I have learned that in my fragile and desperate condition I had envisioned she was undamaged and virtuous and could give me back what I had lost—innocence and purity. Of course this was a deluded thought because I could not emotionally or intimately commit to *any* woman regardless of her age. She was not to be my savior, and I moved on as I had so many times before—alone and isolated.

Financially I was doing extremely well, and I started to help my parents economically in their support of my brothers and sisters, which I didn't know or understand at the time was also *enabling* them. I was gradually becoming the primary caretaker of my grown, adult brothers and sisters, and not just with money but with time as well. If something was wrong, I was determined to fix it no matter what the toll or damage to me was. Some of my siblings had problems that fell on my parents, and I would immediately step in and take it from them despite the anxiety and depression that becoming overly involved in their lives caused me.

I remember when my younger sister needed critical dental care at the age of 19. I found the best orthodontist in the city and arranged, at my own expense, to have her promptly treated.

Additionally, my youngest brother, sixteen years my junior, was misbehaving in school, answering back to my parents, and having trouble socially with his peers. With my parents' encouragement I sought out an academy that I thought could give him the structure he needed.

Another sibling fell hundreds of thousands of dollars into debt, guaranteed by my dad, on a failed business venture. Seeing the dismay on my father's face sent me back to my own memories of abuse, and knowing that the battle royale was about to begin between the two of them, I just went to the bank and, without any specific plan of repayment, took over the debt. This caretaking behavior, I later learned in recovery, was my primary role in the family.

Around that time, I remember, a scruffy, homeless man was always hanging out at the steak shop just a couple of hundred feet from the studios. He wouldn't talk to anyone or let anybody even buy him a cup of coffee. One day I attempted to break the ice with him, and as I looked into this man's weary face I could clearly see and feel his pain. I knew something was strange, that I could feel his pain; how was that possible? I had never slept in the street nor picked food from a garbage can.

Within a day or two "Tom" told me his name and allowed me to buy him fast-food lunches; he also let me give him money for clothes and motel rooms during the winters for the next couple of years. Looking into my eyes, he must have trusted me enough to allow me to help him. Today, looking back, I think what I saw in his face was my own pain. I wondered if he saw in me what I couldn't see in myself.

Love

Chapter 7

Jane

I was almost twenty-nine, and my business had grown considerably. I now had twenty employees and corporate debt of approximately $1 million. My life was either consumed by work or riddled with encounters with women I showed respect to but clearly manipulated or controlled and with whom I would not enter into serious emotional relationships.

On Friday nights, a couple of my business associates would bring beer, wine, and hard liquor to the studios. While I was running recording sessions upstairs, there would be full-blown parties downstairs. Such smaller crowds were fine as long as *I* was in control of everything. In these scenarios I was the one who decided who came and who didn't, what happened, and where it happened.

I was becoming more and more compulsive when it came to my work. If necessary, I'd work nineteen to twenty hours a day, seven days a week. Not being able to take care of myself at age seven, I became a caretaker to everyone else who needed help. At all costs, it seemed, I needed to prove that I was *not* a damaged person and could be like I perceived everyone else: normal. Working so much earned me a significant amount of money and gave me the ability to help people financially, which I could keep in my arena of total control.

My love for tennis continued to grow, and it was the only

activity I did outside of working. There were a half dozen outside courts a few minutes from the studios. Unfortunately, none of the people with whom I associated enjoyed tennis, so one Saturday afternoon I drove down to the lakeside courts to see if I could find someone to hit with.

That trip to the tennis courts would be the first step toward my salvation and to surrendering and accepting what had happened to me in 1959. It would put me on a path to learning how to live and to take back my life, which had been ripped away from me as a child. The next step wouldn't come for twenty-seven years!

While most of the tennis courts were filled, I noticed one in the middle where there were only three players—two men on one side playing against a woman on the other side. Naturally, I asked the woman—who was very attractive—if I could hit with her. Being kind, she let me on the court, and within minutes we were playing doubles.

As the game continued, it became obvious that one of the fellows on the opposing side was her boyfriend—all the more reason for me to want to win the set, which we did. I did have a competitive streak further motivated by being in a position to impress a beautiful woman. All three were really nice people, but I thought the woman was striking, and it really didn't bother me that she had a boyfriend. I would simply go into my normal drill and make eye contact. I quickly learned she was different than most of the girls I had previously met. She wouldn't hold my gaze; she seemed very sure of herself. This was my introduction to Jane.

Jane was pretty—about five foot two, petite build, long, brown hair, beautiful legs, and gorgeous, penetrating eyes. She was nearly five years younger than I was, but, as I was soon to discover, far more emotionally mature. For as much as I was attracted to her, my sixth sense was not ringing off the hook. While I could always appreciate feminine beauty, I made movements toward only those women who gave me the feeling they were at my emotional level, which would usually lead to a noncommittal sexual encounter. Jane did not give off that signal at all. Situations like this were always dilemmas for me. Why waste time on a woman who wasn't going to be just a bed partner? I had no time in my life or an understanding of the capacity to love. If she wanted a commitment, what was the point of pursuing her? Jane, like a few other attractive women I had met, appeared to me to be a dead end. I decided to pursue her nonetheless; I don't know why, but I believe it was because I thought she was someone good, someone wholesome.

After a couple of tennis outings she invited me to her home for dinner. This was not part of my usual routine. I didn't do the "come and meet the family" scene. I'd usually take a woman out to dinner, but pizza with her parents and her sisters was something out of my control, and I avoided anything of that nature.

I also didn't do the "let's just be friends and play tennis together" thing. But I liked her—I really did. My mind was somehow tricked into enjoying the time I spent with her. She was a completely normal woman; *I* was the one who was damaged. A normal man would have found this little courtship to be perfectly natural, but I was not an emotionally or psychologically normal man.

I reluctantly accepted her invitation and dreaded it every minute I prepared for it. What a lovely scene I encountered when I finally convinced myself not to turn around and head back to my car but to be strong enough to knock on her door. As I walked toward the kitchen, I could hear a mandolin being played; Jane and her sisters—five altogether pleasant, kind, and pretty women—were gathered around their father and singing as their mother pulled homemade pizzas from the oven.

I was immediately awestruck by their family closeness and happiness. In some ways Jane's family reminded me of mine, except for a few major areas. One was that there wasn't much arguing, and most of the stories told at dinner were of family fun and time spent together, particularly with their parents at various gymnastic meets throughout the United States. I later learned her father had been a member of the 1948 USA Olympic gymnastics team, and he stayed involved with the sport his entire life. I felt as if I were sitting in the middle of Disney World—you know, the happiest place on earth.

I was always polite, but it was like a group meeting that was too large and over which I had no control; I felt uncomfortable in my own skin. Something always kept me from being 100-percent engaged. Even though it seemed safe, I felt completely out of my element.

Nevertheless, from that evening forward, Jane and I started to date seriously. I would attend many affairs at Jane's and started to take her to many of my family's events as well.

But after three or four months went by, once again I was starting to notice the "break it off" feeling emerging because I could never fully emotionally commit to any woman. It was time for me to make my exit.

There was no doubt that Jane had every quality that would make her a wonderful wife, supporter, confidant, and best friend. I also started to think that she and the life that surrounded her could possibly take me off my twenty-two-year roller-coaster ride. Still, with month four approaching, I was going to break off the friendship and our courtship because, as always, something just wasn't right.

So much of what Jane and I had together was similar to the time I had had with Betsy right out of high school. It was the first—and only—time I had come close to any sort of relationship. I thought that with Jane, unlike with Betsy, I might actually have been closing the gap that had existed for me between sex and love. I didn't know if I could sincerely say that I loved Jane at that time. I certainly *liked* her immensely, but if I was falling in love, it was with the *idea* of Jane. I had come to idealize her and her family. They were just so perfect…or so it seemed to me at that time. The contradiction was that I never felt as though I were deserving of such perfection. That familiar panic was setting in, and I needed to flee.

Jane, however, was different from all of the others and would not let me go away so easily. I rehearsed my exit strategy for a Sunday in December 1980. I had it all figured out. We were getting too serious, and I wasn't ready to devote my life to a full-time commitment. My business had to be my first priority. I rattled off excuses like these in my sleep. It was as if I knew I couldn't let my defenses down because if I did, it would eventually lead to an unimaginable hurt like I had experienced as a child. The flashbacks of betrayal and sexual abuse beyond anyone else's comprehension were not something I was willing to risk going through again. No matter how nice a woman was, the idea of trusting her or letting her get close to me led only to feelings of devastation and loss.

As the day of the breakup approached, I called her and ran through my usual speech. Although she was quite upset, she said, "Well, I want to drop off a gift I bought for the baby." There was a christening that day in my family, and she had already bought a present.

I remember it as though it were yesterday. Her father was a good man, but at times he could be difficult with his daughters, so he wouldn't let her use his car. She had to take public transportation, and since it was Sunday, it took her a couple of hours to reach my apartment. At that time there were no cell phones, and I didn't dare call her house since I was sure that she had left distraught and that her mother was probably upset as well.

By the time she arrived almost two hours later, I was worried sick that something had happened to her and it was my fault because I had broken up with her and had not picked her up for the christening. When she finally rang the doorbell, I was so relieved that when I opened the door and saw her I blurted out, "We might as well get married!"

I cared for Jane very much. Although my future father-in-law would become a positive force in my life and leave an indelible impression on me, I came to discover he was also at times mentally and emotionally abusive toward his wife and daughters. I could not have Jane continue to be subjected to this type of behavior. I felt the need to protect her for the rest of her life. It was exactly how I felt about my own siblings, including my younger brother, who used to get picked on when he was a child. I was a living dichotomy of feelings and traits.

I was an *addict* once thrust into a perpetual addictive cycle by any stressful situation. I needed some form of sexual release, with complete control in the encounter and no emotional attachment.

I was also the *rescuer*—one who could not stand to see another person victimized. Seeing someone mistreated brought up intolerable feelings, and I would do whatever it took to stop them from surfacing. Here were two polar-opposite stances I took, yet the same thing caused both: the sexual attacks I had suffered.

One might think that this is hypocritical. From what I've learned in recovery, this behavior is the cycle of abuse, vacillating between victim and victimizer. Somehow I justified in my mind that I was not a horrible man to these women. I wasn't nasty or rude; I never, ever forced them to do anything they didn't want to do; and when we were in public—and even in private—I always treated them with the deepest respect. At most I thought that my crime, in their eyes, was merely that I wouldn't settle down. For the majority it wasn't a problem; I came as advertised. I did not promise anything I had no intention of delivering. I'd smile, extend my hand in friendship, and then move along. But never, ever, ever would I act abusive or disrespectful.

Jane's response to my impulsive exclamation was, "Are you asking?"

I replied, "Yes," and the deed was done. Everything else felt right, except for the problem I had carried for over two decades. I figured she was so clear in her thinking and so devoid of baggage that maybe, just maybe, she could finally figure out the piece of my personality that always left me hollow, nervous, and even, at times, terrified. For her part she found a person driven to succeed, generous to a fault, and surrounded by a family she thought was a bit gregarious but much like hers. She would later learn in the next couple of years that our family dynamics were extremely different.

Although my family moved to the suburbs, some relationships that my parents began in my former neighborhood lasted a lifetime. Interestingly enough, Jane's family lived a couple of blocks from our home in the old neighborhood, and our parents were friendly. As Jane was one of five girls and I was one of four boys, our parents used to joke, "Wouldn't it be something if two of our children would marry?"

I believe both my mother and future mother-in-law—who became like a second mother to me—thought that the idea would never happen since we had moved to the suburbs when I was ten. What were the odds that I would meet Jane nineteen years later on a tennis court, around the corner from where we had both grown up?

I think the three or four guys I was hanging out with regularly were so taken aback when I announced my marriage that one of them, "Ryan," took action as well—he got married the week before I did! I found out only when I called Ryan for a recording session and his mother informed me that he was at the church getting married. While I'm sure he loved his wife and probably had musings of marriage before my announcement, I felt that he thought the partying and games were over since I had always led the way for our good times, dinner outings, frivolous behavior, travel, and all other sorts of disconnected behavior. I'm guessing that he thought that he might as well get married too.

Ironically, today, thirty-plus years later, we're both in recovery. Ryan's was a different trauma, but he was the only friend from my circle who really understood the difficult journey I started in 2007.

Although I hadn't planned to ask Jane to marry me, having lived such an insane existence for so long, I felt that Jane represented a sense of organization and calm that could ground me and provide me with some roots I had never experienced. What a terrific mom, wife, and friend I knew she would make! Naturally, I would take care of and protect her for the rest of her life. We had come from generations that believed that with enough love, partners had the power to fix each other.

Since we made the decision to marry, Jane and I thought we should do it sooner rather than later. We were married ninety days from the day of our engagement—engaged December 7, 1980 and married March 7, 1981, which was quite a feat since over 500 people attended the service and reception. I worked eighteen-hour days at the studio and record company while doing whatever I could to help Jane with the wedding details.

Jane still is an extremely kind, intuitive woman. We were out one night, and after a nice dinner some two weeks before our wedding day, she stopped and looked me straight in the face and asked, "You are eventually going to let your defenses down, aren't you?" This statement hit the very core of my soul. Jane saw something was wrong with me, something I had been hiding from for over twenty years. At that point she was the first person to get close enough to identify that I had built up walls to protect myself emotionally against something even I didn't understand.

I answered immediately, "What defenses?" Up to that point I had been a constantly moving target no one could ever catch or hit. Jane, I hoped and thought, would stop me from running, but when she made this statement it frightened me to think that someone could see something I couldn't. I could care for and do anything for her, but I could *never* let anybody get close and care for *me*.

One day, early in our marriage, I came home after work and saw that Jane was very upset. She had just had an argument with her father, which left her in tears. I immediately called him. I defended Jane and said it was unbelievable to me that he could get his daughter so upset. I let him know that I was extremely unhappy because whatever he had said to her had brought her to tears. Jane's father knew I was very upset; I heard it in his silence. I ended the call by saying it was usually the father-in-law calling the son-in-law to tell him not to upset his daughter and not the other way around.

While they might have had some other toe-to-toes after my call, he never again did it around me. I think he was embarrassed it was *me* who defended his daughter against *him*. But again my reaction to abuse of any kind was not that of a normal person. It was as if, when I did this, I was fighting back against John and Jimmy, something I hadn't been able to do when I was a child.

Jane was right—I had built a wall of defenses around myself that no one could penetrate, so they could not touch me emotionally. Yet I think we both thought maybe Jane could reach the deep part of my soul that had been buried and blackened for so very long. Decades later, after I entered recovery, she admitted to me that she had thought she would be able to change me and show me why I should let those walls down. We just didn't know that the only person who can change a sexually abused child was the child himself or herself with the support and help of intense therapy and a definitive recovery program.

I recall a seemingly innocent event that occurred some six months into our marriage that put me in such a terror I had a panic attack. A circus was in town, and naturally, since Jane knew how to live life to the fullest, she bought tickets. I was thirty but had never before been to a circus or concert.

As we pulled into the parking lot, my body began to tense up, and I grew extremely nervous. We found a place to park and began walking to the stadium entrance several hundred yards away. After about fifty yards, I became very agitated, and Jane took one look at my face and could see something was terribly wrong with me.

Jane kindly asked if I wanted to leave, and I immediately replied "yes." There were just too many people, and I felt myself losing control. As we pulled away, I felt a cold sweat on my forehead.

I knew this couldn't have made me much fun to be married to, but for Jane this was only the start of things far more severe than not being able to take her new husband to the circus. If the problems of living with me began and ended with nothing worse than a fear of crowds, she would have gladly taken that over what she was going to have to live with over the next twenty-six years.

Chapter 8

Cerberus—Two Lives

Jane was one of five children, and I was one of six, so we talked about having three or four children of our own. In my mind I built a beautiful house surrounded by a white-picket fence, a house in which we were going to live happily ever after, just as on *Ozzie and Harriet*, *The Brady Bunch*, and *The Cosby Show*.

While Jane never knew it, I loved the way she enjoyed life, but I remained in a shell. I always felt out of my skin except when it came to my business; that was where I always had complete, total control. Conducting one-on-one meetings or with a small group of people in a quiet conference room or in the studio, I was the master of my own universe, and I thrived in it.

In contrast, socializing in large groups and even small groups of couples made me uncomfortable. I was even nervous at my own wedding—and not for all the reasons most grooms are nervous—and I failed to take pleasure in this magnificent event that over 500 others enjoyed.

Jane and I were astonished when we discovered that we could not conceive a child. There we were, two of eleven siblings and unable to get pregnant. Jane had scar tissue on her ovaries from a childhood illness, and doctors advised me that my semen count at that time was so low I probably couldn't have impregnated any woman. Ironically, one doctor asked me if I was under any stress or nervous about anything in particular. Of course I said "no."

The Italian culture is one in which male reproduction is all-important, so the tension from the inability to reproduce was like a bomb ready to explode inside me at any time. I couldn't feel anything else once that anxiety set in; it overtook and consumed me. With this, a familiar disquietude started to take over, and before I knew it I started acting out to relieve the built-up nervousness, anxiety, and misery. It seemed that without this process—the chase, the capture, the control, and the release—I was incapable of handling these overriding emotions, of feeling any emotional connection to life and happiness.

The more I loved Jane and took care of her, the further a romantic relationship slipped away, making it increasingly impossible to have sexual intimacy, because my brain understood that sex happened only in a detached relationship. My separate life became one of its own. I had Jane, who I loved as much as I was capable of loving anyone, yet once I would be thrust into a state of anxiety by a stressful situation, panic-related angst would take total control of me. It was as if I were living two lives.

Again, just as had been the case for the twenty-two years before I met Jane, I could not uncover what was transpiring. I asked myself, *What is wrong with me?* Here was a beautiful woman, my biggest supporter and fan, yet I could not totally connect with or trust her emotionally. In recovery, I learned I had no depth of understanding of the effects of the abuse and, at that time, no desire actually to search for reasons, so I would have found it unimaginable and frightening to deal with such high levels of anxiety. I prayed that we would have children. This, I thought, would get me moving in the right direction; Jane would take care of the children, and I could bury myself in my work and then faithfully come home to her each night.

I was living multiple existences. My business ventures had tripled by that time, as I was operating a publishing company and a record company along with the recording studios. I now had thirty employees and was servicing almost $2 million in debt. In my personal life I attempted to play the husband, but I was gradually failing. Last, there was the sex addiction and multiple other dependencies to quiet my system when my nerves felt like they were going to implode inside of me.

Sexually I was what some women had called "passionate," but that was never the right word. Some mistook my aggression for passion. I remember quite a few women saying, "God, it seemed like you were having a heart attack or something." No, that wasn't because I was wheezing and in pain—I was much younger then and in fine shape. What they noticed was that for me sex was a complete and utter physical release from all of my anxiety and stress, like alcohol would be for an alcoholic. I was never a passive partner. As I write this, I stop myself from using the word *lover* because love had nothing to do with it. I was *not* a lover; I was releasing demons that had been living in my heart, mind, and soul since 1959.

My disconnection should have tipped me off to the fact that I had a really serious problem. Sex for me was rather conventional with one exception—to a certain degree I continually mimicked what John and Jimmy had done to me. I would ultimately have every woman in the position my perpetrators had had me: facing away so that I couldn't see their faces, so that they ceased for that moment to be individual people with feelings and personalities.

I also insisted on assuming a superior position as John and Jimmy had done to me, to compensate for my natural reluctance to perform the act. If I had sex a thousand times, it always included those two positions, those two acts done in exactly the ways they were done to me. In every situation I had to be in control, and this was particularly true during sex. Although I had buried the abuse, it was controlling me every day and in every way, and I didn't even know it. In an effort to deny that, to keep that away from my consciousness, I was making desperate attempts at trying to control everything else.

I knew plenty of men who went to strip clubs, but when my anxiety set in I needed to repeat what my perpetrators had done to me. Other avenues of promiscuity didn't satisfy my desperate need to release the fear, compulsion, and tension from my body.

We all know people who fantasize during sex, but unlike most individuals who probably tend to fantasize about new and different people or some famous beauty queen, I would fantasize that sex included real love to try to compensate for the hole in my identity. I lost myself in this dream with whomever I happened to be with, even if it was some woman whose name I'd fail to remember the moment we were finished. I'd pretend that this was my wife, my soul mate, and that as soon as we were finished our lovemaking we would go off and have an idyllic, *Ozzie and Harriet* life together.

But the moment the sex was over I would crash. I didn't love this person; I didn't want to have a lifelong union with her. I didn't even want her to touch me afterward. I fantasized about being normal because I wasn't.

The problem with Jane and me was that, again, I did not *make love*. Afterward, like any wife, she would want to hug me, hold me, kiss me, and love me. But I still needed to pull away. Perhaps I withdrew a little less with her than I had with other women, but I still pulled away, and what wife can find happiness with that?

Another perplexing characteristic from my perspective was that when I was having sex, I felt no love for the woman I was with because I didn't understand love. My introduction to sex had no connection to love or intimacy. That meant to me that *before* I had sex with Jane, I loved her. When we were finished, my love for her returned. But during sex? I wasn't expressing love at all. Women were just inanimate vessels I was having sexual encounters with to escape from my insanity. That's a terrible thing to say, but it was the truth. Love and sex were two different worlds for me. How could I perform the acts that John and Jimmy had performed on me and connect them to love?

Sadly enough, I wanted to commit to loving Jane, but the more I wanted to love her, the more I had difficulty having sexual relations with her. Sex and love became more and more separate in my own mind and my physical life decade upon decade. The introduction of other women into my life separated love and sex for me even more, and Jane was the victim of all of this.

From the moment we met, I had been an incredibly busy, hard-working individual. Now I had the responsibility of trying to be a good provider for the children we planned to have. My being up and out of the house sixteen to eighteen hours a day raised no eyebrows—I had always operated that way ever since she knew me. I still met women the same way I always had, and I still had the radar to identify the most injured souls. Strangely enough, when they asked, I wouldn't lie—I told them I was married. I did what I had to in order to stop the feelings of trauma from returning, feelings I hadn't even consciously experienced during my multiple sexual attacks.

By that time I had become a respected leader in Jane's family. I had already been handling the dysfunctional aspects of my own family for years, which included everything from financial to social problems. I worked hard and was trying to make something of myself. The same could not always be said about some of my siblings. I learned in therapy that this was not their fault; it was the structure my parents had set in motion from our childhoods. I unfortunately failed to realize that helping everyone else was turning into an everyday situation. In reality, I couldn't sit still long enough to realize how these events or any of the other dysfunctional activities in my life were affecting me.

As I learned in recovery, I couldn't sit still because if I did, I would be reminded of the abuse, and that still was much more painful than dealing with all of the dysfunction. It was eating into my own personal and family lives to extremely dangerous levels. Solving crises by rescuing others was the only way I could feel any sense of worth. In my mind, no one would love me if they knew I was such an abused and damaged person.

In recovery I would learn about how family systems function. I had no idea that so many different family schemes exist. I thought most families operated like mine. I would also be guided to learn and investigate my family of origin as well as the origin of my parents' families' and their families' systems. By completing this process I would see why and how my immediate family system functioned; I was told it would be like looking at a blueprint of a building built over three generations.

For one example, prescription drug addiction was handed down from my grandmother to my mother and then to me. While I understand what trauma caused me to abuse prescription drugs and possibly my mother's reason, I don't know why my grandmother had the same problem. I learned in recovery that unless someone in the family steps up and says, "Something's wrong here," the dysfunction and trauma will just continue generation after generation after generation.

Another glowing example learned during this process was that the spouse who was most wounded would more than likely gain control of the family and pass on the same dysfunction from the generation before them.

After studying my parents' families of origin, and from what my mother shared with me, it was clear that between my parents, my mom was the most injured by experiencing her father's abuse. She had been so frightened and harmed by this abuse that she was determined that nothing would happen to her children. Unfortunately this fear would prove to be a detriment in raising her children because this fear enabled most of my siblings, especially my sisters. Her only intent was to protect her children like a mother lion protects her cubs. Sadly, this was the start of decades of our family's living and operating in a very gray and unrealistic world.

I also learned that everyone in the family would play roles and that the parents—either consciously or subconsciously—had much to say about which child would play what role. It was clear that they had given me the role of caretaker, and that wasn't hard for me to accept since I came to feel that role gave me value as a human being, unbeknownst to my parents.

On my eighth birthday, some six months after the abuse had stopped, my mother was preparing my favorite dessert—vanilla ice cream with chocolate syrup. As she reached into the cabinet for the bottle of syrup, it dropped and broke. My body immediately recoiled, and I was in a complete state of frenzy and panic, worried about what kind of outburst was going to come from Mom. I jumped up and retrieved the towels and went to the floor and told her not to worry, I didn't want it anyway.

Lately, in recovery, I learned that this was the beginning of my caretaking, and it began with my mom. Not only did I sense that she needed support and help to get through this episode, but I also felt that if I didn't take care of the situation, *I* wouldn't be able to handle Mom's outburst as it would trigger memories of Jimmy's frightening outbursts.

Based on what I learned in therapy nearly fifty years later about my family's origin of dysfunction and dissociation, and recalling this incident with my mother, I became determined not to pass this legacy of disorder on to my sons. While it was astounding to uncover the reality of my family system, I would be unbelievably shocked to discover that Jane's family, who I thought was perfect, had its own fissures and problems, albeit not near the level of my own family.

In the midst of juggling the stress of my work and new responsibilities of family, I was having yet another personal crisis: I was having an affair with a married woman. Not just any married woman, but a woman I had dated six years before I married Jane.

At that time, "Elizabeth" was nineteen and I was twenty-four. Seven years later, our paths crossed again in the business world, and we picked up where we had left off. Both of us being married didn't present a deterrent. After a short time, I discovered she was also sleeping with another man—not her husband. I could handle her being married and having sex with her husband, but not with anyone else except me. Sleeping with anyone else was a betrayal to me. For as much as I was a completely unfaithful boyfriend and husband, I could never have the tables turned on me. I became filled past the point of capacity with the primary emotion I felt when I had been abused at age seven: betrayal.

Back then I felt betrayed by the trust I had put in John and Jimmy. I felt betrayed by whomever or whatever could possibly be blamed for not having protected me from their torturous attacks—my parents, their parents, other people in the neighborhood, God, whomever.

This betrayal made me an emotional wreck. I later learned in recovery that episodes like these made me retreat into the mindset of a seven-year-old. When it came to sex, love, passion, and emotion, my self-growth had ended the moment I was attacked as a child. I felt devastated by this woman, just like in 1959 when I had been physically violated.

How selfish of me! But seven-year-olds are selfish. Some of the first signs of maturity are the abilities to let things go, to share, to be a fair-minded person, and to lose gracefully. But as much as I could do these things in business, I found it impossible when it came to relationships with women. This woman had taken away my control! What Elizabeth established was that she was in charge of our relationship and that she was out of my control.

This all made sense to me once I entered recovery, especially after remembering Elizabeth's disclosure to me, when she was nineteen, that she had been sexually molested from about age eleven to thirteen by older neighborhood boys; she must have been experiencing all of the control issues that were ruling me on a daily basis. I can't think of anything more devastating than a sexually abused boy and a sexually abused girl meeting in adulthood, both seeking from life the same things that were totally out of their grasp. Since entering recovery, I keep Elizabeth in my morning prayers, hoping that she found the salvation I am searching for.

At the center of my being I had no self-worth. Yes, there are a lot of selfish, egotistical people in the world, but my turn on this classic character flaw had a direct link to the extraordinarily severe sexual abuse that had been inflicted on me. The entire episode with Elizabeth provided me a rare moment of clarity, one I wish I could have built upon. Instead, my self-loathing grew and my waist size plummeted. I was near suicidal despite all that I had in the world for which to be grateful.

Addiction crosses all cultural, racial, and financial barriers. Some people with addictions have it all, and we are left to wonder why they do the things they do. We look at clinical depression the same way and try to apply "normal person" logic to it, and we come up short as we look for answers. Things like this are not, on the surface, logical.

Elizabeth's betrayal suddenly consumed my entire being in every way. I would weigh myself every day and watch the pounds disappear. I stopped eating and lost forty-six pounds; it was impossible for Jane and both of our families not to notice. Anorexia nervosa can have many causes, and stress and post-traumatic stress from my molestations occasionally brought it on.

But I couldn't really link it all up by myself at the time. I put it all on this woman who had cheated on me. On the other hand I was having trouble coming up with a plausible explanation for Jane and the rest of my family. I couldn't tell them about the affair—I didn't want to lose Jane. Despite what I was doing to our marriage, I wanted it all—I wanted a wife like Jane to come home to, and I still needed to act out sexually with other women because of the extreme, oppressive anxiety from which I suffered. I took pride in being a husband, in having Jane on my arm. It made me feel and appear more normal to the world, and other people's opinions of me in that manner meant a lot. I wanted everyone around me to love me for playing this role and playing it well. I couldn't give that up.

But I had to say *something* to Jane. All along—since you don't just lose forty-six pounds for no reason—I had been using all the typical excuses, such as, "Work is really stressful," but the longer things spiraled downward with my loss of sleep, loss of weight, and loss of ability to pay attention, the less Jane was buying into it. I had to come up with something else because people were asking questions. I can remember sitting in my mom's kitchen and her peering at me with such anguish. I wonder now if she was trying to get me to talk about the abuse, if she had any inkling whatsoever that that was the cause of my weight loss.

My weight loss had gained so much attention from Jane that I decided to tell her about what had happened to me as a child. It was less about wanting to unburden myself and come clean and more about hiding my sexual infidelities.

At that point I had not really connected the sexual abuse as a child to the feelings of betrayal I was feeling at the time. I just knew I needed to tell Jane something to stop all of the questions. I could think of no other explanation for the loss of weight that would not have been an elaborate lie, one that I would find nearly impossible to maintain. It seemed to work. Jane was comforting but also very clear, as she had always been.

"You need to go talk to somebody about what happened and see if you can be helped," she said. I went along with this concept because I was backed into a corner, but I knew I could immediately take control of any sessions with any therapist.

Jane was the first person, other than my parents, I told about the perpetrations of 1959, but I barely touched on the details and feelings around John's grooming and the perverted acts he inflicted on me, and I never shared a word about Jimmy's horrific attacks. Even twenty-eight years later—and seventeen years after his death in Vietnam—I was still protecting Jimmy because Jane and her family (and my mom) were still friendly and in touch with Jimmy's mother.

I trusted Jane to be discreet, not to mention it to her family. I kept the story brief and told her I didn't want to go into all of the gory details but that it had happened and it was like a recurring nightmare that haunted me from time to time, and that when it did it sometimes manifested itself physically, just as was happening at the time with my loss of appetite.

The idea of going to therapy had its good and bad points. I knew about doctor-patient confidentiality. He couldn't communicate to Jane or anyone else, for that matter, whatever I told him. I said to myself there was no way I was going to tell another man about the vile sexual abuse I'd suffered as a child, much less describe the events in detail. So with the therapist, I switched back to what I viewed as the core issue of my present problem: I was honestly aware of only the relationship between what I was going through and the betrayal by this woman and was not making any connection to the sexual abuse. If the doctor could help me with that, I'd be all right, right?

I can't remember how I ended up with the particular psychiatrist I saw during that time. He was in his early sixties and probably had gotten his degree in psychiatry sometime in the late 1950s. Looking back, this doctor would most likely not have had any real understanding of or experience concerning the sexual abuse of boys; today's methods and therapies are nothing like the typical protocol at that time, especially for male survivors. Boys were considered only perpetrators, not victims. Research wouldn't come out until the mid- to late 1980s that boys suffered from sexual abuse and sexual molestation just as girls did.

In the few therapy sessions I had, I danced around telling the doctor even what little I had told Jane because I directed the sessions by discussing my feelings for Jane and this other woman. I'd say, "This isn't about Jane. I love her. This is about sexual betrayal by a woman I took care of." With all of my human relationships at the time, I thought of them only in those terms—I took care of people.

Eventually I began eating once again, even though the doctor had solved nothing. My own resilience and self-preservation helped me live through this torrid episode. Some victims of childhood sexual abuse commit suicide or try to hurt themselves, but I was left instead with an all-consuming and uncontrollable addiction. My compulsion gave me something to exist for—I lived to fulfill it and feed it. I was told in recovery that without my addiction I would have, more than likely, done severe harm to myself. In the end I would forget this woman and I would live to feed *The Beast* and act out on my compulsive anxiety disorder once again. Dr. Alice Miller describes this behavior in her book *Thou Shalt Not Be Aware: Society's Betrayal of the Child* as "how we go to any lengths to avoid seeing and having to live with the unbelievable truth."

Chapter 9
Paul and Luke

One day, when Jane and I were driving in the city, she asked me if I would consider adoption. At first the thought of adopting a baby made me nervous; it would be something completely out of my control. After talking it through, however, I told Jane I was all for it. What good fortune to be able to provide a child a wonderful, loving mother like Jane, a fine neighborhood to grow up in, and every opportunity possible—far greater opportunities than Jane or I had had growing up.

Once the word got out that Jane and I were hoping to adopt a child, one of her aunts introduced us to a situation that brought us our first son. I believe God intervened in a very loving way, and soon after we became adoptive parents of Paul.

I prayed continuously for Paul and Paul's birth mother and that, in addition to her physical well-being, she would be okay emotionally with the adoption and was doing it for Paul's welfare. These things do have the potential to go awry at the last minute, which would have devastated us. But everything turned out perfectly—the birth mother came through it fine, the baby was healthy, and there was no last-second change of heart.

I recall Paul, at two days old, being laid in Jane's arms; she started to quiver and tear up, and I did my best to hold her close and hide the emotion welling inside me. What a beautiful baby boy! Paul was a healthy, content, and quiet baby. Somehow I could tell he would turn out to be one of the most loving children God has ever created. I never loved anyone in my life the way I loved Paul. While I knew becoming a father would change my life dramatically, I also felt Paul's birth gave me a glimmer of hope to grab on to, a shining light in my dark and confusing world. Jane and I were ecstatic.

I was not prepared for my increased responsibility for my extended family, as I was becoming a second father to my brothers and sisters at the same time I was beginning a family with Jane. Whatever problem occurred in my extended family, I would do my best to stop the pain. I was taking on too much at once. Work was as busy as ever, and Jane and Paul needed my undivided attention.

The growing responsibilities and worry about my role as supporter of two families began to overwhelm me, and my anxiety grew exponentially. Within months of Paul's birth, in the midst of traveling for business, the emotional burden and stress caught up to me, and I acted out once again. This left me more troubled than usual. The guilt and shame always washed over me immediately upon release of the stress, but now I was not only married but had a son who depended on me as a father. I knew it was morally wrong, but the severe strength of the anxiety and compulsive disorder drove me to the extent that it seemed like I was being taken over by another person. I considered myself a good father, but I still had this part of me I could not control. What was wrong with me?

Perhaps the answer lay in the Bible. I started to pray to God. Maybe if I got closer to God He would guide me from my duality, stop me, and help me understand my self-destructive behavior and actions. I made so many contracts with God; I used to pray, "God, I do ninety percent good—it's just this ten percent bad, so when I meet you, please don't forget the ninety percent good!"

For the next nine months I read the Bible, and at times it

helped. Yet as soon as stress crept into my life, I was acting out once again. While it seemed to me then that I was merely giving in to temptations of the flesh, what was really overwhelming me was the buried sexual trauma rising up with my soaring anxiety. Because even if my love for God, my wife, or my new son was bigger than my fear of reliving the memories of the rapes that controlled me, I did not consciously know what I was up against at the time. Now, even as a father, I would give into the cycle once again, as always set off by the anxiety of any stressful situation.

Since I needed to believe that I was in control of my acting out, I would tell myself that my behavior never upset anything at home. The essence of my survival was control—even controlling my uncontrollable urges, which was a virtual impossibility not known to me at that time.

Jane knew I was never fully emotionally connected, but I don't believe she ever thought it was specifically due to another woman or women, because my behavior hadn't changed from the day she had met me. I was how I was—emotionally unavailable. Had we had a longer courtship, she may have had a more intimate knowledge of what she was getting herself into, and perhaps that might have scared her off—but then again, while she knew I had my defenses up, she never dug deep to find out why. Jane wasn't the first woman to marry someone with the hope of changing him. It rarely works.

It was around that time, nine months after adopting Paul, that we received a call about the possibility of adopting a second child. We had twenty-four hours to make our decision, which was a no-brainer. We both immediately said, "Yes!" We were holding our second son, Luke, in our arms four months later.

What a beautiful baby—blond hair and blue eyes! He was a real looker, just like his brother Paul, who had olive skin and brown hair. We couldn't have been happier or luckier that God entrusted two of his most precious children to us. I experienced the same type of love when I held Luke in my arms that I had when Paul was born. My biggest joy was when they both could walk and I held their hands, one on my left and one on my right. Although they were just babies, I had an innate feeling that they were holding me up when they were by my sides, which gave me a sense of calmness and safety. While not of my flesh, Paul and Luke would become the very *core* and *foundation* of my heart— and my very salvation. This would truly be proven nineteen years later, as they provided unfailing support and strength as I began to take the first step in my journey to reconstruct my broken and disconnected life.

Jane and I were on cloud nine. These two angels God gave us couldn't have come from a man like me and, at the same time, they couldn't have wished for a better mother than Jane, the quintessential, perfect mom with care and nurturing for them that was second to none. Jane read to the boys daily and sometimes dressed them alike since they were only thirteen months apart. I was so happy that Paul and Luke had Jane for a mother.

As quiet as Paul was, Luke exercised his vocal chords at almost every opportunity. When Luke learned to talk, the first two words he put together were "where's Paul?" The boys were inseparable, and even as they grew, Paul was always there as Luke's big brother, and Luke would become Paul's biggest supporter in all his endeavors. Even today it's beautiful to see the respect, care, and love they have for each other. This was greatly due to Jane, who always knew empirical right from empirical wrong without fudging the in-between and without scars and baggage, who taught them how to live life. I could teach them only how to *survive* life, because that was the only way I knew how to live.

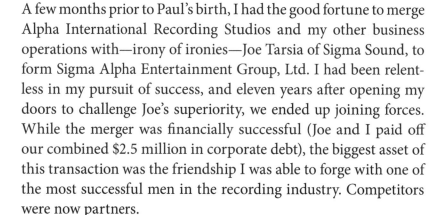

A few months prior to Paul's birth, I had the good fortune to merge Alpha International Recording Studios and my other business operations with—irony of ironies—Joe Tarsia of Sigma Sound, to form Sigma Alpha Entertainment Group, Ltd. I had been relentless in my pursuit of success, and eleven years after opening my doors to challenge Joe's superiority, we ended up joining forces. While the merger was financially successful (Joe and I paid off our combined $2.5 million in corporate debt), the biggest asset of this transaction was the friendship I was able to forge with one of the most successful men in the recording industry. Competitors were now partners.

The merger did not lessen my drive and focus. I now had two children and a wife to support. I pressed even harder, utilizing the tools and skills that had gotten me that far—willpower, single-mindedness, and hard work. Running four companies, from Philadelphia to New York, with fifty employees, put a lot on my plate, but it still wasn't enough.

When an opportunity came to open up a restaurant, I jumped at that as well. I would leave the office at 6:00 p.m. to be at the restaurant by 6:30, work another six hours, and arrive home around 1:00 a.m. I continued this backbreaking program for two straight years. It provided me with the perfect shield against the world. I could avoid feeling anything or dealing with the trouble buried inside me. I just didn't know that, based on my sexual abuse trauma, this frenetic pace was the worst thing I could do to myself. It was a vicious cycle. I would bombard myself with business details, paperwork, meetings—anything to busy my mind and keep it off of the true source of my unsettled nature and anxiety.

Of course, the arduous workload failed to quell my angst and served only to add to my stress. This would ignite my cycle to act out with novelty sex to release the unrelenting emotional pressure. It felt as though I were on autopilot. Each time the feelings were the same. Initially, I'd feel like a ton of bricks was lifted off my back. This was always followed by a combination of guilt, shame, and continued self-destructive behavior.

Jane couldn't have been a better wife or supporter of all of my business endeavors. Nevertheless, as time passed, letting my emotional defenses down with her became increasingly difficult. She supported my entrepreneurial spirit, backed my financial risks, and at the same time cared for our home and our sons beautifully. However, Jane wanted intimacy. She wanted me—all of me—and I couldn't give that to her. I felt myself sinking more into despair with each passing year. At that time, I was forty-four, with thirty-seven years of *Why? What's wrong with me?* and *Can I or will I ever be normal?* While I always had this awareness present in my mind, my understanding never went beyond this level.

Once I completed the merger with Joe Tarsia, I went to California to meet with Mitsubishi, the number-one manufacturer of thirty-two-track digital recording equipment. They were rolling out a revolutionary thirty-two-track, one-inch recorder shortly after our merger.

I made the deal myself, in which we received all the thirty-two-track machines for free so Mitsubishi could use our operation as a beta site to test out the equipment and show it off to any studio that wanted to see them in operation. I thought it was an incredible deal, and so did Joe.

In all business situations, I always felt unworthy. There I was, a man with a twelfth-grade education and keeping a secret I had buried since my childhood that made me feel like I didn't deserve to be in such valued transactions. I was partnering with men such as my Saudi investor who had attended Oxford, and Vladimir, the Russian violinist who had played at Carnegie Hall. The talent I brought to the table was my ability to swing from vine to vine like Tarzan in the jungle. I swung into the studio business, and then when I saw another opportunity, I swung into the record business, and then when that got soft, I swung into the publishing business, and so on. I was not like my Russian partner, a virtuoso musician; what I brought with me were clear-eyed people skills and a business acumen I had gotten from the streets of Philadelphia. Also, just as I had never fallen in love with women, I never fell in love with a business or a business holding. To me it was all just a way to make money and stay in control of my life.

I also never wanted any recognition. When the time came to have pictures taken or to give interviews, I'd send one of my VPs in my stead. The attention made me nervous—I had no control over it, and deep down inside I was somehow ashamed of myself because I knew things about myself no one else did. Someone taking my picture was like someone stealing or looking into my soul, and I couldn't bear that. My only concern was whether the checks cleared.

The music business took a hard hit in the 1990s. The Japanese were able to design recording equipment that could be purchased for almost the same amount of cash a producer or musician would spend for a professional recording session. For about $10,000 you could record as many songs as you wanted in the privacy of your own home. This gave me pause and reason to start to look for other business opportunities as I continued to keep the massive infrastructure going that Joe and I had undertaken. I knew it was time to move on, just like I had known earlier in my life when it was time to separate myself from selling encyclopedias and teaching tennis.

By the early '90s, developments in China were exploding. Although I had raised approximately $5 million in equity for the entertainment company, we were still carrying about $1.5 million in new debt created by the merger. While my personal sexual issues felt beyond my control, I could stay singularly focused on significant and complex business issues. When one door began to close, I pushed another one wide open. No matter what I endured, I would never let anything interfere with my business, which ultimately gave me control of supporting my family and helping as many people as I could and allowed me to continue to stay as far away from the helplessness that I had felt as a child.

One of the investors in the entertainment company introduced me to a Chinese nationalist who had a business plan for developing a device that could use the excess bandwidth of a radio station, called the *subcarrier administration* (SCA). This grabbed my attention but not that of my partner, Joe. He knew only the recording industry—and knew it better than almost anyone—and he felt it was too late for him in his career to move into another industry.

I arranged a significant payout to him for us to separate and decided to move on to create a telecom company that would utilize the backend (SCA) of 43,000 existing radio stations throughout the world to send one-way digital voice messages.

While enticing, the proposition forced me into a situation that would be *significantly* out of my control—flying internationally. Prior to this I had flown, but not often and they were business flights only in the United States. While I experienced significant stress during these trips, most of my domestic flights usually maxed out at two to three hours. Despite the anxiety medication I took to fly, by the time I landed I would be in great distress.

Flying to China would be even more challenging and nerve-racking. I was left with no choice: either control my financial destiny or face possible failure. I later learned in recovery that in my mind, losing control of my finances would have meant losing control of my very existence and could have caused a crippling state of depression and anxiety that I may have never survived. Unbeknownst to me at the time, much more was at stake than just my financial future.

Air travel to Asia became one of many paths this new endeavor created. It was estimated the company would need approximately $100 million to get off the ground and to have a decent chance of succeeding, so I needed to go to China. Other than flying, I wouldn't participate in any physical activities in which I might have lost control. I never rode horses or motorcycles, nor did I snow or water ski. I even eschewed friendships because with human relationships comes the variable of give and take, of the other person having a say, of being a wild card, and so that, too, I avoided.

The first few flights were excruciating. Thirteen hours trapped on a plane was the longest time I had spent alone since the attacks of 1959. With the daily hustle and bustle of my work, I didn't have what people now call *me time*—and I liked it and constructed it that way. These trips allowed me time to ponder my entire life and the thoughts that surrounded my sexual abuse. The grooming, the threats, the flashbacks of the attacks all led back to the acts themselves. I had no place to run or hide; by the time I landed I was so stressed my cycle was in full force.

Over the next four years I traveled the world and became reconciled to the fact that if something went wrong with the plane, it would be over in seconds. Every time I boarded, I would leave written instructions with Jane: "In the event of my death…"

Driven to succeed at all costs, I eventually raised the $100 million and was on the brink of delivering a billion-dollar company. This was quite a far cry from the kid from the old neighborhood in Philly who had never gone to college.

I had become a caretaker for my siblings to the point that I was self-destructing; taking their problems on perpetuated my anxiety level. Only recently I learned there's a term for this behavior as well, one I couldn't grasp at the time: *codependency*. I felt my job was to fix everyone's problems and rescue them from whatever dilemmas they had created or in which they found themselves. With this, ultimately, I was meeting my own needs, since I didn't think I was worthy of caring about myself. Thus I was not the classic needy, clingy person, but feeling needed by others gave me a false sense of power, purpose, and self-esteem I desperately needed. But this was being between a rock and a hard place: I needed to feel needed, but those who needed me—my extended family—never knew when to quit, and if I told them to quit, then I'd be stressed out again. Such cycles are self-perpetuating.

On March 4, 1999, The *Philadelphia Business Journal* listed the top twenty-five biggest deals of 1998 in the city of Philadelphia, ranked by value of the transactions. The telecom company I created was listed sixteenth, with an approximate $198-million transaction value; the giant cable company Comcast came in first at about $2.1 billion.

By February 2002 I was being depicted in the *Philadelphia*

Inquirer as one of the highest-paid CEOs in the city: "Fifty years of age, CEO of an approximately $300 Million Market Cap Public Company," wrote one newspaper. Although I had not actually reached a point of total financial independence, I was free from all debt for the first time in my life, and that felt good—really good... but most of all *safe*.

Being well-compensated, I was able to help my siblings, completely renovate our home, and send my parents on a panoptic trip throughout Europe—something they'd always dreamed of—for their fiftieth wedding anniversary. Before that time they had visited only my father's hometown in Italy. They had never been to California either, so I saw to it that they visited there as well.

Despite all these happy events and financial successes, I couldn't bring myself to buy anything just for me. At the time, I had been married for twenty-one years, and the only things I had ever bought for myself were a couple of business suits and a few pairs of shoes. Anything else I received came from Jane. Many times she would say, "Why don't you go buy yourself something?"

I would always answer her with, "I don't need anything. Just take care of you and the boys." I never felt worthy of anything—clothing, vacations, gadgets, or especially any personal happiness.

If I had a nickel for every time Jane said, "Smile, be happy," I'd be a very rich man. She would say it sometimes when we were driving and I was lost in a trancelike state, thinking about anything from a flashback of the sexual abuse to asking God for help and forgiveness. How could I be happy or smile for Jane when I was endlessly worried about something? I never thought of my own wants and needs other than trying to stop acting out, which was ruining my life day by day.

Around April 2002, the telecom sector went through a momentous correction. Wall Street woke up and realized that the telecom industry was overvalued, and the old economy came storming back. The prior economy operated on real revenues and real earnings, not on potential technological devices or spectrums or what new and interesting wireless networks could bring in a new economy. The handwriting went up on the wall practically overnight; billion-dollar companies were labeled overvalued and overrated and rendered basically worthless. With such titans falling, I knew the company I created would soon follow the same path.

When it came to my business survival, I was never one for sticking my head in the sand. I flew to Europe and told the largest block of shareholders the end was near. I presented the facts; they banded together and took the company through Chapter 11 reorganization. While today the business' value is a fraction of what it once was, it is still in existence.

At age fifty, then, I faced another challenge. While my global telecom company was small compared to the major corporations that crashed and burned around that time, its potential for success would have given me financial independence for the rest of my life. I had over 500 employees working in three countries and had more MBAs and PhDs working for the company than I could count—but I knew only how to survive, not how to flourish. I needed to readjust my focus; I created a company where I could best utilize my business acumen by identifying startup companies and raising the capital needed to grow the corporation.

What I did best was identify companies with efficient management teams that could deliver revenue. So, in early 2003, I started an investor-relations firm and joined a colleague and friend in Switzerland who had all the necessary licenses to raise capital in Europe. He was educated in Switzerland and well-networked throughout Western Europe. At that time, approximately fifty-eight percent of the world's private capital resided in Switzerland, so I thought this would be a profitable venture.

My colleague had an office in Switzerland, and I maintained one in the United States with a staff of two, including me, and a satellite office in London. I went from 500-plus employees to just one. Over the next four years my Swiss colleague and I worked with half a dozen companies; two of them proved to be somewhat successful. But at the start of 2004 I entered a situation that would change my life as I knew it forever.

Chapter 10

Hello, Money and Gail— Goodbye, Dad

In late 2004 my Swiss partner and I opened our business with a simple business plan: I would identify US companies that fell under the radar screens of the big investor-relations firms while my partner would find European investors.

I was accustomed to having dozens of personnel, thousands of square feet of office space, and significantly more responsibility, but I needed only one administrative person to assist me in the US operations of this new venture. The administrative person who came to work with me in this new venture was the person who brought my childhood issues to the forefront of my life.

After opening the office, I reached out to the vast network I had developed over thirty years of work. I was reintroduced to a former colleague who had worked for one of the senior executives of the telecom company I had started seven years earlier. Gail, who was extremely intelligent and articulate, had worked for the company for only about a year before she'd moved on, since she had many things going on in her personal life that needed attention. When Gail walked in on the day of her interview, she took me aback. She had lost weight and was even more dynamic and focused than I remembered. In fact, my former executive had said that she had the potential to be a senior corporate executive if she stayed on track.

Sometimes employees are simply a little green and in need

of some experience. Once they get that knowledge and practical understanding of business, you can see their confidence the moment they walk into a room. I've been around people in business for years, and I can feel in my bones when people have what it takes. The Gail I had known before had potential but wasn't quite there at the time. The woman who stood before me that day exuded professionalism and poise. I remember saying, "Gail, you've really changed. What happened? Did you find God?"

She jokingly answered, "Something like that."

The interview took about twenty minutes. She accepted my offer, which included the real possibility of advancement and opportunity. I sensed an inner strength that I had yet to experience in most of the women with whom I had acted out.

As 2005 approached, we became good friends. We were the only two people in the office, so it was inevitable that we would learn of each other's lives and personal conflicts. My father passed away a few months after she started, and I delivered his eulogy, which Gail helped edit and type. During the months before his passing, she had observed how significantly I was involved with my siblings and their problems while also supporting my parents in any way they needed. While for years Jane had been upset about my over-involvement and wanted me to pull back my support of everyone, it was Gail who really made me understand what I was doing was unhealthy and wrong.

As time passed, I learned that she was in recovery for alcoholism and had been sober for three years. I also learned that the reason she left my previous company was that her father had been dying of alcoholism. While this completely had devastated her, it caused her to realize that she needed help. She was a single mom with a young daughter. Having experienced addiction in my own family, I was fascinated by how this single mother with basically no means or familial support at the time of her father's death went into recovery and turned her life completely around. Gail was quite an amazing woman, and I admired her tremendously the more I got to know her.

When she saw what I was handling she would say things like, "You've set no boundaries," "You can't have the sick people running the family," "You're enabling your siblings," and "You're not giving them a hand *up*, you're giving them a hand *out*, which is destroying both them and you!"

After my father passed away, I took over his position in the family, and it appeared to me that a few of my siblings took his passing as a sign to give up on themselves altogether or to flee our family system. I was now left to do what I had been doing for the last thirty-five years—only alone, without my dad. Nevertheless I was prepared and willing to pick up the flag and carry on.

In the middle of 2006, Gail was involved in an intense legal dispute. Naturally, with my well-honed caretaking and codependency skills, I stepped up to help her, which brought us closer. She had a sister who lived on the West Coast; the male family members had all passed away. With no male survivors from Gail's family and my coming from my family's system, in which males took the roles of supporters, it was a natural fit for me to intervene. Eventually we crossed the friendship boundary. Our sexual relationship served to quell my continuing compulsive anxiety disorder. Gail, ironically, identified many of the codependency issues that would trigger my disorder.

By early 2007 she decided to leave the company and me because she knew I would never leave my family. Over the next two months I tried desperately to replace her. It wasn't easy finding someone qualified who wanted to work for such a small operation. Although she left the business, she would come in three or four times over the next couple of months to help out and keep the books up to date. In addition to losing a key person in the business, I also lost a confidant with whom I had been sharing my daily insanity. Jane had burned out from hearing about all of my extended family nonsense many years earlier.

Through a business associate I finally identified someone I thought would be qualified. She e-mailed her resume, and I had a fifteen-minute telephone conversation with her. Liking everything I heard, I thought she would be fine, but I asked Gail to participate in the face-to-face interview, to give her opinion and to help with the transition. Depending on how you view it, you could say this interview either saved my life or brought it to complete ruination.

When "Elaine" walked through the door, I immediately noticed she was attractive. During the interview it became apparent she was qualified for the position. On the other hand, what Gail saw was her replacement…in every way.

I could see Gail was extremely agitated and was using all her self-control not to storm out of the office. A couple of minutes before the end of the interview she did start to leave (very professionally), but I could see she was extremely upset. I was able to get her to stay so I could talk to her, and she confirmed my suspicions. I told her that her accusations were wrong, that nothing was going to happen between Elaine and me. After all, I had just met the woman! She fired back that it was the perfect storm. Elaine was a single mom who would have needs, and I'd be there to help her through her problems. Once I set about doing that, the rest of the cycle would run its course—we'd end up in bed. With that, Gail stomped out in anger, leaving me to wonder if she would end up being right.

The Terminus of the Veil

Chapter 11
Discovery

Gail had once dragged me to an AA meeting. I couldn't understand why. I mean, I wasn't an alcoholic—never had been. But as a recovering alcoholic, Gail knew I displayed so many dysfunctional signs and perhaps if I could listen to what went on in a meeting, I'd recognize some similarities between my behavior and that of an alcoholic.

Of course this didn't work. I wasn't ready to look at myself, and I certainly couldn't make the connection with my behavior. While the gentleman leading the meeting was talking all about his sobriety, all I could think was, *I'm not an alcoholic. All these people here are alcoholics. What am I doing here?* I could not allow myself to consider that something could be wrong with me. My walls of defense were still as strong as steel.

But as I learned in recovery the next year, I hadn't reached my lowest point of despair, which is what, unfortunately, most victims of severe trauma experience before they surrender to the recovery process.

Gail's goodbye e-mail changed all that.

Paul at college… Jane skiing with her sister in Utah… Luke supposed to be sleeping at a friend's house… Trying to maintain damage control on the phone with Gail… The computer room door open and unattended… Her e-mail illuminated by the light of the computer screen, advertising my infidelities like a billboard to anyone who walked in the room…

Unbeknownst to me, Luke had decided not to spend the night at a friend's...

Three days after discovering Gail's e-mail, Luke finally asked for an explanation. My secret was out. I was no longer the perfect dad. My life was about to be turned upside down and inside out.

Luke wanted answers. "You're my idol, Dad. How could you have affairs with other women? What's going on with you and Mom?"

My heart stopped, and I had only a few seconds to collect myself and answer. Luke was now eighteen, and I was pretty sure he'd had at least one intimate relationship with a very special girl, so he was no longer naïve. In those few seconds I had to make a decision. I could tell him the e-mail was total nonsense, since he knew I traveled extensively and met many women who might have said ridiculous things just like what he had read. If I did this, I thought, I chanced putting him in a box for the rest of his life, always wondering if I had told the truth or if the e-mail were reality.

I could also have asked him to keep it between us men—"Mom would never understand." As John had told me, this would be "our secret." Even though I was extremely unbalanced emotionally, it was clear to me this was not an option. I could not burden one of the two people I trusted and loved unconditionally with a lie. I cared for Luke too much.

It's strange, but had Jane found the e-mail, I would have handled it in a totally different manner. I know that for sure. I would have lied and continued to hide my actions and destructive behaviors. I would have told her the e-mail was fabricated and just attempted to move on. I couldn't do that to either of my sons. With them my love was too pure, too unaffected by all that I had been through. I would learn in recovery, four months almost to the day of Luke's reading the e-mail, that it usually takes a significant event—even sometimes a life-altering event—for a victim of childhood sexual abuse to surrender to the denial of the abuse and the havoc resulting from the attacks. My life-altering event was staring right at me—it was either Luke's life or mine, so at that moment I gave up my life.

I looked straight into his blue eyes and said, "When Mom comes home tomorrow I'm going to discuss the e-mail directly with her."

He immediately calmed down, and I saw his sigh of relief as though the weight of a thousand pounds had been lifted from his back.

Luke's reaction told me I had made the right decision. Affirming what Luke knew to be true after reading the e-mail—his father was an adulterer—was better than creating a lie that would have negated what he already knew. Asking him to participate in my lie—and my life of deception and dysfunction—would have been the equivalent of John's coercing me into believing that "this is what the older guys do." Sometimes facing worst-case scenarios is better than never knowing whether you are in one. I think Luke knew he was in a worst-case scenario.

Up to the point of the e-mail I had been able to keep my multiple lives—my anxiety, depression, stress, and dysfunctional and destructive acting out—separate from what I considered my normal life. Now, knowing the revelatory discussion with Jane was only a day away, I also knew the life I'd known would never be the same.

The next evening I picked Jane up from the airport. As usual she was bubbly and looked cute as a button, wearing a cowboy hat she had purchased during her ski trip in Utah. On the way home I began to explain Luke had read an e-mail from Gail that was very upsetting.

Jane is a good listener. I parceled out the information piece by piece, very calmly, always parsing my words just so but never lying or being disingenuous. It was the hardest thing I had ever had to do. Jane listened but did not ask many questions. Everything was coming out; I held back nothing. No, I didn't go into unnecessary, excruciating detail. When your spouse tells you he's been unfaithful, there are two ways you can approach it. You can ask for every sordid detail so you can twist the knife deeper and deeper into your own gut—which was what I had done years back, when the woman I was acting out with had the affair that caused me to lose all that weight. That woman had cheated on me, and I had to know every single thing about it, asking intimate, sensitive questions so I could feel the deepest depths of depression and could inflict the most pain on myself so I could hate her and wash away the painful illusions of love I thought I had.

The other way to address what is being said is to do so at face value. Your spouse or significant other is telling you he has been unfaithful; what more is there to say?

That was how Jane approached it. She didn't yell or scream; that wasn't her style or personality. She did something far worse. She told me, "You broke my heart," and I knew from how she said it that it was true—truer than true. I had never felt so devastated in my life.

We continued to talk through the night, but I can't recall what was said. As each hour passed I became foggier and foggier, as if someone had injected me with a strong sedative and I was just spinning deeper into an abyss. I had deceived my wife, and now she knew.

There are all sorts of relationships in the world. I know a lot of people who've had affairs, gotten caught or confessed to them, and patched things up, and life went on. I'm not here to judge whether that's right or wrong. We're all wired differently, and we all have different types of relationships. What I did know was that Jane was always a very black-and-white person. Things were right or wrong, good or bad. Unfaithfulness was bad, period. There was not going to be any getting over it.

Once I confessed, that was that. In Jane's world, once you did something like being unfaithful, you no longer lived under the same roof. That was the punishment for infidelity.

I tried to explain to her that I felt something was wrong with me and had been for decades, but she wasn't listening. Frankly, I didn't really understand fully the correlation between the two things myself; I just felt one had some impact on the other. But to a spurned spouse it didn't matter. Again, black and white. When you cheat on your spouse, there's no such thing as a mitigating factor; there are only facts.

I was drowning right before her eyes because I didn't want my life as I had known it to end. I had worked so hard to keep up this façade, this *Ozzie and Harriet* life, and now she was telling me it was over. Jane was taking control; *no one ever* had taken control over me and my life…not since I was seven.

But she had a right. I never really knew she had a right, but she had all of the rights I did, including the right to have her own set of rules, ethics, and morals, and I had violated them. That, in her black-and-white world, was wrong and would cause my departure from our home.

I faced not only being cut off from Jane and the boys but also being removed as savior and caretaker of the rest of the family, a role I relished and played so well. How would all of those people survive without me? I was everyone's lifeline. In fact, I *needed* to be everyone's lifeline; otherwise I was nothing to myself. What would happen to all these people and their needs now? What would happen to me if I no longer had all of them to need *me*?

Now both Luke and Jane knew I'd been unfaithful. While I had mentioned to Jane that my sexual abuse experience as a child may have played a role, I didn't say any such thing to Luke. I was in no condition to handle that discussion, nor did I really know how to couch it, because I had only certain inklings about it as it was. It haunted me—especially the sexual attacks from Jimmy—but I couldn't connect much more beyond that at that point in my life. Jane knew about it only superficially from when I had confessed it to her twenty years earlier, when I dropped all that weight during the collapse of the addictive relationship I'd had years earlier.

Jane called Paul at college to tell him I had been unfaithful and she was thinking about separating. I wasn't thinking about separating, but for once in the marriage *I* was not in control. Jane made it clear to me that I was being asked to leave the house. In keeping with her personality, she kept it from being an ugly scene, but that didn't matter to me. My life as I knew it was ending, and I wanted to die.

Chapter 12
Descending Into Hell

I'm sure Jane was dissatisfied with the way I was with our sexual relationship, which I'm also sure left her unfulfilled. I believe her dissatisfaction was more about how I was not providing the type of love she wanted and needed. She said she wanted intimacy, something impossible for me to comprehend much less deliver. Unlike me, Jane would never go outside the marriage to fulfill her needs. For Jane, infidelity was wrong, and that was that.

Jane wanted to cuddle. She wanted to be caressed and loved. When she would lay her head on my chest, it felt like an anvil crushing me. When she'd stroke me lovingly on my chest it felt like an army of ants crawling all over my body. When she placed her hand behind my head and attempted to massage my neck gently, my brain could think only of how John and Jimmy had touched me in a similar way. When she would wrap her leg around mine in bed, after twenty seconds I couldn't bear it. My mind would flash to John's pinning my legs down as a child.

While all these physical actions reminded me of the sexual abuse, I still didn't connect my sexual behavior as an adult to those attacks. Although these physical affections were what most people would consider pleasurable feelings, they made me feel agitated and nervous, and I had a hard time masking my reactions. Even though I wanted Jane to love me and I wanted peace and harmony in our home, I couldn't tell her how I felt or make her understand. For that matter, I didn't understand why I felt that way either.

Two days after our entire world fell apart, Jane and I went to a marriage counselor. Jane was understandably hostile throughout. I believe she went through the motions for the sake of our boys; she showed up but without true desire for any real understanding other than what she faced on the surface: the affair. During our first session the counselor asked about our backgrounds and childhoods. Jane gave a fairly nondescript account of hers, and then I described mine. Simply as a way of being factual, I mentioned my childhood sexual abuse but not in great detail. But once I briefly mentioned the abuse, the therapist slowly raised her hand and said she wasn't qualified to discuss that topic, but she could recommend another psychologist. She *strongly* insisted I see him as soon as possible.

I went to the psychologist. Jane, however, stopped seeing the marriage counselor, especially since her annual vacation trip with her sisters was just a few days away. I couldn't believe it. Our lives were falling apart (due to me), yet she was preparing to depart for a vacation with her sisters.

Of course Jane hurt. But working with a counselor meant trying to fix what was broken. For her, it didn't work that way. For her, you simply moved on. I later learned in recovery that at the time, moving on was the only way Jane knew how to protect herself. The fact was that both of us thought the only one who had issues was me. Jane wasn't the one who was broken, just her marriage. I'm not saying she's perfect—no one is, but this wasn't about picayune things like disliking the way another person played with the silverware or chewed gum. Marriage was about monogamy, and I hadn't been monogamous. I felt Jane was punishing me by asking me to leave, by not reconciling, by not understanding me, and by not wanting to enter therapy with me.

I remember talking to Jane on her vacation and hearing her sisters yelling in the background, "We're on our sister trip! Come on! Get off the phone!" and "why does he want to talk to you now?" This was so hurtful to me; I didn't know what to make of it. I think I would have had an easier time with it if they would have let me have it, but instead they were acting like I didn't matter or exist. Jane's family handled crises very differently than my family did. I was literally in a fetal position, barely able to function. They were all out partying, trying to help Jane forget me and my deceptive behavior.

Jane's sisters felt the best way to help her out was simply to grind their heels into me and kick me while I was down. I can understand their emotional need to circle the wagons around their sister; if it had been one of my siblings I would have felt and done the same. But I was perturbed at them, particularly because of their hypocrisy. I had extended myself to every one of them above and beyond the call of duty over the previous twenty-six years. Shouldn't that have counted for something? How quickly, I felt, they forgot. I desperately needed them or *anyone* to see beyond the infidelity, which at that point I had only begun to understand. How could they think that was who I really was? I wasn't some good-for-nothing man they hated and regretted their sister Jane marrying; I was someone every one of them could have turned to in times of need. They didn't see I was wounded and needy, but how could they? I had been hiding and protecting myself since the age of seven.

On Jane's return from her trip she said her sisters had told her, "Ask him if this was only the first one." I exploded. I was feeling so many emotions right then. I was needy for people to understand, and I was aching for comfort and support. I also felt anger toward my fair-weathered sisters-in-law.

I uttered the truth. "No, this wasn't the first. It was probably the *thirtieth*, and there were probably another seventy or eighty women *before* we were married!"

I regretted saying it as soon as it came out of my mouth, but after Luke had confronted me with that damning e-mail, I'd decided I could no longer live in such excruciating turmoil. I didn't know how I was going to put my life back together or find salvation, or if that was even possible.

To accelerate my departure from the house, Jane had a condo set up for me in less than two days. I couldn't sleep for the next few nights, so I'd get up around 3:00 a.m. to start moving my things out, so as not to create any more emotional harm to the boys. I didn't have much to move, just some suits, shirts, and pants. I was more concerned about the contents of my desk, so over the next few days I took my files to my office so I could keep track of my family's finances.

No grass grew beneath Jane. She put our estate home of over twenty years up for sale within a month. It reminded me of the time my parents put up my childhood home for sale some time after they learned of the sexual abuse. It was, forty-eight years after the crimes committed against me, and my wife was fleeing the scene of the many crimes *I* had committed against her.

I didn't really care about any material things and supported her decision to sell our home. My only concern was that we acted as one when it came to the boys. I told her, "No matter what happens between us, the most important thing is the welfare of the boys." She wholeheartedly agreed. We may have been at our lowest ebb at that point, and I knew she disliked me on many levels, but at least she wasn't going to allow the boys to become collateral damage.

We were separating, but Jane didn't need a lawyer—a recommendation from one of her sisters. What she really needed was an investment banker. I had always taken care of Jane financially, and I always would. There was never a question as to what the right thing to do was. I loved her to whatever extent I was capable.

I arranged a meeting with a banker, one with whom I knew she'd feel comfortable and would trust. I prepared a twenty-page document detailing what I would give her then and for the rest of my life. These pages also provided for Paul and Luke's welfare and their needs through college and grad school, which I took on as my sole obligation.

Jane was given a few days to review the document with the banker I recommended. His response was that he thought it was extremely generous. In so many ways money never really meant as much to me as it might have to other people concerned about acquiring material things. For me it represented freedom and control to be able to take care of myself and as many others as possible.

I was deeply depressed. Feeling insurmountable pain, shame, and guilt, I accepted my fate, left my home of twenty-six years, and found myself alone in a rented condo, wishing I had never been born. My first two months in the condo were like being in another world. Saying goodbye to my sons had been one the most difficult events I had ever experienced in life.

I was completely isolated, lonely beyond comprehension. Not seeing Jane and the boys each night left me devastated. I just couldn't fathom that I wasn't going to wait up for the boys to come home at night and see them again the next morning. I became very efficient at mobile-phone texting, which up to that time I hadn't used at all. I had Elaine from my office teach me so I could keep in close communication with Paul and Luke. An evening wouldn't pass without texting the boys good night. I would keep their text responses for weeks and view them sometimes two or three times a day and acted as if I were simulating a conversation with both of them.

I was so lonely. I had nowhere to run or hide. I had always made myself a moving target—I hadn't thought of it that way, but it was accurate. Work and suppressing my compulsive anxiety disorder and addiction were occupying most of my life. It was all about keeping in motion, making sure I didn't slow down and stop; that would mean having to think about what I was doing and why. I was trying to outrace the world around me, but I was also trying to outrace my own thoughts. Now the moving target had stopped, and the depression was crippling me.

Somehow I continued to work throughout this whole debacle, although not at my usual pace or efficiency. I have no idea how I carried my workload, but I believe it was due to my fanatical work habit, which I would learn in recovery was yet another addiction caused by the attacks. I was probably worthless as a businessman during those darkest of days, but I showed up, and, as Woody Allen says, showing up is eighty percent of success. It was also the only arrow in my quiver when it came to trying to get the bad things off of my mind, although this time it was far less successful. I mentally drifted back to my home over and over again.

The three most-important people in my life now knew of my indiscretions and imperfections, but it was my sons I never wanted to know of my weaknesses; knowing that hurt most of all. Every dad wants to be on a pedestal for his sons. Husbands and wives may bicker and may see each other at the very worst, but most children think their parents can do no wrong. I was far from perfect, and now the boys knew it. For all I had accomplished in my life—the successes and the money I'd earned—I felt it was all worthless because more than for money or for anything else, I had done it to earn the respect and love of my sons. Now I felt they would never look at me the same way again.

The boys lived with Jane, and I was in the condo alone. Jane wanted them to accept this transition so they wouldn't hurt or feel sorry for her or me. She wanted Paul and Luke to feel this was a natural progression, and she urged them to visit me.

I knew they wouldn't come, however. I understood this from the boys without hesitation or reaction. I knew my living at the condo only intensified their feelings over our separation, so they avoided coming. It was fine with me; I was their dad, and I should go to them as I had for the previous nineteen years. I would see them at least once a week, on Thursdays, when I would go to the house to take care of the family finances and make sure everything was okay. While seeing the boys on Thursday evenings was something I cherished, I would break down uncontrollably as I pulled out of the driveway.

How could this be happening? I was the leader of my immediate family and my extended family and, at times, supported my wife's family members—all while running multiple businesses. In all of my sordid, self-destructing, dysfunctional life there had been nothing I hadn't kept under control. I had been able to manage so many different lives and at such high levels, but now my entire world was falling apart.

During many of the nights I spent alone at the condo I reflected on when Jane and I were engaged and that one evening when she had asked, "You are eventually going to let your defenses down, aren't you?"

I had shrugged and said, "What defenses? I don't have any defenses." I had refused to acknowledge what was surrounding me and coming between Jane and me or anyone attempting to get close to me—that twelve-foot-thick titanium wall a thousand feet high that *nobody* was going to get through.

My sons were different; they never asked me to let down the walls erected from the violations that had occurred some forty-eight years prior. Our love for each other provided me with a sense of security I had never experienced. I could care for and protect them. I could be in their lives in every way possible. Even when I left, even when they learned I had done something terribly wrong, my sons gave me the hope, love, and reinforcement I needed so desperately at that time.

While Luke did not understand why I had done what I had, he hugged and held me tight the night of my departure. Both of us had tears in our eyes. He said, "Dad, you'll always be my hero, and nothing will ever change that." This statement gave me immense strength and encouragement. I wanted to heal for myself, but I wanted Luke to know I was the man he thought I was.

Paul, who, his entire life, had had the innate ability to understand and care for people way beyond his years, left me with the most touching statement. After an in-depth talk, I hugged Paul and said goodbye. As I was leaving the room he stopped me at the door and said, "Dad, you'll help more people in your life than you'll hurt." This loving sentiment is something I will carry with me for the rest of my years.

But how could I have hurt the three most important people in my life? What in the world drove me to that point?

Recovery

Chapter 13

Therapy

Dr. DiCesare, the psychologist recommended by the marriage counselor, was a specialist who counseled adults who had gone through the trauma of childhood sexual abuse. Talking to Dr. DiCesare was extremely foreign to me; this man was attempting to unlock decades of deeply held secrets. I'd have to let my defenses down to another man and discuss the unspeakable, but at that point in my life I had nowhere to go. It was clear that my forty-eight-year roller-coaster ride had come to a halt and I was forced to get off.

The first time I had revealed the molestations to Jane, I was simply using it—using anything—to barricade her from the truth: I had been sexually acting out. I knew Jane, and I knew she wouldn't ask many questions if I told her answering them made me feel uncomfortable. The psychiatrist who had counseled me twenty years earlier never knew of my sexual abuse so could not have linked it to my behavior. I had explained to him that my weight loss was strictly the result of the betrayal by another woman. I played him just as I played everybody else in order to remain in total control at all times.

This time I was seeing a specialist I couldn't play. This time there would be no conning. I was a beaten man and at my worst; I wasn't emotionally strong enough to try to figure out how to manipulate this doctor, as I had in 1987 with the first therapist. I couldn't think of a good diversion tactic; the truth was all I had left in me to say. I had nothing left to lose.

The next two months were a living hell. Between work and attending twice-weekly therapy sessions, each day I was in bed by 7:00 p.m., curled up in a fetal position. Additionally, both my sons were in college, and I still had to provide not only for them but for Jane as well. I had retired Jane twenty-seven years earlier when I'd asked her to marry me, as I'd seen no reason or need for her to work. We were going to marry and start a family, and her complete and total care was my responsibility, which I cherished.

I did everything in my power to make it until Friday each week. Once I made it to Friday night, I would just physically exist through the weekend. I was getting out of bed only to eat something once a day. Over the next four to five months I was full of fear and trepidation that Monday morning was coming too quickly. The emotional trauma was enough for me to ask God to take me in my sleep. I truly wanted to die. I always had a bit of a morbid side, which I would learn in recovery was due to the trauma of the sexual abuse. I still can recall how each time I stepped on an airplane I'd talk to Jane and the boys as if it were for the last time. I wasn't the pilot—I was merely a passenger. I was relinquishing control, and I didn't *do* that—thus my anxiety. I couldn't fly a plane, but still I didn't trust a trained pilot to do it for me either.

Deep down inside, the only two people I ever really trusted were my sons. Everyone else, even the trained professionals in their various crafts, were suspect. Never had I actually wanted to die before…not until now. I contemplated suicide, but I simply couldn't do it. Mostly I thought of Paul and Luke finding me alone and gone, knowing it hadn't been an accident or the result of natural causes. What a horrible thing to foist upon your children. I would ruin them for life if I hadn't already done so. However, I did learn in recovery there were survivors who *did* take their lives once they were awakened to how sexual abuse had affected their entire worlds.

The other issue was a moral one. Though it was an oxymoron, I always tried to remain a religious man, although I didn't wear it on my sleeve. I *negotiated* with God. I knew I did some good in my time thus far on earth, and somehow I tried to reconcile the bad with God. But while it may be one thing to alibi marital infidelity, how do you alibi suicide?

I would toss and turn and stare at the ceiling in a cold sweat, unable to sleep as I pondered these life-and-death, philosophical issues. Flashes came to me in abundance. I remember sitting in my Catholic-school classroom, hearing, "You cannot get into heaven if you take your own life." The nuns would constantly advocate that other sins might be forgiven, but not that one. So I gave myself up to God. I asked Him that if it was His will, would He be so benevolent as to take me as I slept, with no action on my part that would damn me to hell or injure my sons? I suppose that was not in His plans, or else He had truly forsaken me at that time of need in my life.

Since my life with my family had ceased to exist, I had nowhere to turn, and there was no one to listen. So I began more in-depth conversations with Dr. DiCesare, as he was the only human contact in my life. I stopped my game playing; I gave him control over our sessions. He asked, I answered, and I held nothing back.

Did it feel good? It felt like surgery without anesthesia. I would rather have had someone pull my heart through my chest while it was still beating. It hurt so badly to go through it, but those were his instructions. He drew me out and got me to talk, and he never made me feel horrible about myself. I suppose he'd heard it all before, and indeed he had. Unlike the other mental health professional I had seen, this doctor was specifically trained in this particular area. He wasn't going to hear me out and simply say, "I think you should just go back to work and forget it. With the passage of enough time, you'll barely be able to remember it happened." No, I was getting up in years, and after decades upon decades I still hadn't gotten over it. I would soon come to learn it doesn't work that way.

After my confession to Jane, the years of support and care I had given her family suddenly meant nothing to them. Although I had assisted in certain situations with a few of Jane's sisters and their children, I now became an instant outcast to her family. I received *one* supportive phone call from a brother-in-law, for which I was grateful. Yet even he was spooked after he learned it wasn't just an affair but decades of dysfunctional and dissociative behavior. After that, surprisingly, the only other person in Jane's family who initiated contact was my mother-in-law. She was as comforting as my own mother. Jane's mom was an extraordinarily loving, kind, and thoughtful person; she believed it was just impossible for me to have had these affairs and acted out with such disconnected behavior.

My mother-in-law said, "It couldn't have been you, Pete. It must have been the devil." While this eighty-five-year-old great-grandmother had little understanding of mental health, her description of "the devil made me do it" could be likened to what Dr. Donald Kalsched, an expert clinical psychologist, describes in his book *The Inner World of Trauma*. Dr. Kalsched depicts what happens to a child who experiences the level of trauma that I did: "When a child's innocence is deprived, a *diabolical* spirit is created."

The more I saw Dr. DiCesare, the more it became apparent to me that the sexual abuse I had suffered had a lot to do with many if not *all* of my adult caretaking, controlling, and sexual behaviors. This may have been easy to deduce for a trained professional, but the recognition came slowly for me. While he still had not rendered a final opinion, he probed me with questions that led me to believe he was assembling an analysis along those lines.

When I shared this information with Jane, her initial reaction, unfortunately, was that I was "looking for an excuse" and that Dr. DiCesare was providing me with one. Furthermore, while Jane had given up on marriage counseling, she seemed to resent that I was still in counseling and trying to find answers for my actions, which she had already decided on and was sure were just deceptive. Dr. DiCesare even asked if she wanted to attend my sessions, but Jane declined.

As I lay awake each night, still asking God to end my misery, I wondered if Jane had begun to tell her family about the content of my sessions with Dr. DiCesare. I feared the worst, and the reality was only slightly less than that. When I confronted Jane, she admitted that, when pressed as to why I was going to a psychologist, she told her family—discreetly—I had been molested as a child and was talking to a therapist about the sexual abuse I had experienced. Her disclosure made me feel extremely exposed and vulnerable. I thought maybe one of her sisters (or even all) might reach out to me to see how I was coping, all things considered. None did. Now they knew the deepest, darkest truth about me, yet there was no understanding.

The fear of being abandoned once I told someone of the attacks had been with me since age seven. While I realized Jane's family would view me as the man who had hurt and deceived Jane, I struggled to understand why none viewed my dozens of infidelities as out of character for the man they knew. After all, I had given shelter to some of them, enrolled some of their children in school, and always offered my help, sometimes to my own detriment. You would think it would have dawned on them that my behavior did not equate with what they knew me really to be and they would recognize something must have been terribly wrong. Yet nothing mattered but exclusion and extracting punishment if only by cutting off all contact. Now, to make it worse, they had this embarrassing information about me, which I had kept secret for forty-eight years.

I thought only the worst of everyone because they did nothing to prove me wrong. All those years I had felt like trash because John and Jimmy had treated me like trash, and now I felt like Jane's family thought I was trash as well.

I know if this had happened to one of them, nothing would have stopped me from reaching out and seeing if there was anything I could do to help.

An incident shortly after they learned of my childhood sexual abuse convinced me any contact with Jane's sisters was completely finished at that point. I happened to call Jane on her car phone to make sure she had received a wire transfer. Unbeknownst to me, two of her sisters were in the car when we were talking on the speakerphone. When I discovered later that they were there and hadn't even uttered a hello, I became very upset. That evening, on another call with Jane, I asked her, "Don't you think it's ridiculous that your sisters didn't say hello?"

Her answer was, "Come on, Pete. Don't you think it's a little awkward for my sisters?"

It was explained to me, once I came out of denial and surrendered to what had happened to me as a child, that the emotions of rage, resentment, anger, and betrayal would send me into uncontrollable reactions. I immediately snapped back, "No, Jane, I think it's a little awkward for a seven-year-old boy to be raped and violated multiple times, more than I would think a couple of fifty-something-year-old women wouldn't say hello to someone who was not only in their lives for almost thirty years but who had occasionally helped them with problems and situations they had in their own families!" When they'd heard my voice, all they were thinking about was my cavorting with a woman, yet I was reliving the trauma of John and Jimmy's abusive, sordid sexual attacks every day in my therapy sessions.

Their silence made me realize they were no different from most of the world when it came to understanding the effects of sexual abuse on a child and how those attacks created the adult I had become; not even three decades of knowing me made a difference. I started to think that if Jane's family thought and felt I was a leper, then I guess most of society would think that and worse. What had I gotten myself into by opening up about this? I later learned in recovery that many children who found themselves in my awakened position as adults, especially men, still continued to live in denial and just carried on with their suffering.

Our separation was unfathomable to both of our families, to our many friends, and to our so-called friends. Those who showed themselves to be less-than-true friends immersed themselves in our despair. The expected gossip from the catty women in the neighborhood and from the boys' school was in full bloom, discussing the misfortune that had befallen my family and me.

Jane's cousin told her about an incident that had happened fifteen years earlier between me and her neighbor's daughter. While the story she told was twisted in its content and not the whole truth, no one at that point was listening to me.

This cousin asked me to help out this young woman by giving her advice concerning her career path. An appointment was made, and a young woman in her mid- to late twenties showed up in my office with her resume. Within ten minutes she moved the conversation from her resume to her telling me that, for some reason, her husband neither understood her, nor was he giving her attention or affection. She even went so far as to say their sexual relationship was nonexistent.

The conversation was kind of strange, but I started to tell her she probably was wrong because she was a bright and attractive woman. Our meeting finished with my giving her my office phone number and saying if I could be of any other help to call. By her second call she greeted me with "hey, boyfriend," leaving me to think she was making sexual innuendos. After a couple conversations I suggested dinner, which she quickly accepted.

Here was an obviously willing participant who was going to relieve my tension and—without my knowing at the time—continue to feed *The Beast* of addiction engraved in my brain. I truly felt I had developed a sixth sense about this type of woman from the time I was seven, and this woman wasn't even being subtle—a blind man could have seen where she was coming from. Three things a married woman doesn't want to do to a man in my condition is say her husband isn't paying attention to her sexually, greet him with "hey, boyfriend," or accept his dinner invitation!

At dinner I learned this woman was looking for attention and affection—emotions I clearly couldn't deliver or comprehend. After dinner we ended up at my office, and I understood very quickly that she needed *just* attention, which wasn't what I wanted or needed. As soon as her signals changed and were clear to me, I regrouped before I had done anything untoward. No one ended up the wiser, and no one ended up hurt.

Now that Jane's cousin had learned of our separation caused by my extramarital affairs and told this woman about them as well, the woman's response was something like, "Oh, he hit on me too." My first thought was if this woman had been so appalled by my behavior, why did she wait over fifteen years to disclose my indiscretion? Why hadn't she told Jane's cousin the next day? It was clear to me why she hadn't. At a minimum she had been an equal or willing participant. But now that I was down I was being scrutinized in every way and by *everyone* possible—this is the essence of gossip.

It would have been one thing for an old encounter to come out of the woodwork, but it was another for this woman, who I'd never been with, to create even more havoc in my life. That was just cruel, probably crueler to Jane than to me. I learned in recovery that many people—like Jane's cousin and this woman—covet the idea that they have lived ideal, perfect lives. Therefore, when people like me fail at life, they step up and show how well-adjusted they think they are compared to the injured.

Every family has its good and its bad points. In recovery, I was learning that neither of our family systems was truly healthy. In Jane's family system, though it was healthier than mine, you were still either good or bad; you didn't deal with emotional trauma, and there definitely was no gray area. Not only was my family's system built in the gray area, but we also chose to ignore our caches of family secrets, my childhood sexual abuse one of the biggest. I believe the reliance on keeping secrets more than likely came from my mother's side, because her parents' generation had been surrounded by secrets. I suppose it was no great leap for her to embrace the pediatrician's recommendation that my sexual attacks not be discussed with me.

I believe today that my mother was afraid her father would have blamed her for having let me out of her sight. Was that a fair assessment? I don't think so. My mother was a good mother and a stalwart protector of me. If she'd been out carousing or drinking, not taking care of her children, then maybe my grandfather would have had a point, had he known what had happened to me. My mother was not irresponsible, especially given the era and the type of neighborhood in which we lived. Perhaps in today's culture parents are a bit less trusting, but a lot of that has to do with neighborhoods today being nothing like they were back in my childhood. Today, more often than not, both parents work, and people move in and out constantly; there are fewer roots. No sooner do you get to know the people who live across the street from you than they are transferred a thousand miles away. Back in my day, Sam the butcher was Sam the butcher who lived in the same neighborhood all of his life, and everyone knew him. Neighborhoods back in my day were cultural enclaves in which everyone took care of each other.

For years I had heard Jane's sisters talk about a certain woman from our neighborhood they thought might have been sexually violated. Of course, every time this conversation arose I would say to myself, "If they only knew…" In any event, one of the sisters took it upon herself to call this woman, to tell her Jane and I had separated and I had been sexually molested and raped as a child. What was she thinking? I may be able to talk about this now, but when I had just begun therapy I was not in a state of mind where I wanted others to discuss the horrible, distorted sexual attacks from my childhood.

Unbelievably, this hadn't been done to embarrass me; it was worse than that. This sister had always wanted to know whether this woman had been molested. Somehow in her mind she must have thought, *If out of the blue I tell her Pete was molested as a child, maybe then she'll open up and admit she was also. Then I'll know.* It wasn't that she was hoping to draw the woman out so she could help her in some way; she simply wanted to know if the gossip had been true. This phone call by this particular sister truly cut me deep because I had provided more support to her than I had to any other of Jane's sisters, particularly during a traumatic and lengthy crisis in her and her family's lives.

I don't know if this woman was one of the others from the old neighborhood who had been molested, but I do know I had not been the only one. That much I had gleaned from my mother around the time I had been confronted about John. But I never knew exactly how pervasive it all was. Had only John and Jimmy menaced children? Or had there been other pedophiles sexually assaulting children back there, back then? Had it been limited to boys, or were there girls as well, perhaps even this woman? I didn't know, and I wondered if I actually wanted to know. I was still frightened and felt completely out of sorts discussing anything related to my sexual attacks.

My sessions with the doctor were torturous, and the reaction I was getting from Jane's family was everything I dreaded it would be. No one was sympathetic, only negatively judgmental—everyone except my sons.

During one of my many phone conversations with Jane about

the details of our separation, another one of her sisters happened to be in the car listening to my call on the speakerphone. Jane and I were discussing a legal matter that wasn't being handled properly, and right in the middle of our conversation, with a quick chuckle, her sister blurted out, "My daughter just graduated from law school—we can ask her."

This was the same daughter I'd held in my arms when she was just a few months old; I'd graciously opened up my home to this beautiful baby and her family for the next year of her life. How inappropriate to ask my niece to negotiate a point of our separation! What would I need my darling niece to do that I couldn't do after having been in business for thirty-five years? But in Jane's family system there was nothing too serious that couldn't be handled with a nervous chuckle. Anything was better than addressing trauma. This statement floored me, but it was in keeping with their family system of not dealing—really *dealing*—with anything unpleasant. They could make light of just about anything going on in or around their lives—or worse, just simply avoid the issue altogether.

Another sister—one whose son I had spent a significant amount of time counseling and offering direction concerning his career—would struggle for days making a simple financial purchase because of an innate fear of never having enough money, which unfortunately was a driving fear in her life. Yet, concerning this most serious life decision, she felt qualified to advise Jane, "That part of your life is over. It's now time just to move on."

This was another direct family way of not addressing an unpleasant or difficult situation. Better just to "move on" and run away from it.

And finally this advice from yet another sister: "What you need, Jane, is a good lawyer." Sitting in their parents' kitchen twenty-seven years before that, she had announced that the brother-in-law, "Frank," who had a gambling problem, should never be spoken about again in their family. He was weak and not of good character, and that was that. At that moment I'd glanced across the room and I had seen my future father-in-law nodding his head with approval, as if saying, "That's my daughter. She clearly knows what's right and what's wrong." At that instant I said to myself, "If this woman ever found out I had been raped, she would cast me out as well."

Twenty-seven years later, that was exactly what happened. The casting out came not because I had been raped but because of the emotional fear and inability of her and Jane's family to try to understand and to connect how the sexual abuse trauma I suffered had caused my deplorable behavior.

If either of our family systems would have been healthier, perhaps we would have all understood that Frank's family dynamics most likely contributed to his downfall. I learned in recovery that children usually model the systems they come from. Frank's father was a habitual gambler, so it should have been no surprise that Frank had modeled his father's actions. The difference was Frank's father could manage his gambling behavior while Frank couldn't.

While my sisters-in-law are still to this day the most decent people, with significant integrity, I've ever met, it took me two years of intensive therapy and recovery to understand that they had reacted to me and had treated me the only way they knew how. To go to my underlying problem—the sexual molestations—and to understand and attribute my deplorable behavior to the sexual attacks was never going to happen. They would have to go to a very unpleasant and dark place, and their family system made that an impossibility.

Jane's sisters had received their roles in their family the way my siblings and I had received ours. One sister mimicked the role of her father, seeing life in terms of right or wrong; another one took the role of her mother, had low self-esteem, and at times endured the same emotional problems as my mother-in-law. Two sisters married at age nineteen. I'm sure these two women loved their spouses as much as they could at their relatively young ages. But after two years of recovery and therapy—after having learned about family systems, origins, and dynamics—I think a part of their decisions to marry so young had to do with their desires to flee their family system.

Unlike my brother-in-law, who had run away—I'm sure he'd been thoroughly traumatized by the rejection and his debt—I decided to stay and deal with my unmanageable life.

I hope one day my brother-in-law's two wonderful children will come to learn and understand that, more than likely, a significant piece of their dad's gambling problem was actually caused by his being a victim of his own father's gambling habits. He was not a man of real malice and probably had no real understanding of why he was such a compulsive gambler.

Another woman from our neighborhood, a supposed friend of Jane's, took delight in being emotionally vicious. It seemed her primary task in life was to let everyone know she had proof from a reliable source (a person who was welcomed in both our homes) that I had had an affair with another woman, which had prompted Jane to ask me to leave our home. If that vindictive, jackass of a woman only knew I wished what had happened had been *just* an affair!

This entire episode in my life—my estrangement from Jane and the boys made worse by the swirling gossip and family damnation—was without a doubt one of the lowest points in my life. Everywhere I turned, I felt another kick to the ribs. The therapy hurt, many of my friends turned out not to be *true* friends, and all of the extended family I had done so much for had turned their backs on me. More and more my sexual molestations became exposed; parts of me I had never wanted anyone to learn about came out in the open. Instead of finding comfort, support, understanding, and love, I found most people taking only glee in my demise and letting me know how imperfect I was. I hated mankind at that point, and every day was just another prayer that I die in my sleep.

Chapter 14

Path to Healing

The ongoing weeks with the therapist were both enlightening and overwhelming. The doctor was very deliberate and spoke very slowly and carefully to me, almost as though I were a child. A few weeks later, he explained to me that he took this approach because on an emotional level I *was* a child.

After approximately two months of extensive therapy two times a week, I received my first diagnosis. I was spellbound by what Dr. DiCesare had to say. He was describing everything I felt, who I was, and what I had been going through for the last four-and-a-half-plus decades. It was as if he had been there all along, riding along inside of my head, taking notes so one day, when I was ready, he would be there to explain it all to me.

First, he told me I had been suffering from post-traumatic stress disorder due to my childhood sexual abuse. From the age of seven I had developed an obsessive-compulsive disorder focused on sexually acting out. This came from the early sexual *over*-stimulation and trauma, which also caused an extreme anxiety disorder in my young brain. Post-traumatic stress disorder is the result of dissociation and unresolved anxiety. It develops when one experiences life-threatening or perceived life-threatening trauma; hence anxiety that goes unresolved.

In all my sexual experiences over the previous forty-eight years I had been trying to take control in order to master the sexual abuse that had happened to me. This effectively made it impossible for me to have a truly loving experience, since there had been absolutely no love or care involved in what I had suffered. The obsessive features were really my trying to process what had happened to me as a child. By age seven, the link between relationships and sexuality had been severed. In my damaged mind, sex and love were separate and could never be combined. While I grew physically and mentally over the years, the abuse left me so traumatized and frightened, all of my emotional development and growth had stopped in 1959.

What a resounding prognosis to understand! How could any part of me be only seven? Everyone who knew me thought I was a man's man, as did I. I'd never asked for anyone's help in my entire life. I was self-made, self-reliant, and successful.

My attackers had taken away my childhood and sentenced me to a life of never being able to trust anyone or develop a loving, sexual relationship with a woman. In order to survive their vile abuse I'd had to block out feelings as my only defense, which in turn halted my ability to experience or *share* feelings. The psychologist stated that although all of this was extremely traumatic, it pushed me to unnerving extremes in my business life, causing workaholism. I developed a sense of power in controlling my success, which in turn controlled my destiny. I learned how to dissociate my feelings from myself. Since the feelings resulting from the molestations at such a young age were too powerful to handle, if I didn't block out these emotions I would have been destroyed or possibly even caused harm to myself. While I was somehow able not to go completely insane, I still put all of my feelings, emotions, and issues about my attacks away in a metaphorical box.

The sexual abuse had ignited circuits that were supposed to lie dormant until I reached my late teens. I shouldn't have known anything about these circuits, but by the age of seven my assailants had completely burned them out. I discovered through my reading, a clinical psychologist who stated sexuality is like Pandora's box—there really is a proper time in human life when one can safely be exposed to its sensations. Exposure to sex at age seven is much too soon, and being introduced to it by manipulation, abusive betrayal, and rape just magnifies the tragedy.

It was strange for me to hear about such things in medical terms. Issues like "when is a person old enough to become sexually active?" always seemed to me to be more religious or moral or ethical issues. But Dr. DiCesare said there were biological and psychological issues as well, issues that went beyond societal judgments and morals. What John and Jimmy had done to me was as physically wrong as it would have been for them to have started pulling on me in order to stretch my bones so I would become taller before my body was ready to do so. They forced themselves on me in more ways than I could ever have imagined, and considering I had no proper expert intervention to mitigate the damage they'd inflicted upon me, I had been doomed to a life of dissociation and depression.

Dr. DiCesare was straightforward. I had been introduced to sex by despicable and vile sexual attacks. Therefore, the more I cared for and loved Jane, the further I drifted from her. Subconsciously I just couldn't see treating her in such a manner. It was like I was protecting her from the aggression I had been subjected to. Sex was dirty; sex was bad, aggressive, and violent. My body craved it when I needed to soothe my anxiety, but that didn't make deception right in my mind. How could I exploit this wonderful woman, the mother of my beloved children? The more my anxiety about this grew, the more stressed and thus self-destructive I became.

While the diagnosis was quite alarming, it was also a relief, for I had been trying for years to connect the dots to understand what was so wrong with me. There was not a day in my life that I didn't think about the abusive sexual assaults, especially Jimmy's violent, distorted attacks. Each memory would create anxiety as soon as it entered my mind. I would try to put the visions of the attacks out of my mind as quickly as the thoughts arose.

Of course, after hearing all of this, I had plenty of questions. How could I not trust my wife? Why couldn't I be emotionally connected to her? She was my best friend, my biggest supporter; how could it not be different with her? Why had I separated from her physically and mentally over the years?

Dr. DiCesare felt the only thing that separated my childhood sexual attacks from out-and-out torture was the fact that I hadn't been tied up. Hearing the word *torture* was very disturbing, and while I hadn't been bound, I thought it might as well have been torture. For any person who had to endure so many decades of torment it could just as well have been classified as that.

He did state it wasn't unusual for a sexually abused child to have been violated by more than one predator. What was somewhat unique but not unheard of about my circumstance was, although being groomed by John was more the statistical norm, I had also been bullied and sexually violated by Jimmy. To have two distinctly different types of perpetrators—one kind, one cruel—both at age seven completely obliterated my psyche. The doctor explained that some children who are attacked as I had been grow to be abusers themselves, although it's a smaller percentage than one might imagine. Some become addicted to drugs and/or alcohol, some become addicted to sex, and many develop other self-destructive behaviors that cause lifetimes of misery and heartache.

While I needed to act out sexually to stop a crushing anxiety attack, I also carried an enormous amount of guilt as an adult that I hadn't been able to protect myself from my childhood abusers. Initially, Dr. DiCesare wasn't sure if I could ever experience intimacy and love with sex until I could experience it with a healthier mind. No doctor can tell any adult who was sexually abused as a child an exact time when he or she will be able to learn how to live with what happened, simply because they have no true understanding of whether the violation left him or her so wounded that letting down defenses is an emotional impossibility. I had a long, steep road ahead of me, but Dr. DiCesare was encouraged that I was committed to trying.

Something profound that Dr. DiCesare said was that I was now free *not* to act out because I was conscious of how my anxiety disorder would send me into an automatic cycle, whereas before I was merely compelled to relieve myself of the anxiety. He taught me all of the triggers and reactions that would cause my cycle to start: anxiety, stress, and then, ultimately, self-destruction. He felt that my dissociative state of mind was one of the most severe he had ever seen because I would be driven by the anxiety to act out with a woman one afternoon and then attend a family function the same evening as if nothing had happened in between. Once I fully grasped the psychological and clinical damage, I would also need a spiritual connection to help me heal from the severity of my childhood nightmare.

I was getting an analysis of my lifelong problems, which was an entirely new education about what I had gone through and why I acted as I did. He taught me that a sexually abused child couldn't start to heal or grow emotionally until that child—now an adult—started to talk about the abuse and the role it played in his life. One must come out of denial about the events of the sexual molestation.

The first step in my recovery was to accept that the sexual abuse had happened. In order to do that he felt I should finally describe the acts in detail. It was extremely difficult for me to talk about what had been done to me and even harder for me to talk about what John and Jimmy had forced me to do to them. I sat silent for three or four minutes in his office before I could begin to tell another human being in detail what had been done to me. Getting through this exercise, while it was extremely difficult, made me slowly start to feel as though a weight were lifted from my shoulders.

This was especially true when I learned about addiction, eating disorders, dissociation, and other complexities of adults who were sexually abused as children.

As we went on, my mind began to grow clearer in a way I had never thought possible. Once I began to learn the effects of my childhood sexual trauma, I had a thirst to know as much as possible. Many nights I would wake at 2:00 or 3:00 a.m. to write a note—"ask the doctor" or "go online and find books on the topic of sexual abuse in relation to male children." During my initial sessions I took extensive notes daily.

One out of about twenty books I found really spoke directly to me: *Beyond Betrayal* by Richard B. Gartner, PhD. I couldn't put it down. It took me about four hours to read it cover to cover. It was the first book I had ever read completely in my life. Prior to recovery I had been too wounded and did not have the attention span to read a book. I highlighted points of interest throughout like a college student cramming for an exam. It captured me so vividly; it was as though I were reading my own autobiography.

Another helpful book was *Childhood Sexual Abuse: A Survivor's Guide for Men* by Suzanne Nice and Russell Forrest. In it the authors state, "One of the greatest struggles you may face, as a victim of childhood sexual abuse, is learning *not to blame yourself* for the abuse. Regardless of how many times you may have heard, or been told, that the abuse was not your fault, you may still have difficulty believing this." Inadvertently, the abuse caused me to think I had to earn people's love by taking care of them. Caretaking and rescuing people provided me with my only sense of decency, as I feared I was such a damaged and abused human being I felt I was not of any value or worthy of love. This put an extreme amount of pressure on me as well as Jane and anyone dear to me, because I was always working to stave off my omnipresent feelings of self-hatred for what I felt was my fault.

Dr. DiCesare suggested I bring Jane in to attend one of our sessions even if I had to drag her. He knew from what I had told him that I loved her as much as I was capable of loving, and my anguish about the breakup of our family gnawed at me terribly. He felt that, were I to explain his prognosis to her alone, she might think I was merely making up excuses for my behavior or trying to put one over on her, which was far from the truth.

There are times when men and women hang gender clichés on one another, and I knew that Jane, after the initial shock, was battered by her friends and sisters, who told her that all men are dogs. One friend even told her, "That's what men do, especially Italian men—they cheat." She advised Jane not to believe anything I told her.

She reluctantly agreed to come to an appointment. Dr. DiCesare made it clear to her that my problems were not somewhat the result of my childhood rapes—they were *completely* the result of my childhood rapes. With no prompting on my part, he stalwartly came to my defense, although he did emphasize to her and me that only *I* could initiate my recovery. There would be no magic pill that would make me all better, nor would it be anyone else's responsibility to help me get well, if getting well were even possible. That was all on my shoulders.

Jane never actually disagreed with the doctor's assessment. It was as if she were looking at a math problem and agreeing with all of the numbers in the equation, but when the sum came at the end, while she could not disagree with it mathematically, she needed to disagree with it emotionally. As the doctor would rattle off symptom after symptom—he's distant, he likes to be alone, he needs to always be in control, he hates to be touched, he hates large crowds, and he fears anything out of his physical control—Jane just sat and nodded in agreement. Yes, that was Pete. The analysis Dr. DiCesare put forth was that when you put that all together, along with my explicit description of what had happened to me as a child, I was a textbook case of a survivor of childhood sexual abuse.

Jane said, "Okay, yes. That happened then [the molestation]. But I believe that after that he made choices."

The doctor sympathized with Jane's inability to see his point but nonetheless continued. "You can call it *choices*, but you'd have to understand that these perpetrations that occurred at the age of seven caused a biological addiction and a distinct dissociative state of mind within Pete as an adult, and people who are addicts rarely, on their own, know how to stop."

"You're telling me that, as a wife, you want intimacy. What I'm saying to you is if you want intimacy with Pete, you have to go down into the abyss with him. He's in a terribly dark hole and has been there for just about his entire life."

Jane immediately interjected, "Well, I can't do that."

I could see the doctor's wheels turning. "Jane, when a person says they can't, what the therapist hears is 'I won't.'"

Jane replied, "Look; I'm sorry the molestation occurred, but it's been discussed. It doesn't have to be discussed any further."

He replied, "That's not really so, because if you want intimacy, you have to feel and share with Pete the same pain he's feeling from it."

Jane repeated, "I can't do that."

Although the session with Jane didn't go well, Dr. DiCesare and I continued my recovery process. He told me it was apparent to him that Jane simply couldn't handle my situation. She couldn't or wasn't ready to deal with it. Of course that angered me, but then, perhaps, she deserved the benefit of needing more time to understand something even I had trouble comprehending. I looked at how hard it was for *me* to grasp and come to terms with it, and I was there! I had been enduring it my entire life. How could I have expected someone else, someone who had never lived it, someone who had been betrayed within her marriage, to identify immediately with my trauma? I craved and desperately needed her understanding, but I wasn't really sure if I would ever receive it.

My entire personality, good and bad, had been completely created from the violations. In some ways it made me the business success I was—which I resented hearing—and it made me the constant giver, the one who had to go above and beyond in order to feel loved and to feel deserving of love. It was also my inner demon. It was behind every moral and immoral decision I had ever made.

The manifestation of the sexual abuse could have come out in many different ways, but for me it was primarily a sexual compulsive disorder, along with a myriad of other emotional and even physical issues including insomnia, which had started at age seven after the attacks and continues to this day.

One odd physical effect that drove Jane absolutely mad was my excessive yawning. We would take drives to the Atlantic City shore, just sixty miles away, and I would be yawning constantly the whole way down. This was the focus of many arguments between Jane and me for many years. Jane could not understand (nor did I, frankly) how I could be yawning so much after getting enough rest the night before. Once I would start to yawn, it wouldn't stop.

What I discovered later during my therapy and constant research to understand and deal with my condition was the book *Victims No Longer* by Mike Lew. In it he states, "Survivors are often amazed that they find themselves experiencing wave after wave of yawning, one yawn following the last uncontrollably… There is evidence that this type of yawning is a way that the body releases muscular tension and works its way through the physical part of emotional recovery."

This further illustrates how earlier professional intervention could have identified and helped me deal with the multitude of puzzling habits and tics I had developed as a result of the sexual abuse. From the time I'd been raped as a child, I'd been damned for life. I should have received proper treatment the moment the attacks had been discovered, but that never happened. Perhaps, had that happened, I might have been spared decades of suffering. The people who meant the most to me in the world might have also been saved from the hurt I caused them.

I finally had the dots connected for me. I was now determined to fight back, to try to salvage what was left of my life. The problem was that Jane wanted a sanitized, all-fixed-up Pete, but she would have no part in helping make me so.

Unfortunately, Dr. DiCesare said Jane's unwillingness to participate in my recovery would hinder the healing process. This would also marginalize the possibility that any improvement in my condition would include the things Jane wanted from me. In other words, while there was no guarantee I could ever be helped—even if I could restore myself in some way—it would be unlikely that Jane and I would have a storybook ending together if she didn't participate. She would always be tapping her foot, wondering why the method was taking so long, and I would be resenting her for removing herself from that process—not a good combination.

At least the path for me was clear now. Only when one knows the prognosis can one begin to heal. I now wanted to heal—with or without Jane.

Chapter 15

Understanding *The Beast*

Many people get a second opinion after an initial medical diagnosis, so I sought a second opinion concerning my mental health and physical addictions. I was learning it was indeed a mental and physiological condition. I wasn't addicted to sex just because I liked sex. Frankly, one might even question how much I truly *did* like sex. I don't think alcoholics really love alcohol all that much after a while. In recovery I've talked to people addicted to drugs who rhapsodize about the first time they got high, but they also admit it hasn't been that good the thousands of times since. I was having sexual encounters to relieve a compulsive anxiety disorder that was paramount to anything else in my life.

I was referred to Dr. John J. O'Connor, one of the pioneers in the field, for a second opinion. He had been dealing with sexual abuse and addictions in young boys who had grown into emotionally fractured adults for over twenty years.

Dr. O'Connor was himself a victim of severe physical abuse as a child, and he overcame difficulties most people would have thought insurmountable. To my surprise we came from the same neighborhood; he had grown up in the Irish section whereas I had grown up in the Italian section. While I felt an immediate connection to and comfort with him, his diagnosis was eerily similar to that of Dr. DiCesare. Oh how I had hoped that just maybe there might have been a brighter, easier prognosis. Where was that magic pill that would fix me and bring my family back together?

Dr. O'Connor confirmed that, besides needing intense therapy, I also needed to be with a group of survivors who had experienced similar childhood trauma. It seemed impossible to me that such a community could exist. How could there be a community of abused children who had grown into damaged men? How could they find each other? How would they come together? And why? Worst of all, what about my issues with intimacy, socialization, loss of control, and crowds?

I explained everything that had happened to me, and Dr. O'Connor reassured me he had treated hundreds of men like me. Dr. O'Connor immediately sensed how devastated I was that I had lost my family, my home, and my control, but he looked me square in the eyes and said, "You don't realize it now, but you had to lose everything to become teachable."

Since at that time I had lost it all and had no defenses left, I could begin to suffer, to feel the pain that had been inflicted on me as a child. That pain would help me reconnect with myself and take me from where I was, hopefully, to a place where I could finally retire that pain and damage for good. Maybe I *could* learn how to love and learn to live without shame, fear, guilt, or addiction.

He was very clear that the sexual betrayal and abuse had affected me sexually, physically, mentally, emotionally, and spiritually. In his opinion, it would be nearly impossible for me to heal if I weren't participating and sharing my recovery process in a community of men suffering as I was.

We went into significant depth about my extended family and the worry, concern, and caretaking behaviors that I had grown accustomed to over so many years. Dr. O'Connor was also clear that, other than needing intense therapy to understand how the molestations created so much havoc in my life, I needed to learn how my family system contributed to my dysfunctional behaviors. While he awakened me to understanding family systems, I still had only two experiences to compare and understand how such systems operated: I grew up in my family system and spent twenty-six years in Jane's before entering recovery.

Although Jane's system was not truly healthy, I came to realize my family's system included much more dysfunction and distortion. Five out of the six of our marriages ended in divorce, and three of the six siblings were involved in multiple marriages and divorces. In addition to this, my siblings and I suffer from various addictions and maladies: food addiction, drug addiction, prescription drug addiction, abuse of alcohol, nicotine addiction, and, in my case, even sex addiction.

I truly feel that Jane's parents and my parents were four people who adored their children and would have done anything within their power for any one of them, and actually did the best they could. No parent is perfect; no parent always does the right things and always makes the right decisions for his or her children. But it was now obvious to me that the eleven children from both families hadn't received adequate nurturing or developed true understandings of life's realities. What I learned in recovery—which is just about universally agreed upon—is that a child's brain is significantly formulated from birth to age twelve (http://www.childdevelopmentinfo.com/development/piaget.shtml). Therefore, while our parents, like millions of other parents around the world, did what they thought was best, there were definitely disconnected and unclear messages given. One might ask why this could have occurred, but what I've learned is it was because the generation who raised them had their own dysfunctions, and our parents simply repeated those maladies.

Dr. O'Connor recommended that if I studied and researched the origin of my family, I would probably see what we deem both *good* and *bad* characteristics being repeated generation after generation after generation. In studying my family's history, I realized my parents had been raised by the GI Generation, who were unified by the accepted phrase "sacrifice for the common good." This was not a very emotionally healthy foundation for my parents' generation, which was called "the Silent Generation"—the majority of people who were born and lived through the Great Depression. Its characteristics were defined as grave, fatalistic, and expecting disappointment. Again, one would have to say, not a very healthy outlook on life.

This Silent Generation gave birth to the largest generation in the United States: the baby boomers. Including Jane and me, all but one of our siblings were boomers. On a percentage basis, this generation has had more divorces, addictions, and unsettlement than the generations before it. One would only have to trace the emotional development from the GI Generation to the Silent Generation and then to the baby boomers to see how we got to the point where we are today.

My main focus of study and need of understanding of the last three generations was my parents' generation—the Silent Generation. It was difficult for my mom to help me understand the events of 1959 because I believe she was still reeling from learning that Jimmy—one of her closest girlfriend's sons—had committed the same carnage upon me as had John. While my mom would eventually come around, I needed someone now! I needed to know if it were possible that my aunts and uncles knew what had happened to me in 1959 and that all of these adults together didn't know what to do, therefore nothing was done. I had always had a close, warm, and loving relationship with my aunt Josephine, who was also my godmother. When I asked if I could come to see her, all she knew at the time was that she had heard I had had an affair, which had caused my separation from Jane.

When I showed up that night at her home, I had lost a significant amount of weight since she had last seen me. I was ashen and very emotionally unsettled. While she told me that she had no idea about what had happened to me in 1959, I'm sure it was clear to her that evening I was in an emotional crisis. I talked, and she listened. She not only encouraged me to talk but also invited me back, to continue to help me work through my confusion concerning the events of some fifty years previous. She became an integral human connection to the process of my recovery over the next two years. She was supportive and understanding. I look back over those two years and often wonder where I would be today if my aunt Josephine hadn't been able to understand me or even be tolerant of what had caused my abhorrent sexual behavior.

I'm sure when this seventy-eight-year-old great-grandmother had held me in her arms at just twenty-three herself—a young, beautiful, engaged woman—she'd had no idea I would ring her doorbell fifty-five years later, needing her emotional support as much as I needed air to breathe.

My mother could have chosen someone other than my aunt Josephine to be my godmother, but just as I believe God intervened concerning my son Paul, I truly believe He knew I would need someone to be there for me fifty-five years after my birth. He knew my aunt Josephine would listen, understand, and give me the love I so passionately needed at that time.

As Dr. O'Conner and I continued our sessions, I desperately wanted answers to certain questions. I told him I would never do anything out of my physical control because I feared being incapacitated. I wouldn't care if I was killed, but I was extremely fearful of physically risking bodily harm to myself, regardless of whether it brought me happiness or joy. I participated in none of the physical activities my wife and sons would on our many vacations.

Dr. O'Connor explained, "You were so traumatized by the sexual abuse that you were actually afraid to try anything in life that wasn't in your total control, because feeling out of control was a trigger for the memories."

I also had issues with normal physical contact. To this day I've never had a facial or a massage. The thought of someone touching me is still an unfathomable event that I could never let happen. By being so traumatized, I had been sentenced never to develop or experience intimacy or emotional trust. Even watching a loving, romantic scene on television or in a movie would make me very uneasy and nervous. Now I knew why. My childhood trauma left me fearful to experience emotional vulnerability because I would be terrified that if I experienced it I would fall apart. It was self-preservation.

I continued to seek more and more information to fully understand my condition and what I would need to do to heal—if that were even possible. I returned to Dr. Gartner's book, *Beyond Betrayal*, in which he solely addresses and deals with the effects of male childhood sexual abuse and the results for the child as he grows into adulthood. I was so taken by his studies and work in the field that I was determined to meet him.

The majority of what he wrote hit so many chords and feelings and covered so many aspects of my personal experiences that I felt as though he had interviewed me before writing his book. Early on in the book he wrote, "For example, a seven-year-old might obey a teenage neighbor who invites him to his home, simply because he's older and authoritative." Was it possible that Dr. Gartner had been there in 1959? Obviously not, but if you were me, you could see why I couldn't put the book down.

I e-mailed Dr. Gartner on a Friday afternoon, and he answered me the next day—a doctor helping a total stranger on the weekend! By that Monday I had scheduled an appointment with him in New York for the next week.

Dr. Gartner asked me to explain what had happened in 1959; I wanted to do so since I was thirsty for knowledge of how these attacks had molded my life. After about twenty minutes he sat back in his chair and spoke in a very calm voice, giving me his insight into the clinical and psychological damage that had confused and devastated me for almost five decades. He said that my perpetrators had created the destructive behavior that would put me in a trance, and from that I would deduce that the only time I could calm myself down was when I was acting out the way I had been abused.

What I still wanted to understand was how a child could become an addict at such a young age. Dr. Gartner explained that the sexual abuse had created a significant form of unnerving fear. I was so terrified of having an emotional life, afraid that if I felt something emotional, it would become too overwhelming for my psyche to handle. Unfortunately I was unable to turn to my parents for help because I was too afraid they would holler at or hit me for letting it happen. Once raped at seven, with no family to turn to, there was no chance for me to continue any normal human emotional development. All of my behaviors were in the service of self-preservation.

I could understand the earlier diagnosis that the abuse had caused post-traumatic stress disorder as well as severe anxiety, but I still couldn't understand how, at seven, the molestations had created such overpowering sexual compulsions as well.

His best way of explaining it to me was to say that after the attacks I still had a desire to live, which was not the case with every childhood rape victim. Along with this, the attacks made me want to feel in control so I wouldn't have to feel the powerlessness of being so violated, but such thoughts of control are unrealistic for someone who was just seven.

It's a paradox that someone with a compulsion feels he's in charge of what he's doing, but this may be the *only* time in his life when such a person feels in complete control, even if that control is merely an illusion. As I grew older, I found other things I could control, such as my businesses. Making money also gave me a feeling of control over the people around me by making them dependent on me. In bed I would also always try to take control, but again, my control over my sexual *compulsion* was the biggest illusion I ever had—I had no such control.

As it related to the clinical component, Dr. Gartner was certain that when such a young child is so traumatized, he has to act out because the compulsive behavior tranquilizes him no differently from a person with obsessive compulsive disorder (OCD) who compulsively checks things or counts to soothe himself or herself. *Sex* would soothe my tremendous anxiety, even if I didn't understand why I had the anxiety in the first place or why it soothed me. Dr. Gartner explained that the human body secretes certain opioids during stress. Opioids, related to opium, have a tranquilizing effect on the body. During my childhood sexual abuse my body had released these chemicals to allow me to survive the trauma. It's a built-in survival mechanism that had been activated during the attacks.

Unfortunately for me and *hundreds of millions* of sexually abused men and women, these opioids are very addictive because they are so effective in calming down the nervous system that the body continues to desire them. What a baffling situation! I thought that if I didn't produce the opioids to help me get through the trauma I wouldn't have survived. The release of these chemicals allowed me to live through such a vile perpetration until I would be able to make some sense of how to handle such an atrocity.

The natural way to produce opioids is through reaching a threshold of stress, at which point a cycle would begin for me. I'd feel anxiety and then seek a way to relieve that anxiety and not have it escalate to an intolerable level. My body knew that secreting these stress-reducing hormones would accomplish this. Thus my body would tell me to look for situations that would make it release these opioids. What better way to look for stress relief than sexual behavior, which caused my body to produce them in the first place? It had always worked.

I discussed this process in great detail with Dr. Gartner. He explained that children face stressful situations just like anybody else. The issue is one of degree. A child may have a nightmare or be punished by parents and not allowed to go out and play with friends, which at the time seems like the end of the world. Think about your own adult-sized problems. You may be able to step back from what ailed you last week and be able to laugh about it now, seeing in retrospect how small and insignificant it was. But at the time it was happening, it caused traumatic stress that produced opioids in your body.

On the other hand, we've all heard of post-traumatic stress disorder (PTSD). It's not associated with a child being grounded for bad behavior or that sales report you failed to get done on time last week. It's associated with the most extreme catastrophes a human can experience: war, witnessing a murder, narrowly escaping death...rape. Post-traumatic stress disorder is a serious condition. The body produces opioids just as it does during times of everyday stress, except that during an enormously heinous experience the production goes into hyperdrive. Normally your body regulates these opioids so the amount produced reflects the amount of stress being experienced.

People who suffer post-traumatic stress disorder often become addicted to opioids and thus seek out similar situations that recreate the original stressful experience: soldiers beg to return to duty, people take up skydiving; crime victims want to become cops; nurses choose to work in emergency rooms.

But what happens when such people do not produce large amounts of opioids? They lie in bed all day, unable to move. The problem is that society chastises the person lying in a fetal position in bed and applauds the skydiver.

The truth is, both have been damaged; it is simply that both bodies are reacting differently. One is producing exorbitant amounts of opioids while the other lacks production and experiences depression. A small amount of opioids is healthy and fine. An overabundance is unhealthy because, like opium, it can become addictive.

When a young boy is exposed to massive amounts of opioids during a major trauma, his mind and body have not developed enough to allow him to be able to reason through the situation that is happening to him. Thus, because of the extreme immaturity of the mind and body of a child, his situation is actually far worse than that of an adult rape victim or any adult victim of any major trauma because he is far less equipped to integrate it or make sense of what is happening. His behavior becomes patterned unconsciously, and he becomes stunted in his emotional growth.

There is a reason we have different suggested drug dosages for people of different ages and weights. A full-sized adult may take two ibuprofen tablets for pain or fever, but that dosage could kill a newborn. Basically that was what happened when I was raped multiple times at age seven. It was as if I had been shot up with heroin and while it did not kill me right then, it did cause an addiction, as it would in most children.

What Dr. Gartner emphasized to me was that, for most men with these compulsions, conscious thoughts and desires don't have to occur—the cycle is automatic.

"If you were betrayed as a boy," he said, "especially if it was repeated betrayal, you may have been programmed to expect betrayal as a natural part of life. You don't even think about it. Your responses may include unwanted impulses to the current world around you. Right now, do you act from your own impulses, thoughts, and feelings? Otherwise you're responding as you did long ago.

"With all of these inputs telling you that you're being betrayed, you'll have a hard time thinking rationally, knowing what to believe, relaxing, enjoying, and nourishing your relationships. All men who have experienced childhood sexual abuse struggle with this predicament. They wanted different things, for example to live or feel without shame or guilt, yet their minds' automatic reactions gave them something else. Taking charge isn't easy, especially if you've been abused. It's a constant struggle. It's almost *impossible* to lead a happy and more satisfying life when your mind refuses to cooperate."

Dr. Gartner stated, "A belief system creates a moral compass that allows us to navigate life. Sexual abuse is a major betrayal of a boy's belief system. Without a belief system, you are a candle in the wind. Without purpose or reason, you'll be either passive or impulsive. The solution won't come easily. You'll most likely have to push yourself through uncomfortable, lonely landscapes to discover purpose and reason."

Dr. Gartner has given in-depth thought and purpose to taking charge of your recovery. This was what I wanted to do. I wanted to leave my old behaviors of mistrust, stress, loneliness, anxiety, and addiction behind and take command of my recovery. I wanted to stop living my life as a victim! I wanted to *heal*! I wanted to *live*! I wanted to feel *worthy*! I wanted to *love*!

"Recovery must be deliberate," he said. "You must decide you want to be better, and you must be willing to work toward that goal. Recovery won't happen on its own. Remember, you are rewiring your brain, making new connections to old, split-off feelings and memories. The only way the brain can be rewired is through experience. You will learn by living and doing. You can improve your reaction to unwanted, dissociated feelings or memories, your understanding, and your insight, and adopt a positive attitude. As you learn to accept them, you'll probably find you experience the memories less frequently.

"The reward isn't one big prize at the end of your journey. It's a new way of experiencing and living life. The ultimate reward is loving the journey itself."

I don't know what provoked or led Dr. Gartner to study, learn, and write about male childhood sexual abuse. Yet I do know that other than making a living as a writer and a psychologist, God gave him a calling to reach out to do his work so that men like me could learn to understand why they lived lives of fear, isolation, torment, havoc, and addiction year after year after year.

Through his work and studies he has given me the answer to the question I had pondered for almost half a century: why was I so sexually compulsive? As I sat before him, I made a vow to take his work and his results and push on with my recovery. I believe his diagnosis and message were sent from God through him to me. I thanked Dr. Gartner for everything—his book, his professional counseling, his support, and his time—and I encouraged him to continue his outstanding work, which gives adults like me a reason to live and to understand what havoc our sexual molestations have caused in our lives.

The clinical analyses of Dr. DiCesare, Dr. O'Connor, and Dr. Gartner were devastating to me and left me extremely despondent. I wondered out loud where Jane fit in all of this. Outside of everything that had happened to me, she was (and still is) my best friend in the world. I didn't want to lose that. There was nothing that depressed me more and sank me into a bluer depression than my loss of Jane and the boys.

Dr. Gartner said, "Being intimate means allowing another person to know your innermost nature. It means relinquishing caution, defensiveness, and self-concern and being openly honest with your thoughts and feelings. Being intimate is a complex challenge if you were sexually betrayed as a child. The prospect of intimacy may be unendurable, even if it's by someone you love, like, or trust. If you're unable to be intimate, you are apt to feel isolated. The more cut off you feel, the more you may despair."

Dr. Gartner continued, "Emotional intimacy seems to meld two souls together in love. But being sexual isn't necessarily being intimate."

Understanding emotional intimacy was a goal I hoped I would achieve with Jane as I moved on with my journey.

Chapter 16

Journey

What a painful and complex journey! When my life and world came to an abrupt stop, the resulting isolation and depression overwhelmed me and crushed me.

So what could I do? I could do what a vast majority of people with addictions do—I could go back to my vice. I could either return to my old behaviors, which were very familiar, or work on moving forward by creating new behaviors. If I were going to create new behaviors, I would have to start to think—and live my life—as if I were going to be a survivor of and not a victim of my sexual abuse traumas.

Now, for the first time in years, there was no legitimate reason for guilt—at least as it pertained to being unfaithful. I had been asked to leave my home. My wife and I were legally separated. Technically I *could* date. But I had never really dated in the classic sense. Dating is about building a relationship that could lead to identifying a partner with whom one could fall in love and start a journey as a couple. Sexual relations are a part of this process, but for me it had always been the *only* part.

Although I had often taken women out to dinner and drinks when I was single, it was merely a prelude to sex—or at the very least a setting of the table for eventual sex. I never really had a true female friend. In my mind men were friends and women were solely for sexual relations and to relieve my stress-induced anxiety attacks.

Over the many years and all of the things we had gone through together, Jane became my best friend. Ironically, our diminishing sex life helped to foster an even stronger friendship. The more I liked Jane, the more she became my closest confidant and supporter—my *rock*—and the less desirable I found her sexually. When she and I had relations, I needed to dissociate myself because I cared for her, and sex to me didn't include caring. I wasn't connected, and Jane could feel my detachment. She had emotional needs, and physical sexual technique or frequency can never fill the void of the lack of loving emotion.

Now armed with the understanding of how my childhood sexual abuse had made my life a complete shambles, I had to decide to continue whatever life I had left either living in my old behaviors or doing one of the hardest things a human being can do: changing my very *nature*. I decided to work on changing my nature. I now had been opened up to a psychological analysis by three doctors of what had been going on inside of my brain and body since those dark days of 1959. It was like when people first find out that they have cancer. A frequent initial response is, "I wish I didn't know. I wish I could just die from it and not have to go through the knowledge that something is eating away at me and killing me."

That was how I now felt about sex. For the first time, I truly knew I was using sex and women to manage my compulsive anxiety disorder as a result of the sexual abuse I had endured as a child—and it made me depressed beyond words. I thought of myself as nothing more than a heroin addict shooting poison into my veins. How on earth could I enjoy it, even for the moment it was happening, knowing full well now this was what was going on inside of me? Once my denial was gone and I was *conscious* of my behavior, it made it more difficult to go back into denial and into my old behaviors.

The next day I saw Dr. O'Connor and told him of my decision of wanting to work on changing my nature, but I told him I felt sick, the worst I had felt since entering recovery. He said the reason I felt worse was that I had now hit a *new* bottom. Now I knew what I was doing. Now I knew I was exploiting women by having relations with them solely in order to fix something broken inside me, and it made me sick to my soul.

From that point on I gave up on having any sexual activity whatsoever. This was not a specific edict from any of the doctors; it was something I felt I needed to do as much as I had formerly felt I needed to act out to soothe my extreme anxiety.

Some people close to me had sniped that I was using my childhood sexual attacks as an excuse for my philandering, that I wasn't accepting responsibility. Well, if they thought that was the case, I would certainly prove them wrong by my approach to my own recovery. I was going to try to take control over the one thing I could never control in my entire life. I decided that part of my recovery would require me to control my own body, and its addiction to the opioids it would secrete prior to acting out, by abstaining from sex—any form of sexual release—and avoiding stressful anxiety situations until I had reached a point of solace and normalcy.

Part of my journey to recovery was for me to accept that Jane was still my wife. Although she had asked me to leave our marital home and had given me no indication she would ever fully forgive me—and no assurances she would let me return and be her husband again—if I didn't begin to think of her as my wife, as the person I should have been faithful to, then how could I ever imagine we could possibly be together again? I needed to remain committed to Jane—whether we were together or not—if there were ever any hope for us to reunite or for me to control my compulsive behavior.

Furthermore, I was now committed to honesty and working hard on my recovery and connecting wires in my brain that had been disconnected for decades. By and large I had been a decent husband with the exception of one glaring area of deceit. Now I swore I would forevermore be *completely* honest with Jane. There would be no asterisks in this vow. I needed to gain back her trust and love. I needed to work hard in my recovery process in order to fix my physical and psychological maladies. I had to do it so I could prove to her I could change my behaviors by changing my nature, which, Dr. O'Connor stated, "could be harder than changing the mouth of a river."

The night I left my home for the last time, Jane and I felt it was important to give the boys a straight talk on what was going on. As they sat on the sofa, I gathered all the strength I could muster and said, "As you already know, there are some things Dad has done that were not right—and there is an explanation for what happened, but I'm not ready to talk to you about it yet. I just want you to know that in some ways I am not the man you think I am today, while in other ways I am *exactly* the man you always thought me to be."

Over the next month I continued to visit the boys, often taking Luke to basketball practice just as we had always done. We'd talk, but more often than not we both tried to keep it light. I was going either for therapy or to my group meetings nearly every day, trying to understand more and more of what was wrong with me and what I'd have to do in order to get myself healthy and well.

One day I went over to the house a little early to pick up Luke for basketball practice. Paul was home from college, so I wanted to see him as well. It was dinnertime, and Jane was cooking pasta. Paul had a friend over for supper, so we couldn't speak freely.

Living alone was not agreeing with me, and like quite a few times before, my stress and anxiety were causing a bout of anorexia nervosa. I had lost nearly twenty-five pounds that I really could not afford to lose. Jane took pity on me and offered me a home-cooked meal, which I couldn't refuse.

I'm not the world's most careful man. I tried to help Jane with dinner by grating some cheese. I made a bit of a mess—nothing horrible, but cheese flew around, and some spilled on the floor. Jane got upset, and I humbly cleaned it up.

After dinner, Luke got into my car to head off to the courts. He was unusually quiet for a while before he opened up a conversation. "You know, Dad, you could have been a bit more careful with the cheese, and on the other hand, Mom went a little overboard. She shouldn't have made such a big deal about it."

It suddenly occurred to me—Luke was confused about how his mom and dad could ever get back together if little things like this were such major events.

When I brought Luke home after practice, I pulled Jane aside and told her, "Look, I think it's time the boys know exactly what's been going on with me concerning my needed therapy and recovery program. I promise I'll be delicate, but I think I'm ready to handle it now, and the longer we go about withholding information, the more they'll just be making up scenarios inside their own heads, most of them off the mark."

Jane had been deathly afraid to tell them. She said, "Oh, so now you're going to tell them, and they're going to feel sorry only for *you*."

This showed me the depths of people's ignorance about childhood sexual abuse and its effects carried throughout an adult's life. Jane had been given the opportunity to learn all I knew, but she'd run away with her hands over her ears, unwilling to deal with it. One of the things I'd liked about her family when I'd first met them was that they seemed so happy all the time. What I came to learn was that they simply suppressed everything. Feeling blue? Change the subject and put on a smile! I guess if that worked for them, that was fine. It didn't work for me, and it was the opposite of what I needed from a partner, especially then.

"Well, Jane, I've been to three doctors, and they don't agree with you. The boys are going to realize it's not their journey but mine, and if they don't understand that, I'll make sure they do. What happened to me as a child is a part of my life, and it's the reason my sexual behavior was so horrid and why they woke up one day and learned you had asked me to leave our home. I've discussed this with Dr. O'Connor, and he said I should tell the boys together with you at home, or I could bring them to his office and explain what happened to me as a child with him."

Jane got defensive. "No, no, no, Do it with me."

Paul's friend was gone, so we called the boys down for a heart-to-heart talk. I said, "Listen, Paul and Luke; I'm going to tell you something that happened to Dad in my childhood that's not an excuse for my deceiving your mother, but it is an explanation."

I began slowly, because there is no easy way to tell your sons you were raped when you were seven. As I was nearing the end of my story, Luke slammed his hand on the table and said, "Well damn, Dad; that explains it. All my friends think you're a terrific and caring dad. They love coming over to our house because you make them feel so welcome."

It was clear in Luke's mind that something so traumatic had to have occurred for me to be acting out in a way he could never have imagined.

I reassured them I was deep into my therapy and recovery work and was trying my best to get better. Paul immediately turned to Jane and said, "Mom, you have to go with him."

Jane said, "Oh, I'm available to Daddy."

Not quite so—she went to one session but just couldn't deal with or understand how completely disconnected I had been my entire life. It wasn't her fault; the odds against her understanding were a million to one. The words *molestation, sexual abuse, rape, addiction, therapy,* and *recovery* would send her into a tailspin, as, I learned in my recovery, it does to many people. As I dove deeper into my recovery, I started to think if most people couldn't think or talk about sexual betrayal and abuse, how was I going to live with it or work through it?

As time passed, the boys would ask me questions about how I was getting along in my therapy and recovery, what I had learned, and what I was working on to get well. They seemed genuinely interested, which made me smile and feel loved. They're both so good and so kind but intellectually curious as well.

At times I would tell Luke, "You saved my life," because his discovery of that e-mail I had left exposed on my computer had given me a chance to learn how to live.

To Paul I'd say, "You understood my trauma and what I would need in recovery by asking Mom to go with me." He was the first member of our family who truly did understand. What more can any parent ask for from his or her children?

Back in 1959 I was just a boy going about life like many other children, making friends and excelling in school, a happy child growing and thriving in what I felt was a beautiful world. This came to a crashing end when I was marked by two pedophilic predators. As an adult, I found myself angry, resentful, and upset about the vile perpetrations. I thought, *What if I hadn't been molested? What if my attackers hadn't taken my trust, my heart, and my soul at such a tender age?*

I recall my first two years of academic achievements and wonder if perhaps I could have gone to college and achieved even greater heights in my career. Perchance instead of being sentenced to a workaholic's life, I could have enjoyed a career and a normal, happy relationship with my wife. To be told the traumatic betrayal left me so terrified that I had never grown emotionally since 1959 was unfathomable. But even worse, I realized it was true. To be told I had never trusted women and had feared emotional attachment to the point of cutting myself off from that need was remarkably accurate. I understood I had been so terrorized by their abominable acts that I was too afraid to experience joy or happiness; learning my only purpose in life was to take care of others because I hadn't been able to take care of myself at age seven was spellbinding.

After the denial, anger, and isolation, I began to realize I had no other choice but to start to learn to accept the hand I had been dealt. For whatever reason, this was my destiny, and I needed to stop asking why. If I was ever to have any peace or happiness, I had to start dealing with who I was—a victim of severe sexual betrayal and abuse as a child that had led me to become very emotionally damaged, disconnected, and self-destructive as an adult.

I had already lost everything—my family, my home, my standing. How could I try to recover at age fifty-five? How many years did I have left? Why not die and avoid going through all this pain and work to recover from a situation I had never caused?

After allowing myself to be eaten up inside, losing significant weight, and going through life in a fog, the answer slowly began to arrive. There was no way for me to go through the horrific events and the decades of duress that had followed without knowing or feeling there is a higher power. Such a power is there for everyone, at all times, regardless of religious beliefs or whatever horrendous experiences a person has endured.

That higher power for me was God and Jesus Christ. It doesn't matter what faith (if any) you practice; God is there for everyone on this earth. A higher power emerges as you understand who God is to you. Just when I thought the suffering couldn't get any worse, a light began to shine. It may have begun as a small one, but that light was showing me a path from despair and toward hope.

Rabbi Shais Taub of Pittsburgh, Pennsylvania has worked in the field of trauma and addiction and is the founding co-director of the Jewish Recovery Community in Milwaukee, Wisconsin. He wrote a small passage concerning the death of Amy Winehouse that I feel epitomizes my own personal thoughts on the need to connect with a higher power to insure my path on my journey to recover. He states: "One of the axioms of recovery is that the addict is beyond human aid and that's why addicts need a 'higher power' to live. You can call that hocus-pocus. I call it an everyday reality. There is no fact more real to me than the idea that no human power can stand up against the power of addiction. Sometimes I think of it as a giant black hole that can devour the light of a thousand suns and remain just an unfathomly black as if no sun had ever shone at all. It is an insatiable vortex that mercilessly consumes every iota of strength that human power can muster. We throw love at it. We throw loyalty at it. We scream at it. We bargain with it. We fight it. And when we just can't fight it anymore, we swear to ignore it, to never let it hurt us again, that is until it pulls us back in."

Like it or not, I had to learn to start to heal. This was a truly humbling position for a man like me because for the first time in my life I had to surrender my control and eventually my defenses—the only two ways I knew how to survive. How in the world could I do this? I had to learn to like and then love myself first, and then take significant actions concerning my mental health. I had to place my recovery foremost in every aspect of my life so I could start the healing process. But this was as foreign to me as learning to speak Chinese. I never thought about doing anything for myself. I never felt worthy of anything materially or emotionally. This was so difficult for me to grasp that I gave significant, serious thought to quitting recovery. It seemed these were things I couldn't do—they were too far out of my reach.

So, in order to get to where I wanted to be, I had to do something I had never done before. I had to ask for help from God on His terms and not on my contract terms. It's been said in recovery that the spiritual piece is the first piece the child loses from the attacks and the last piece that will come back to light. I believe this to be true because I had tried so hard to pray my way to health but to no avail. I first needed to learn and understand the psychological and clinical effects of the molestation before I could feel and draw the spirituality back into my heart and soul. I experienced my first miracle of recovery when I sensed a glimmer of spiritual light within me.

Facing Myself

Chapter 17

I Get a Little Help From My Friends

Dr. O'Connor was extremely convincing when he made me start to think that maybe I did have value. In learning the manifestations of the sexual abuse, I had to accept that I was psychologically scarred and clinically addicted. Dr. O'Connor gave me a brochure, *The Cycle of Addiction;* its contents fit like a glove.

I would feel extreme anxiety concerning any matter, especially when it came to my siblings, my business, and the fact that I wasn't worthy of Jane and her clear understanding of empirical right and wrong. These emotional events placed me in stressful predicaments, creating far more fear and panic than any one situation actually merited. Rather than getting outwardly flustered or emoting, I would start to go into a trance.

Throughout most of this cycle, the vivid memories of the sexual abuse came rushing into my brain. I had to stop this feeling or the stress would drive me insane. The only way my brain knew how to dissipate such stress and depression and to relieve the extreme anxiety was by acting out sexually. Sex was such a strong release that I would lay almost paralyzed when I was finished. It wasn't the encounter but the *effect* of the encounter that soothed my angst.

During my early months of therapy, I started to better understand Dr. Gartner's statement from *Beyond Betrayal:* "… for sexually abused children, these thoughts [of acting out] don't have to occur, the cycle is automatic." I was finally beginning to understand that these trances controlled my life.

In another of his books, *Betrayed as Boys*, Dr. Gartner wrote, "All forms of early trauma can powerfully affect later character development. Reactions to sexual abuse are influenced by his developing personality, his family, and cultural context, his physiological resources and the external events in his life."

When I first entered psychotherapy, I still couldn't work on healing for *myself*. I was trying to recover for my *family*—my two terrific sons and my wonderful wife. I clung to this thought. Over time I came to understand I had to do it for me primarily and not them. This wasn't my concept; it was Dr. O'Connor's. He tried to drum into me that if I couldn't care for or love *myself*, I would be of no use to them *or* me.

By my third month of intensive therapy with Dr. O'Connor, I began to understand more readily what he was teaching me. It seems a rare occurrence that a patient agrees to break himself or herself down into a malleable pile of clay, fully open to new thoughts, patterns, and actions. It takes time, and it can be extremely frustrating and tedious for the patient as well as the therapist. But quite simply it is the only way to start the healing process.

I started to learn the actions necessary for me to overcome the severe sexual abuse I had so long suppressed. I also learned why the only way I knew how to fix my anxiety disorder and dissociative state of mind—through sexually acting out—was neither healthy nor effective.

Dr. O'Connor reinforced my learning about the triggers Dr. DiCesare had taught me about as well—the ones that would set me off into my cycle, specifically my dissociative state of mind. The start of any anxiety or stressful situation was a trigger. While there were many things that caused me anxiety, a significant trigger was dealing, for thirty-seven years, with my siblings and their life issues and trying to fix things that went wrong in their lives, especially when those actions would cause my parents great despair. Every time I picked up the phone and heard one of their voices, a trigger would go off. Somehow, in order to begin healing myself, I had to let them go. I had to let them work out their own problems so I could be of *any* real value to *anybody*.

Yet how could I stop caring for them and fixing the sorts of problems that I had been handling my entire adult life? Even after losing Jane and the boys, I was still carrying out these brotherly (actually fatherly) duties daily for my mother and my siblings.

My therapy was teaching me that continuing this cycle—and I was learning that *everything* is part of *some* cycle—simply enabled my brothers and sisters. And for as much as I would get upset with their needs, I now knew I had just as much reason to be upset with myself. I was the enabler, and this behavior had to stop. It didn't work well for me or my siblings, and it definitely wouldn't help the next generation of our family. Each time I interceded on anyone's behalf, it did not allow them to grow; it did not make them stronger. It had the opposite effect, and there was plenty proof of that.

In our own minds we envision that when we help someone, we are like good parents running alongside our child attempting to ride a two-wheeler for the first time. We are the temporary replacements for their training wheels, and once we've held them up and they've gained their confidence and skill, they soon ride off on their own, leaving us smiling in their wake.

We assist them in their times of need, but sometimes the people we help never ride off on their own. Every time we try to let them go, they call us back, pleading that they cannot continue under their own power. Thus we continue to cling to the wheel of their life's bicycle, running alongside them, wheezing as we lose breath, leaving our own freedom behind. We enable them to go through life being carried by us. They careen from crisis to crisis created to some degree by themselves and largely contributed to by the system in which we were raised, always knowing that someone will be there to fix things up and make them right.

As the recovery process taught me, my behavior of over-caring and over-involvement was indeed *codependency*. While I had subconsciously been resenting the needs of my siblings for years, what I never knew was that I was equally codependent upon them. I needed them to need me! Without their crises, what value would I be to them? But when the phone rang with a new problem, it would consistently trigger my cycle. It was all about cycles, and all of these cycles were destroying me.

Rabbi Shais Taub describes the devastation of codependency in the Huffington Post as: "For those who have only observed the chaotic drama of addiction from a safe distance, let me tell you that the concept of it being a 'family disease' is painfully true. The insanity of 'active codependence' is just as gruesome a spectacle to behold as the addicts own downward spiral. To watch a life wasted trying to stop the unstoppable is something that can just tear your heart out. We learn that all we can do is carry the message of recovery, which is that if the addict can find a higher power, they can live a long, happy life. And if not, well, no other power in the universe can stop this terminal disease from running its course."

During the fourth month of recovery, an event happened as I was boarding a flight for a business meeting in Europe. I received a call about a cash disbursement for one of my nephews. For once I firmly disagreed with the solution being suggested for this latest problem. In reaction to my own firmness, this change to my well-worn behavior and what would have been the beginning of another of my cycles, I immediately felt overwhelmed by severe anxiety and stress. I had done what the doctors had told me to do, but I didn't immediately feel better—I felt worse. At the same time I had an eight-hour flight ahead of me, and I boarded the plane in a state of great despair and agitation.

Why did I feel bad? Why did I feel guilty? After all, I had just straightened out everything following my father's death, which was no small feat since one of my siblings had put my parents' entire estate into a chaos nobody believed could be fixed. It took me fourteen months to repair everything, including yet another cash infusion. But now that everything was fixed and on track, my mother was going to start the maddening cycle of dysfunction all over again by distributing money for frivolous reasons.

By the time I landed in Europe, I was sweating, stressed, and extremely frustrated. As if on reflex, everything I'd been learning in my therapy sessions was starting to make sense. I hadn't slept a wink on the plane. I tried to read and to prepare for my upcoming business meetings, but in reality I was in a wakeful trance that kept me alert and restless for the entire flight. After landing I went straight to the hotel and finally got some sleep. I wanted to share my experience with Dr. O'Connor back in the states, but due to time-zone differences and my schedule I had to wait eight hours before he would arrive in his office.

I knew I couldn't return to my cycle of sexual release in order to bring me full circle; relapsing now could put me in a state of despair that would cripple me far worse than it had done for all of my adult life. After decades of caretaking, I finally made a decision I had never thought possible. I called my mom, who knew I was in recovery, and told her I had thought about it long and hard and had decided to step back from running the affairs regarding her and Dad's estate.

I further expressed that it was unhealthy for me to continue in our existing family system. I couldn't do it and heal. Every one step I would take forward in recovery would be negated when I would have to make decisions for my siblings or mother and end up stepping back two. I needed to separate myself from my siblings and what remained of my father's estate. I could tell my mother wasn't exactly thrilled with my decision, but she said I should do whatever was going to help and support my recovery process.

I wondered how long I would have to go on like this, how many days, months, or years it might take before I would be healthy enough to reenter my extended family system. Or perhaps that would never be in the cards. When you have done something for as long as I had in one fashion or another, you never think of life differently. It was like retirement. I've seen so many men say they were semi-retiring, go fishing or whatever for a while, then come back to check on things at their old businesses in order to stay active. Oftentimes they found they were indeed replaceable, even though they had never imagined that. Maybe this would be for the best. While I was so focused on how I was being crippled by all their troubles, maybe I was the one who had been crippling them, not allowing them to stand on their own and learning to work out their own problems. I was learning that each person holds some responsibility for what happens in a relationship.

For the first time in my life I had taken a stand for *me*. Effective immediately, my younger brother would be taking charge. All questions regarding money and operations would be directed to him.

My next call was to Jane. Her reaction was stunned silence. Jane had been asking me to set boundaries regarding my extended family for over twenty-five years. She didn't want it for her own sake, but, while not fully understanding to what degree it was harming me, she knew it was a cause of great distress in my life. All Jane wanted was 100 percent of me, for me to be in the moment and fully alive when I was with her. While I was still unable to give her the emotional connection she so desired, obviously this was one of the many other issues that took me physically away from her as well. For as much as I could have told her about this action simply to regain her confidence—I wanted so much for us to reunite—I wanted her to know I took this step for *me*, solely for my need to get healthier.

The call to my mother and turning the family affairs over to my brother—combined with my sexual abstinence during this episode—were significant actions that told me I truly wanted to heal. I wanted to recover from all the lost years of torment, misery, and havoc.

I had at least five or six people I met through my business career whom I considered close friends. I was told in therapy that these people weren't really my friends but people I could control emotionally. Sure, there was mutual respect and camaraderie, but for them to be *really* my friends, they would have to know who I was, and for them to know the real me, I would have to tell them about the events in my childhood.

I resisted this next step for over a month. How could I tell these people who viewed me as a driven and successful businessman that I had been molested and sexually abused? After all, they thought I had only had an affair. Opening up that much seemed unfathomable. How could I speak of such atrocities to men I felt knew me only as a man's man?

To make things worse, one of the six people was a woman with whom I had only recently developed a working friendship. "Mary" was an extremely successful, intelligent, and talented business executive. While Mary was the newest individual in my group of friends (not quite two years), she knew as much about me as the others—but Dr. O'Connor explained to me that *no one* really knew who I was.

I respected these people enormously. My initial thought was that their opinions of me would change dramatically. I thought they would say something like, "Pete, how could you have let that happen? You're so strong. You've traveled the world and completed complex business transactions that we all admired." And now I was going to bare my soul to them? What would they think of me? But I felt compelled to follow Dr. O'Connor's direction because I was committed to healing and really wanted to feel emotions of joy and happiness, and not just compulsive anxieties and addictions.

I began with one who had been a friend for over twenty-five years. "Steven" was a graduate of Penn's Wharton School of Business, considered the top business school in the nation. He was probably one of the smartest men I knew. As intelligent and business-savvy as Steven was, I always felt he led his professional and personal lives with his heart. In other words, as my Jewish friends were apt to say, "He was a mensch."

When I started to stutter as I told him my story, I could see the hurt and empathy for me in his eyes. I explained, as I would to the others, that it had been recommended to me by Dr. O'Connor to tell him of my childhood ordeal in order to help me heal emotionally from the abusive sexual attacks I had suffered.

As I was coming to the end of my story, Steven hugged me like a brother. He said he knew all the things I'd done for my family and other people over the years, and he admired that I could live through these atrocities and still become the man I was. A tremendous load came off my shoulders with that hug. Steven told me he'd always be there for me and nothing would change our relationship. In fact, he felt this disclosure would only make it stronger.

I wanted to speak to Mary next, but she was going to be out of town for several weeks. That left four men—all with extremely strong, masculine, and successful backgrounds that made disclosing something so vulnerable all the more difficult.

Maybe this was what was intimidating me the most. I still associated this…this thing, this horrible childhood experience, with masculinity, with sexual orientation, with inner strength,

strength of character. I kept blaming myself somehow. I hated this part of me, and I kept saying to the seven-year-old Pete, "*Get up! Fight them off! Beat them! Don't let them do this to you! Don't be a victim! Be stronger than them!*" It didn't matter how much the doctors told me the sexual abuse wasn't my fault or how much they echoed there was nothing I could have done about it at the time. The sexual molestations still stood for something within my mind. They somehow demeaned my self-image. I still could not make myself love the seven-year-old Pete, which meant I couldn't make myself love *me*. And if I could not love myself because I knew what had happened to me as a mere boy, then how could I expect anyone else to after they learned my secret? I was engulfed by self-loathing and embarrassment.

Even after Steven embraced me and made me feel loved and respected, the thought of facing this same situation again frightened me immensely. At some point, someone in my life was going to let me down; someone was going to tell me I was no good, I was a fraud and a weakling, someone to be laughed at, scorned, or pitied. I would no longer represent the man I believed that person thought I was. I envisioned they would view me as something else, something far less. I feared what had happened to me at age seven would negate everything I'd accomplished since then.

I felt the most difficult person to confront would be a man who had been my friend the longest—almost thirty-five years. "Sam" and I were friends and colleagues; we had watched our children grow from babies to adults. His children were all married with children of their own. He had even stood for my son Luke at his confirmation.

I respected and loved Sam to the extent of which I was capable. He was born near my childhood home and had lived in an Italian neighborhood similar to mine. He had earned a college degree and had been a successful banker and a flourishing residential builder.

To describe the vile acts perpetrated on me was excruciating. Over the years, I'd noticed that Sam had a tendency not to look a person directly in the eyes when he spoke. However, during this conversation, his eyes were fixed on mine, and, seeing how painful this talk was for me, I think I saw a tear welling in the corner of his eye. Once I finished, Sam made me feel incredibly relieved that I had unburdened myself to him. Not only did he embrace me, but he also made it a point to touch base every couple of weeks either to catch up or get a bite to eat.

The hardest part of these talks was figuring out a way to get the story started. Once I got going, the next hurdle was trying not to be vague about what happened. I related the story exactly as it had happened so I wouldn't have to clarify any misconceptions later. I gave this exercise my full effort; I desperately wanted to be honest. I'd been told I had to be committed to my recovery or else I wouldn't succeed. Dr. O'Connor's words reverberated in my mind; I knew from my business dealings that I couldn't approach recovery—or any other endeavor for that matter—half-heartedly and still expect a fulfilling return on my investment. I had to be committed; I had to work hard on completing these tasks as suggested. I owed it to Paul and Luke. I owed it to Jane. I owed it to myself.

One by one I met with and spoke to the others. I was beginning to realize how much they really cared for me, and it wasn't just about the business we did together. While they were all in a bit of shock, they were each extremely comforting.

The youngest one, "Bob," I'd basically raised in the business world from the time he was eighteen. While Bob was extremely kind and very hurt that I had been so brutalized, the first question he asked was, "How can we get these sons of bitches?" It was just a sign of how overwhelmed he was that I was so hurt and fractured. I explained to him that revenge was not something that would help my recovery—besides, Jimmy was dead.

Mary finally returned from her business trip, and it was time to speak with her. Mary would be the first woman other than the women in my family—my mother, my wife, my godmother, and my mother-in-law—to whom I had divulged these attacks. Mustering the courage to speak to her made me feel like I was in the deep end of a lake and trying to churn through miles of water to get back safely to shore. I was far, far out of my comfort zone and perplexed as to how what I was about to say would be received. Would she be as understanding and as comforting as my male friends had been? Or would she be a wild card, hitting me with an attitude or with questions I wouldn't be able to see coming? This was the out-of-control feeling I had run from my entire life. I was about to reveal the most sensitive and personal information about myself, and I was uncertain of the outcome.

After a few minutes, Mary could see it was getting difficult for me to talk. She placed her hand on my forearm as if to tell me it was okay and she understood. In fact, she understood more than I ever could have imagined.

By the time I was through explaining what had happened, Mary told me she empathized because someone very close to her had been through the same trauma. For the last twenty years she had watched this person live out most of everything I had just disclosed to her, both psychologically and clinically. I was working on my next corporate project with Mary when my roller-coaster of insanity had come to a halt. I now wonder where I might be today if she had shut the door on me then. I had already lost my family and home. I believe losing my career could have left me totally and completely in ruination. I will remain eternally grateful for Mary's kindness, support, and consideration, and I look forward to our friendship for the rest of my years.

I had now shared my darkest secrets, secrets I thought I would surely take to my grave. It was painful beyond words, but it proved to me a higher power was indeed watching over me. Where once

I thought I had no real friends, I now discovered real friends who cared about me, loved me, and respected me. They now knew who I really was, and they still felt bonds with me. In fact, our bonds were strengthened because I trusted them enough to share this darkest part of myself with them, something I had never been able to do before.

By speaking to my new friends, I had broken my pattern of denial and had overcome another hurdle in my recovery. The next challenge I was asked to face was about changing my behaviors. While I thought at first the worst part of my recovery was over, I would soon discover the work had only just begun.

Chapter 18

I Die Daily

To help and support the change in my behaviors and my way of life, it was recommended I should adopt a twelve-step program very similar to the Alcoholics Anonymous (AA) program. I attended Survivors of Incest Anonymous (SIA) meetings. When most people hear the word *incest* they think only of a family member violating a child in that same family. I was to learn in this group that the broader definition of incestuous violations and betrayals of a child includes those perpetrated not only by family members but also by coaches, teachers, neighbors, or anyone else who has "groomed or gained the trust and or love of a child." Through the SIA group I learned that approximately ninety-two percent of all victims of childhood molestation knew and trusted the people who sexually abused them.

I began to work through each of the twelve steps with Dr. O'Connor. You can read each self-explanatory step, but there was a significant amount of work I had to do to understand fully the meaning of these steps and how to implement each one in my everyday life. These twelve steps outlined the framework on which I built my road to recovery.

Once I started the healing process, I almost felt the same way I had when my predators sexually abused me. I felt like I was stuck in that same mousetrap. I couldn't go back to my old behaviors—I'd learned not only how to avoid them but also how self-destructive they were—and I couldn't go forward until I could be taught how to trust someone emotionally. To accomplish such a feat, I would have to let my defensive walls down—walls that for years had been my only protection in order to survive life.

After months of therapy, Dr. O'Connor thought I was emotionally ready to start the twelve steps of SIA. He felt at this stage of my recovery I fully understood the psychological and physiological damage I had suffered and I was ready to restore my spirituality.

I was nervous, though. After all the hard work and feelings of isolation I had gone through by that point, I couldn't take the possibility of failure. It would be too painful, and I would have to begin my recovery all over again. But I took a deep breath—and, buoyed by Dr. O'Connor's belief in me, I plunged in and began to work the following twelve steps into my life:

> **Step 1:**
> *We acknowledge that we were powerless over the sexual victimization, and due to the wounds caused by it, our lives had become unmanageable.*

It took the total devastation of my entire world before I would admit my life had become unmanageable. To admit I was powerless over my compulsive anxiety disorder and addiction was to give up control, and that did not come easily to me. After I was sexually abused, I never wanted to feel powerless again, so I manipulated every situation into my command and into my comfort zone.

I had no choice but to admit I was indeed helpless. It was time for me to stop my lifelong juggling act. What helped me through this first step was to pray for the following:

- **Honesty** to admit that my life wasn't working.
- **Open-mindedness** to making changes.
- **Willingness** to change.

As I worked through step one, I came to grips with the realities of my life for the first time. I had obsessive traits, and I now realized if I had persisted in living my life as I had in the past, my world would have continued to be unmanageable. This step put a halt to my over-controlling efforts and gave me the permission to quit, to let go, and to acknowledge there existed areas in my life where I was not in total control, nor would I ever be.

Step 2:
We have come to believe that, with a loving higher power's support, we can restore innocence and hope, and continue healing. We can thrive!

If I were to recover, faith in my personal higher power wasn't an option; it was a must. More and more over the passing years I had turned to the Bible and had gone to Mass regularly, seeking understanding of who I was and why I had acted out sexually the way I had. Even during my darkest hours I had made that ninety-percent/ten-percent pact with God, promising Him that if He could possibly forgive my sexually compulsive behavior, I would give to Him all else that I had within me to give; I would dedicate my life to doing good works.

Those who were raised Catholics, especially in the 1950s, were taught that God was all good and caring. However, to be in His graces, you yourself definitely had to be good. I felt like I had succeeded over the course of my life to *be* good…ninety percent of the time. Was that enough? Was it enough for God to give me some sort of comfort to get me through the other ten percent? Now I was making a commitment to Him and to myself to use all of my power—power I owed exclusively to Him—to right the wrongs of that other ten percent. I needed His guidance and mercy to make changes so I could be whole again—whole for the first time since I had been seven.

During my worst, most-isolated moments when I was first separated from my family, the pain and despair were unbearable; they consumed my very existence. What I desperately needed was for God to help me or at least like me enough to help me with the pain and loss.

The second step taught me I needed to trust that a power greater than me was going to start to work in my life. When my despair had reached its lowest point, I started to sense a connection to a higher spiritual power. I realized I even tried to control *God* by making my pact—my ninety/ten formula. Who was I to do such a thing? But that was how sick I was from the sexual abuse and betrayal. That was how much I had sought to manipulate the world around me. I had even tried to mold my vision of how God would work to my own personal agenda!

Dr. O'Connor said, "Religion is for people who are afraid to go to hell. Spirituality is for people like you who've been *in* hell and are seeking a way out." I was responding slowly to this feeling of spirituality. I could sense and feel a connection. The second step began teaching me that God was not only all good and caring; he was also a forgiving and loving God—even for people like me.

I needed help to be the person I wanted to be, the person I thought I *could* be and not the damaged, sexually abused person I had been made to be. I allowed God into my heart, and once I did a feeling of spirituality began to bring me closer to God more than any Mass or Bible reading ever did. Once God was in my heart, my perpetrators had to move out of the way in order to make room for Him.

Step 3:
When we make a decision to align ourselves with the guidance and support of a loving higher power, we are no longer alone.

I always felt somewhat religious. I especially thought I had a true love for and connection to Jesus Christ. But it was always on *my* terms. Yet it began to become clear to me that He felt He could bring me even closer; He even had my sons help me in the process. I had to believe He loved me so much, He knew I would never hurt my son. So when I chose Luke over myself by admitting to him the damaged life I had been living, whether I knew it then or not, at that moment I made my decision to turn my will and my life over to the care of God.

My life was completely in shambles. It was time for me to relinquish control and let God try to manage the mess I'd been juggling for forty-eight years. I finally came to the conclusion that I couldn't barter with God and I had to surrender my will and every part of my life to His care if I wanted to recover.

I had struggled with the effects of my childhood molestation and rapes all my life and had never been able to come to terms with that abuse. I had to learn to trust in God, and if I did, I would no longer feel the need to carry the burden myself. With this step I began to feel God's presence, which in turn helped me feel I had the right to live a normal life. My self-confidence began to grow—only this time it was being built upon a solid rock, not a false front I was wearing for the world.

Prior to working the third step, I felt unworthy of almost everything and very much alone. When a child is sexually abused, his or her senses of value and self-esteem are stolen and crushed, and it usually leads to self-destructive behaviors. I was determined to align myself with God and put an end to my harmful actions and feelings of seclusion.

The most important concept I took from the third step was that I didn't have to act out the urges and sensations in my body. Instead, I could learn how to control them through my thoughts and with God's help, along with the help of my support groups.

Step 4:
Bravely and gently, we inventory the victimization and its effects as well as our strengths and challenges. We have no more secrets from ourselves.

Even though I had been molested and I realized how those events had ruled my life, I had to take responsibility for my own actions, which had hurt many people, especially Jane. My denial had kept me blinded my entire life. My low self-esteem had kept me ignorant about the worth of my life. This step was particularly hard for me because it was very demanding. Upon coming out of denial and processing what had happened to me, I had a significant amount of resentment and rage over the abuse. It made me a caretaker for everyone else but me.

In therapy, I was taught that resentment could end my life. If I didn't ask for God's assistance to help me nourish myself—which I so very badly needed—I would never be able to turn my anger into forgiveness.

I knew immediately that if I didn't try to work this step regularly I would allow negative emotions to cloud all the progress I was making. The key seemed to be to try very hard to live in the present by working actively through recovery rather than choosing to dwell on the past. The mantra I had to repeat to myself was that I was working toward being comfortable in my solitude. Once I started to reconnect to my spirituality, this became more and more achievable.

I took two phrases from the fourth-step prayer and included

them in my daily meditations: "light a candle within my heart" and "remove the wreckage of the past." These two lines became my touchstones, elements I could embrace and understand when so much of what I was going through put me through the gamut of human emotion.

Light a candle within my heart. Yes, God; I'm letting you in. There is this dark spot within me that no one else can see because I've buried it my entire life. It scares me, yet I keep going back to it, and when I go there I do terrible things because that dark place makes me feel small, insignificant, and unworthy. Light a candle there, God. Take that terrible, frightening place and make it warm and bright. Prove to me that every place within my heart can be safe and warm so long as I allow you to be there with me.

Remove the wreckage of the past. Take the ugliness out of me, God, and let the rest of me heal. Take those terrible acts and toss them out of my memory. Rebuild me, God. Exorcise these demons, and cut this darkness out of me. Let me live again.

Step 5:
We share our inventory with a loving higher power and a safe person. We own our strengths and challenges and unburden our shame. We have no more secrets.

Most people might think a person with a sexual compulsive disorder or a sexual addiction has no care or love for God or Jesus Christ, judging simply by his or her actions alone. For me—and I believe millions of other survivors of sexual abuse—this is far from the truth. I so desperately wanted a connection to my higher power, but I began to learn that any true spiritual relationship with God had been severed since the time of my *first* attack. So, once I reached step five, I admitted to God all of my actions and wrongs in my life and came to learn a few very important details:

I couldn't change the past, I couldn't change other people, and I couldn't change God's will. The only thing I could change was *me*.

By that time I had told six people outside of my family about the sexual abuse and my self-destructive actions during my adult life. Yet, in accordance with this step, I continued to reach out to people to whom I felt close—as close as I was ever able to allow myself to be. I continued to confide in the people I worked with and shared time with, letting them know who *I* was.

I looked around at my world as I had built it and saw many people who had been parts of my life for a very long time. These people thought they knew everything there was to know about me. Those who remained in my life did so because there must have been something about me they were drawn to. At times I felt I had been conning them—they knew only the artifice I showed them. I was like an actor who really got into the role by taking it to such an extreme that I too started to believe I was the character they thought I was. But we were all wrong.

The most basic aspect of my recovery was for me to come to grips with *me*—the good and the bad. Next, it was to filter into that the totality of my personal history—again, the good and the bad. I was at once the helpless seven-year-old, a business maven, a loving father, a husband—I was all of these things. I could no more deny *one* of them than I could deny *all* of them. I did all of those things, I had all of those things happen to me, and all of those things contributed to who I really was.

We are all like this. Each of us has his or her own demons, although each of our demons is unique. My demon made me do terrible things I had kept from my family. My demon kept me from forming the sorts of bonds and relationships that make life truly rich and fulfilling. I had allowed my demon to set me apart from everyone else; it kept me from trusting people and letting go. Now what I had to do was find the people who had been victimized by *my* demon, even if they themselves did not know it, and tell them the true story. This did not mean I had to reach out to every new person I met. It was about all the people who were already in my life in some fashion. I was surprised by how many there were. Perhaps I took a lot of them for granted. I certainly know I kept them all at bay, letting them know only the part of me I wanted to show.

Did these people know there was something a little off about me? Sometimes when a person is suppressing a deep, dark secret, they get paranoid about what people think. They wonder, *Why did he make a joke like that? Does he know about the abuse? Can he tell just by looking at me?*

Pretty soon that paranoia degenerates into imagining everyone is looking at you, whispering about you, standing in the shadows of your dark place and judging you, laughing at you. It creates the stress trigger, and I had known only one way to fight that demon—by acting on my destructive behaviors.

Now I had to address the triggers by stopping them before they even began. Part of the process of doing this was to continue to let people know what had happened to me and how it helped create who I was and why I had acted as I had. Yes, I was confessing to much bad behavior—the philandering—but I was also explaining the manic control freak in me, the man who was uncomfortable in crowds, the man who could never let down his guard.

By sharing my trauma, I gave a deeper understanding of myself to anyone who cared to learn. Each time I disclosed more of me, it was extremely difficult, but nearly every single time the overall reaction was positive. By offering up my true self, I was bringing people closer to me.

In this step I came to grips with all my deep shadows. While I felt my life had been derailed as a child, once I was out of denial I needed to admit my actions were wrong and hurtful no matter what had been done to me.

In my daily meditations I included the following prayer, which helped me immensely: *God, I understand that you already know me completely. I am now ready to reveal myself to you openly and humbly—my hurtful behaviors, self-centeredness, and negative traits. I am grateful to you for the gifts and abilities that have brought me to this point in life. Take away my fear of being known and rejected. I place myself and my life in your care and keeping.*

Step 6:
We become willing, with a loving higher power's help, to replace the effects of the victimization with respect, compassion, acceptance and self-care.

In step six, our emotions are allowed time to develop with our new experiences. Working this step with Dr. O'Connor gave me a trust in God that I had no choice but to accept and embrace. I could not change merely on the strength of my own willpower. I had already tried that for decades to no avail.

Now I am relying on God to give me the strength to resist my defects. I realized a feeling of safety in this step. I didn't need to act out. I wouldn't die if I didn't act out, but in actuality I started to feel stronger because I knew God was helping me along my way to recovery. Surrender was the key that opened the door to a new life. I was entirely ready to release myself from the grips of my own pride and control, to no longer depend upon myself alone, especially since I now knew I couldn't do it without God or the fellowship of my groups.

I could feel the difference in my personality reflected in my attitude toward others. As each day, week, month, and year passed, my confidence grew. I could feel and see the change in me, and it's definitely because of God's presence.

There are four lines from the sixth-step prayer I include in my daily meditations:

Help me receive your inner working and change. I want to turn my back on yesterday's ways. I want to truly desire change, lasting change. So, quiet my heart, make me ready!

Step 7:
With the help of a loving higher power, we begin to replace the effects of the victimization with respect, compassion, acceptance, and self-care.

This is a very difficult step at best for an adult who has lived for decades accepting a victim mentality without ever knowing why. I learned that shortly after my first attack I had lost all respect for myself. I had to recognize that I had no control over the perpetration, but I also had to learn how to stop living the life of a victim. Through the grace of God I needed to accept both of these realizations and live my life differently.

Deception and betrayal were major factors in my abuse. Once betrayed, I could not have cared less if anything good happened to me. I constantly lived with the feeling that I did not deserve anything good or positive in my life.

I believe the meditations and affirmations I say each morning, combined with my prayers in the evening, slowly enabled me to start to let my defenses down so I could let God come into my life. I had always wanted God in my life, but with this step I could learn how to replace my victim mentality with care, love, respect, and acceptance. So, with God's love, I could release the diabolical spirit implanted by my attackers and begin to learn to care for and accept myself.

Step 8:
We make a list of all the people we have harmed of our own free will, especially our inner children and ourselves, and become willing to make amends to them all.

I had to stop thinking simply of the harm that had been done to me and think instead about the harm I had done to others. At the top of that list were the three most-important people in my life:

Jane, Paul, and Luke. All Jane ever wanted was emotional trust. Unfortunately, this was something I not only couldn't deliver but didn't know *how* to deliver. I have apologized profusely to her, but in reality, saying "I'm sorry" to her just wasn't enough.

I've written letters to my sons with the hope that my behavior hasn't hurt them beyond repair. They were the cornerstones of my salvation and recovery. I owe them so much. I sent a letter of apology to my mother-in-law, who, even after learning of my behavior, gave me support and love during some of my darkest moments.

From this point forward, my personal list was strewn with women from before and after my marriage. I contacted as many as I could find. A few commented that they just thought I had a problem with commitment but had never understood why. A few thought I just had an overly strong sex drive. One seemed so interested in the journey I was now on that she offered to help me reach out to others who were also survivors of childhood sexual abuse.

What this entire process taught me was that I had been blessed all of my life to be surrounded by a lot of wonderful, soulful, spiritual people but had never realized it. God had given me blessings, yet all I had done was think about what I felt was missing from my life. I realize now that my life is like the scene at the end of *The Wizard of Oz*, where the Tin Man, the Cowardly Lion, and the Scarecrow all find out that what they've been seeking are things they had all along.

As far as my inner child, I have stopped blaming myself for my sexual abuse, and I've put it at the foot of where it belongs—with my perpetrators! So, with continued work and my fellowship with other survivors, I will work out many other issues concerning my inner child.

Step 9:
We make amends to such people except when to do so would result in physical, mental, emotional, or spiritual harm to others or ourselves.

There were definitely more than a few women I chose not to or could not contact—ones I had dated before I had married Jane. While I know I always behaved like a gentleman, I know without doubt a few of the women could not understand why I had ended our relationships. It would make no sense to cause them any more emotional pain by reentering their lives simply for the sake of my own personal journey.

One example was the first girl I'd ever dated seriously. We went steady, and I placed her on a pedestal that put insurmountable pressure on her until she made that one mistake of betraying me, perhaps out of the frustration I had caused. I couldn't connect sex and love, and she had no way of understanding why; nor had any of the women I dated before my marriage. If I knew then what I know now, I would never have caused so much emotional turmoil for some very caring and thoughtful women I had encountered in my life. By contacting some of these women, I felt I would just be relieving myself of an abundant amount of guilt, but in the process I would be hurting them once again.

Step 10:
We continue to take responsibility for our own recovery, acknowledging, sharing and replacing effects as we become aware of them. When we succeed, we promptly celebrate it.

Dr. Gartner told me once that I and only I could be responsible for my recovery. "Recovery is a decision," he said. My experience with recovery is that it is an extremely difficult journey. With that being said, once I started to see the sun, smell the flowers, and feel friendship—all things I had blocked from myself for decades—I wanted more.

To experience more of those feelings, I needed to continue with significant hard work and a commitment to my recovery process. I wanted serenity in my life. To have that, I had to face my sexual abuse and take responsibility for my own behavior. This was a total and comprehensive battle. I had to be forced into recovery just to understand and especially to admit to the many things I had done wrong. I learned very quickly that to admit a mistake made me extremely vulnerable, just like when I was a child being sexually violated. This was another blockade to my personal development and had been for almost fifty years. The inability to admit fault and to accept responsibility prevents many of us from achieving success. I had always associated it with weakness, but taking on personal responsibility and acknowledging fallibility is a show of true inner strength. I was ready not just to *pretend* to be strong in a macho, stubborn way but truly to *become* strong by showing my humanity.

Step 11:
We seek conscious connection with a loving higher power for guidance and courage to thrive.

The phrase *conscious connection* rang so very true for me. I had tried to achieve this for decades. I knew my actions were wrong and immoral. As I have stated, I would attend Mass and read the Bible often. Growing up in a Jewish neighborhood, I even tried to pray in a synagogue for the understanding and hope to stop my destructive and dissociative behavior.

What I learned is that this spiritual connection was impossible to reach until I could understand the psychological and clinical damage the attacks had caused. Somewhere around the sixth month of my recovery I fully understood what those sexual assaults had done to me.

So many times I would try to reach for spiritual peace and end up withdrawn and isolated and feeling like this was an impossible task. Because I had returned to prayer and meditation and was able to be part of a fellowship with other survivors, I began to feel a real connection with God for the first time in my life.

Step eleven asked me to push myself to believe there was something in me and around me that was good and powerful. I needed to seek it with a new, learned passion. I constantly sought His help to assist me in connecting with Him. Two pedophiles had caused my darkness, not God; God had given them free will, as he had given it to me. By connecting with Him, I could truly understand the difference between my life as a victim and my life now as a survivor, clearly having the belief that I was no longer alone.

Step 12:
Having established conscious contact with a loving higher power, we reach out to other survivors and practice these thriving principles in all our endeavors.

During the tail end of my first year in therapy, I had brought three others into recovery. I was thrilled that they, like me, would have the opportunity to heal and reclaim their lives. It's funny, because during my entire career I was involved in communications, music, the telecom sector, and the expansive technology field of the Internet—all businesses that reached millions of people. Now I was reaching out to people but on a far more personal basis.

I'd never bared my soul on the records produced in my studios, as some of the artists and songwriters I worked with had.

I'd been the cool customer in the executive office, sealed away from the passion going on below me in the control room and in the studio. I'd really had no interest in hanging out with those guys, getting drunk or getting high. I'd wanted to make a buck, to succeed, to make my family proud of me, to make *myself* proud of me. But there was no real personal touch, no intimacy at all.

During my recording days, much of the music coming out of Philly was referred to as *soul*. It's a word like *love*—bandied around a lot in songs but often so overused that it begins to sound trite and meaningless in the wrong hands. I had no idea what having soul really felt like. I'm not talking about dancing or having a good sense of rhythm. My soul never developed. It was buried alive at age seven.

What makes great soul singers stand out is their ability to reach into their guts and pull out raw emotions that are so genuine listeners know they're true—no pretense. Soul comes from gospel, from heartfelt church music, from praising God, from bringing real troubles to Him, and from asking His grace to help soothe a troubled spirit.

Just as I did not have a real, heartfelt, emotional relationship with God, neither did I have one with anybody around me. I had built up boundaries out of necessity so God couldn't touch me, nor could anyone else. In order to break down my own defenses I had to reach out beyond myself, beyond my own newfound relationship with God, to other men and women who had been through the same sort of hell I had been through.

You can't just save yourself. The apostle Paul said, "I die daily." I never quite knew what he meant, but I now believe it to be this: with an addict, each day is a new beginning, a place to start or a place to end. The good works you did for yourself or for others yesterday are gone by tomorrow. It is my duty to be there each day for someone else. By doing so, God is there for me. I bare my soul to others, and I bare my soul to God. As I do this, others share their troubles with me but in a good way, a spiritual way.

For years I took on the problems of my extended family and so many others for all the wrong reasons; I enabled them and crippled myself. Now, when I reach out to other sexually abused men and women, I am doing it for all the right reasons. I am squaring myself with God, and I grow stronger every time I do it. I am surrounding myself with strength and love, not stress and anxiety.

While the crimes perpetrated against me ultimately caused me to lose everything dear to me, I became determined to reach out to as many sexual abuse survivors as possible to help them avoid experiencing the same loss. I wanted to awaken them as I had been awakened.

The Free Dictionary defines *spirit* as "a vital principle or animating force within living beings." Sexually abused children are robbed of that spirit. By following these twelve steps, I am affirming that I deserve to have my spirit and my life back.

Chapter 19
Groups

Following our intense twelve-step work, Dr. O'Connor admitted me into his men's group. To help me feel comfortable as a new member, Dr. O'Connor asked for the members to do their weekly check-ins and to share the traumas they had experienced and their effects on their adult lives. One by one the members introduced themselves, checked in, and explained in detail their personal traumas, the events that had left them much like myself—dissociated, disconnected, self-destructive, and looking for answers.

By the time it was my turn to speak, I felt an extraordinary kinship with these men. Previously I had always felt out of my skin in any group setting outside of my business world. And what could be worse for a man like me than to be in a collection of people where everyone was discussing traumas similar to the one I had been burying for years? Yet in some way I felt connected to these strangers—a feeling I had never experienced, even with people I'd known for thirty years.

When it became my turn to disclose the darkest moments of my life, I won't say it felt comfortable, but I will definitely say it felt safe, safer than when I had revealed myself to my family and my closest friends, as I had previously been guided to do as part of my healing process. In this group there were no hidden agendas; no one who was going to use what I said in order to hurt or humiliate me.

After I finished my story, there was a moment of silence before Dr. O'Connor resumed speaking. In that moment I sized up the men around me and guessed they were in their early thirties to late fifties. The room was full of human wreckage, extreme loss, and pain. We were all victims of actual weapons of mass destruction. The stories I'd heard were about lost careers, addictions, broken families, divorces, irreparable damage to spouses, even a suicide attempt—the kind of devastation that loss of innocence, rape, and other forms of emotional and physical attack on the defenseless can cause.

Dr. O'Connor introduced us to a series of group exercises in which we would be asked to confront our demons in order to heal. He also gave us assignments to do on our own in between group sessions. During these exercises and open discussions I discovered that childhood sexual abuse and trauma affect all walks of life. These were men of different races, socioeconomic backgrounds, intellects, and cultures, but we all shared one terrible common denominator. Most of us had learned to compartmentalize what had happened to us. We were able somehow to bury our secrets—and our pain—deep inside ourselves, as we *limped* through life. The wounds from our traumas may not have been easily seen—we weren't on crutches or in wheelchairs—but the emotional damage inflicted on us was very real, and without treatment our wounds would continue to grow and eat away at our souls until they crippled us on the inside.

Our group was made up of men who were more like bridges in need of repair. When I read about the bridge in Minnesota that collapsed in 2008, I thought, *Why are people still driving over it? Don't they know? Isn't it crumbling right before their eyes?* No, no it wasn't, and neither were we. Like that bridge, we were crumbling *inside*. Just as it took trained engineers to see that bridge was about to go, so too only a professional could discover, through the use of psychological tools, that we were emotionally broken, falling apart in all sorts of ways, a micro-hair away from not existing—gutted of our childhood and innocence.

I came to learn that another debilitating factor hindering recovery is that most of our families really didn't want to know, hear, or talk about the trauma or the results. Admitting and addressing the situation could change *their* lives as well. Many families can't handle the reality of the ordeal and don't know what to say, so they agree to live in denial along with the wounded person. Now in recovery, we as struggling survivors have lived through enough consequences and pain that denial was no longer an option.

For the first time in my life I found myself sitting in a room where more than half of the men were as wounded as I was. There were four men in the group who, like me, had been tormented their entire lives over sexual abuse and betrayal they had suffered as children. Over the next year I attended weekly group meetings with them and even became friends with a few outside the formal group. Several of us would also attend our twelve-step group meeting for sexual abuse survivors on weekends. These meetings were also eye-openers, depicting what an epidemic male and female childhood sexual abuse had grown to become over centuries, and the wreckage it caused to an adult's life.

While I was learning a great deal at all of my therapy sessions and group meetings, I sometimes resented that I had to attend these meetings in the first place. I almost felt like they were a punishment, like I was seeing a probation officer or being forced to go to rehab for some crime I had committed. Why did I have to do this? Why at times did it make me feel like such a bad person? For despite coming to terms with what was the root cause of my adult issues, I was forced to face the manner in which I had acted out. There was no room for denial, but there was, blessedly enough, room for understanding.

At other times I would be angered, thinking, *If only I had been protected more or watched more closely, I would never be in this position or sitting in this room.* But I had crossed this path so many times before, thinking I could will it away, pray it away, or wish my life had been different. I just had to give in and accept this had happened to me and it was and would be a part of my life forever. I would have to learn how to live with the sexual abuse and at the same time learn how to heal and survive it.

No form of therapy makes it all go away. There are no do-overs in life. Our pasts are our pasts, and they cannot be erased. The past influences our present and our future and directs them as if we are not conscious. But we have the power to heal from the past if we so choose, if we are able to gain control of our lives and learn how to live in the here and now.

I may have achieved many of the business objectives I had set for myself and may have experienced financial success, but now I needed to create a new set of goals to help me heal and experience a healthier, more complete life.

The community group became a pivotal part of my recovery. We all had each other's phone numbers; we could call a group member if we just needed to talk. Since Dr. O'Connor projected my recovery could take five to seven *years*, I found these men would become more than my support group—they would become my lifelines. Dr. O'Connor and these men became my path and my friends, a pipeline to my spiritual healing from God as I understood God to be.

Four of the six friends in whom I had confided about my sexual abuse outside of therapy remained very supportive as well. The others were all very sympathetic, but what I felt would eventually happen did happen. They had their own lives and their own families and no real understanding of the effects of child sexual abuse on an adult's life. One by one our relationships returned to what they had been before I had told them—friendly but professional. They weren't the people I needed to reach out to when I woke up in the middle of the night in a cold sweat, or when I wanted to curl up in a fetal position in the middle of the day when I considered all of the years I had lost and the splintered family I had left in my path. I think the information for a few was just too overwhelming to comprehend. I don't believe they could grasp that this could have happened to the man they knew.

Sam—the friend I had known the longest—never gave up on staying in touch with me. While I knew he was a true friend, Sam was also, ironically, experiencing his first grandson's turning seven a few months after I told him of my childhood trauma. One night, when we were out to dinner, he told me how terrific and wonderful his grandson's birthday was, but in him he saw the innocence and anxiety of a seven-year-old. I believe Sam could see and understand how his precious grandson could just as easily be victimized as I had been, and that would frighten anyone.

My youngest friend, Bob, who had wanted revenge, never stopped calling to ask how I was—and if I were traveling, he stayed in touch through e-mail or phone. Bob wasn't afraid to talk about my recovery and was definitely supportive throughout my journey.

Within six months of my disclosure to Steven (the mensch), he asked me to move my business operations in with his, and over the next two years we had many heartfelt and supportive dinners and talks.

Mary also stayed close, as she was just an extremely understanding, caring, and loving person.

Although I had Steven, Bob, Sam, Mary, my community group, and my SIA group meetings, Dr. O'Connor now told me I needed a sponsor, someone in the recovery process as well—albeit further along than me. He explained that the sponsor would be there for me anytime I felt depressed or about to relapse and go back to my habitual ways of dealing with my burden and my pain. The sponsor would be my go-to person who would be there for me wherever and whenever. What a responsibility! It sounded like a full-time job with no pay and lousy hours—and it would be a gift from a total stranger. There must be a special place in heaven for anyone willing to take on such responsibilities for another human being.

Going through the twelve steps and the journey through recovery is not an easy process. With a sponsor, however, I could have someone just a phone call away to discuss any issue that might have threatened to take me out of my zone of recovery.

I approached this sponsorship selection somewhat unconventionally. Because I was so wounded, instead of finding one sponsor, I found myself clinging to three. Perhaps I thought I was so lost and wounded that one person alone couldn't handle me. I trusted these three people not only with my recovery process but also with my life.

I befriended two men and a woman who became like my brothers and a sister to me. Paul, Jeff, and Annie were the epitomes of the program's mantra about giving back and helping other members.

Paul had also been violated as a child, but his violation manifested not in sexual addiction but in alcoholism. He started drinking at age thirteen and entered Alcoholics Anonymous (AA) at age twenty-five. Paul has been sober for over thirty years and has recently been able to face his core issue—childhood sexual abuse at the hands of a group of older boys and a Sunday school teacher. In recovery we maintain anonymity, so I won't use his full name, but he knows who he is, and I thank him from the bottom of my heart for all his support and understanding during our time together in recovery.

My close bond with Jeff was due to two major reasons. The most unfortunate one is that we were both violated at age seven. The second is that I feel he saved my life. During the first six months of recovery with Dr. O'Connor, I just couldn't sit still. I didn't know how to live alone or even be happy with myself. Jeff taught me a most valuable attribute that kept me sane: how to live in solitude. He would come to my condo and would call me constantly because he knew I couldn't handle being alone. Slowly, after many conversations and a few visits, I started to believe and feel that, for the first time in my life, I could live with myself. How do you say "thank you" to someone who taught you to live with yourself when you didn't even think you were worthy of living?

Annie was the first female in my entire life who became one of my closest and dearest confidants. I was able to look past her physical beauty to become emotionally intimate and see one of the most compassionate and caring women I ever met. Sexually abused at age four, Annie had been in the recovery process for many years but still found significant time and patience to help me through my many wounds, especially since I had no room in my heart to be compassionate to myself.

It's been said in recovery God awakens us only when He feels we are ready and can handle the unfathomable trauma. I often wondered why He waited until I was fifty-five. I believe it was because not only did He think I was ready, but He also knew I needed Paul, Jeff, and Annie to guide and support me through my journey.

Schism

Chapter 20

What About Jane?

In the beginning of my recovery, after hearing and agreeing with my psychological and clinical diagnoses, Jane would be accepting for a couple of days. Then she would eventually revert to not truly understanding how the sexual abuse attacks had created both my actions and who I was. Her personal therapist even suggested I had so much work to do in recovery that she would be better off having *no* contact with me for at least a year. She'd been advised not to let me talk to her about my abuse, recovery, or anything else that had to do with my past.

Like anything else, there are disagreements within the professional community regarding childhood sexual assault and the resulting dysfunction of the victim. Jane had every right to go to her own therapist; I respected that, although I can't say I agreed with this particular opinion. Her therapist suggested two options. One was that she could model forgiveness for her children by reuniting, or she could show our children there were consequences for my actions by going through with a divorce.

Based on everything I was learning, I didn't think this therapist truly understood the behaviors of a child who was sexually abused and was now living as an adult trying to deal with the manifestations of that abuse. Jane's therapist—as I did in my early recovery—was addressing only what was in the forefront: the affairs and not the sexual abuse that had caused them and the decades of dysfunction. This advice put a wall between Jane and me right when what I wanted and needed more than anything else was for us to grow *together*, not *apart*. It's funny I find myself saying that, because we were both trying to grow, and in many ways I believe we were and still are, yet my therapist felt the best way for me to grow was to share and go through my recovery with Jane and reunite with her and the children. Jane's therapist was telling her the opposite.

I was supposed to show Jane how I was recovering through actions rather than words. But if recovery can take five to seven years, that's a very long time to wait to see if I would or even could recover. Therefore, at times Jane would get frustrated and would ask, "Why don't you read a book that tells a man what a woman wants?" My heart would break for her when I'd hear this kind of statement. She truly didn't understand how much damage my predators had caused me. I couldn't find the answer in a book any more than I could will or pray the abuse away. There was no way for me to go *around* the pain in recovery, I had to go *through* it!

Jane felt wronged; she *had* been wronged. I had been terribly unfaithful to her. She felt betrayed, and she had every right to feel that way. For my part, my recovery involved my learning to understand *why* I had treated her and myself the way I had and for her to learn it as well.

Just as I was still in pain from what had happened to me when I was seven, Jane was still in pain from my deplorable sexual behavior. In that sense, what John and Jimmy were to me *I* had been to Jane! I had betrayed her. I had broken her trust. The things that women wanted most—safety, security, faithfulness, and intimacy—I could not provide.

But there was no magic book, just as there was no magic pill. Would she ever be able to trust me again? Would she ever be able to trust a *man* again? I don't know. Could I get over my tactile/intimacy issues? If I couldn't, could Jane live with me that way? If not, what then? Would she seek intimacy with another man? How would this entire experience mark the way she would go about the rest of *her* life?

Thinking about all this made me melancholy. I loved her, and I knew I always would. I found myself wondering sometimes whether I actually did want her to find someone else who could give her what she needed. But that's like a man on his deathbed telling his wife, "Feel free to remarry. I don't want you to be alone. I want you to be happy." It's a lot harder when you're still around.

As I was going through therapy, I was abstaining from any physical contact with women. I was starting to feel and understand what love was meant to be, but I wanted to experience that feeling only with Jane. I was healthy enough to realize that acting out would not solve my loneliness or quell my anxiety or stress, but my healthier attempts at life, coupled with Jane's resistance to reconciliation, left me more alone than ever. I was very confused and hurt.

Jane and I were still married, and as hypocritical as this may sound, there was still a front we were putting on for the rest of the world. I had been discreet when I was in the fire of my addiction. Jane didn't know about it, nor did any of our mutual friends. The picture of an all-American, nuclear family had been intact—at least as everyone had seen it but me.

But how was Jane supposed to pull off dating now? I supposed—and I actually discussed this with Jane—she could be equally discreet, keeping me and the boys and everyone else in the dark. But the emotional stress for Jane would have been significant, and if I had ever found out, it would have torn me up inside.

When we talked about the possibility of her seeing other men, Jane more or less agreed with me. She did tell me she felt lonely and in need of companionship and intimacy but did not feel comfortable dating. However, at that point Jane did not see a future with me either. Not only was she understandably hurt and having a difficult time forgiving me, but I also couldn't provide her with what she really needed—true love and intimacy.

At those times I felt Jane should just move on without me, break it off forever legally. I could feel her frustration. She didn't want to hear it, professional advice or not. Part of her still thought my childhood attacks were an excuse for my abominable sexual behavior and for what I wasn't able to give her in our marriage. Not being able to accept this didn't put Jane at fault. This part of it was not her journey; it was mine. Jane, like millions of other spouses, found it almost impossible to understand that someone in a relationship or a marriage could be so disconnected.

In recovery, working the twelve-step program, I fully understood how deeply I had hurt Jane. Saying I was sorry, guilty, and ashamed of my actions was not really going to help Jane. In the beginning of my recovery my only thought was to try to convince Jane to take me back and to resume our life together with our two beautiful sons. I tried everything I could to reassemble my family. I bought books for Jane to read to try to make her understand, as crazy as it sounded, that my acting out hadn't been about her but about me. One of the books I gave Jane was Marie H. Browne's *If the Man You Love Was Abused*. While she agreed it depicted me to a T, Jane said the book was really just all about me and what I had gone through and not what *she* had gone through.

After meeting with Dr. O'Connor and me during a couple of my sessions, Jane learned there was no way I could have been emotionally connected to our marriage. He told her that I was completely incapable of being emotional or surrendering my defenses to her or to any other woman for that matter.

As time went on, I imagined how much this statement probably cut to the very core of her heart. Now that I understood my own hurtful actions, I didn't ask for her forgiveness, but I hoped and prayed she would find peace and happiness as she moved forward. To her credit—since, unlike me, she knew how to live life—Jane had built a group of friends and activities that kept her fairly busy, but I'm sure her mind rarely drifted too far from the devastation I had caused her.

While I had been a very broken person since age seven and had sworn off marriage for years and years prior to meeting Jane, it was Jane—and the person she was—who at least brought me to the point of saying, "She's perfect in every way… Let me at least try." I think she would say we're *both* glad we at least tried, because if we hadn't come together we would not have had Paul and Luke. I believe I can speak for Jane and me when I say that the boys provided us with the greatest joy in our lives.

The deeper we progressed into our individual therapies, the more aware Jane and I became that the odds of our reuniting were not good. The information I read stated that over seventy percent of marriages involving adults who were sexually abused as children ended in divorce once the dissociative behavior of the survivor was brought to light—a percentage much higher than the national average.

While I missed Jane, I truly believed that after twenty-six years of marriage to me—a victim who had victimized *her* emotionally—she deserved to be happy.

Paul and Luke, like most children, didn't have a choice. They were thrust into this complex situation against their wishes. In my mind, I'm sure if the boys had had a choice of whom to pick as a father, they would have passed over someone like me, who was so damaged from abuse, and I wouldn't have blamed them for doing so. I prayed daily that my sons would come to understand fully that what had happened to me as a child was not a choice I had made and that my love and caring for them were eternal. For as much as recovery is about my doing what is best for me, in my heart I know I am also doing it so I can be the best father I can for Paul and Luke.

Part of my recovery was learning to like myself and eventually even *love* myself so I could be emotionally fit to live a normal life, first for me and then for the boys. As I got deeper and deeper into recovery, I truly felt I wanted to learn to feel worthy and to understand I had a right to live a happy, normal existence. But without a doubt, my love for Paul and Luke was also a significant driving force in my healing.

Positive visualization became a big part of my process. I would go to sleep each night imagining that one day my sons would see I was getting stronger and that by demonstrating the courage to address the abuse that had caused my abhorrent behavior, they might understand how and why that behavior had come about in the first place.

Now that I'd come to grips with the fact that my horrific childhood sexual abuse had set my life into an irreversible cycle, I also needed to take responsibility finally for my actions that caused so much pain to my family.

Chapter 21

Mirrors

As time went on, my recovery and its process became my life. I was determined to make things right in my world, and if that meant taking on rehabilitation with as much determination as in my business life, then so be it. I was driven to seize control of my life because in actuality I was *fighting* for my life!

I had been in intensive therapy for almost a year, about as long as it had been since Luke found the e-mail. It had been forty-nine years since the sexual attacks sent my world careening out of control. I had a lot of time to make up and a lot of insanity to overcome—not quite twelve months of "sobriety" versus a lifetime of chaos. I was learning how to become healthier and more connected to my feelings and life itself.

Even though I was never an alcoholic, alcohol was still something I used to quell the anxiety and to help me deal with the flashbacks of the attacks—but it also lowered my inhibitions, and I always had to be in control of my mind and body from there on out. Therefore, alcohol was dropped from my diet.

When I first entered recovery, I was prescribed antidepressants for the severe depression I was in, but I gradually weaned myself off of them as well. They were good for me as a stabilizer and a bridge, but I needed to do everything on my own. If I were in control and I had the support of my group, I was no longer anxious or depressed, so I no longer needed medication to keep me calm.

At that point in my recovery it had been eight months since I'd cut off all contact with my mother and my siblings. Their life situations had caused me a great deal of stress and anxiety, and that, I was afraid, would cause me to act out and return to my old behaviors. The separation from my family caused some initial pain for all of us, but I think it helped them (and me) in the long run more than it hurt.

I may not always need this distance that I established between my extended family and me, but at that time in my recovery I had to set boundaries for my own health and well-being. I truly love my mom, brothers, and sisters, but I was following the advice of my doctors, who viewed it as an issue of gaining the strength to reestablish my family relationships and not allowing their worlds to cripple me.

Likewise, if Jane and I ever reconciled, I would need to set the same boundaries with her family. By entering recovery and surrendering to how the sexual abuse I had endured had shaped my personal interactions, my relationships with family and friends were forever changed.

I say these things not from a condescending position or a place of superiority. I have an addictive personality and a terrible compulsive anxiety disorder created by my childhood trauma, but I am trying to deal with them directly, one day at a time. Taking those calls from my family and going to events with Jane's family are things that someday I may be able to handle, but at that point I was not strong enough.

I learned in recovery that based on the way I had been sexually violated, I had to look at my life and the way I was living it, and I needed to avoid any situations that would spin me out of control emotionally.

Once I began to understand that my family dynamics had contributed to my struggles—and to the plight of some of my brothers and sisters—I decided to write a letter to my mother and my siblings, telling them that while I was certain that Mom and Dad loved us very much and had done the best they could, things did not turn out so well. The way we dealt with problems and issues that arose—even the way we interacted with each other—was not conducive to living a healthy life.

I was stunned when one of my siblings called me in a rage and told me that "just because *you're* a faggot" it had nothing to do with our family not being emotionally healthy. The outburst stung and hurt me deeply, but I realized—and would come to understand even more in therapy—that by questioning the stability and soundness of my family, I had made each of us take some responsibility for the dynamics that existed, and that was a situation my brothers and sisters were not prepared to accept.

While it took some time, eventually my mother would be the first in the family to agree that maybe what I was learning in therapy and trying to communicate to our family had some merit.

My sibling's angry retort was another harsh reminder of why survivors of sexual abuse are hesitant to come forward. They believe speaking up will cause family breaks and their silence, however painful, will keep the family intact. To recognize that something terrible happened to a brother or sister—and to admit that the support to help the injured sibling may have been lacking—causes the other siblings feelings of guilt and anger. In essence, admitting that a brother or sister is flawed is an acknowledgment of their own shortcomings. I believe this dynamic is even more evident when a child is molested by a family member.

I continued my one-on-one and group sessions with Dr. O'Connor. There was also my SIA group that included both men and women. By that time I had also begun seeing another therapist, Allie Miller, who was counseling male survivors of childhood sexual abuse. Feeling that although I had definitely developed some strong ties to my brothers in Dr. O'Connor's group, I figured I might also be able to grow and understand even more—and even more quickly—the effects of the attacks by joining a group that focused solely on how our childhood sexual abuse affected us as adults. Over the next two years Allie, more than any other therapist I had seen, would provide me with a feeling of safety and understanding to speak about those dark moments and to further emphasize that they were not my fault and should not be my burden.

I was gaining insight into what made me tick, or, in my case, what made me tick incorrectly. It was fascinating, although I rarely had the opportunity to intellectualize it. I left those meetings and those sessions and went home to four walls and waves of self-doubt. Solitude was my enemy, and it would have me fearful that I would seek comfort in my old, familiar behaviors. Yes, that would make it all better—at least that was what the old Pete would have thought, and there was always that old Pete buried deep inside me. He was the damaged one, the one with all the wrong answers. He was the one I was trying to avoid and to conquer, but I also had to accept that he would never die until *all* of me would cease to exist. No alcoholic who has been through rehab says, "I'm cured." The operational term is, "I am in recovery. I am still an alcoholic." So too am I still a man struggling with a severe sexual compulsive disorder. I had to learn to accept this.

You realize as you go through this process that it's really not a matter of *wanting* to go to these types of meetings but *needing* to go. It's not a matter of being in the mood for them or thinking, *Hey, this might be a good idea, something I really should think about doing for myself.* Instead I felt like a significant part of me was dead, and I feared the rest of me would die if I didn't get help. That's a strong motivator for anyone.

Early on during my time in the groups, I suffered frequent panic attacks when I was alone. I would compare it to a person going through withdrawal from narcotics or alcohol. What I learned from the groups was that the first thing I had to do when this happened was to pick up the phone. So much of what was triggering these attacks was loneliness, being in a room with only myself, my guilt, and my thoughts of the abuse or even the recovery process itself at times. We're taught to pick up the phone because the most natural inclination is to do something negative to take the pain away, which for me most often was to act out sexually with a woman. That had been my narcotic in the past. Now I needed something else that wouldn't take me off of the positive path I was on toward mental health.

My weeks became programmed. Monday through Friday I had my business, which kept me busy up to ten hours a day. I had my group meetings and my private counseling sessions that I would attend after work. It was very hard coming home to an empty condo, but the work and the sessions were supportive and at times life-saving.

The weekends were long and lonely, but Paul, Jeff, or Annie would pull me through and carry me when I couldn't carry myself.

Another challenging part of my recovery was the never-ending activity of being called upon to recount all the things I had been through and all I had done. I must have shared the details of my attacks by John and Jimmy a few dozen times. I also had to discuss openly the episodes of my life, my years after age seven when I acted out and was disconnected from any emotional bond or intimacy. I had to dredge up every demon I had ever had, and I had to face them and deal with them. It wrung me out completely. I felt so bad about how I had brought so much pain to my family.

Once you start recovery, it usually gets worse before it gets better. I'd had panic attacks before while in crowds, but they were nothing compared to what I was experiencing in recovery. Back then I would run from a situation or avoid it entirely. I didn't ponder or face the nemesis inside. But in therapy I couldn't run or avoid the demons or the disconnected feelings or actions they created. I had to take a hard look at myself, and it frightened me and made me sick.

In recovery you're taught not to look away. You're taught to embrace the pain and try to understand it. The "feeling bad" part is a major piece of the process. You're *supposed* to feel bad. If you don't feel terrible at some point, you aren't really understanding or going through true recovery; you're still in denial.

There were times I wanted to quit. The recovery process was extremely hard. I was distraught emotionally and, at times, drained physically. I felt exposed, forced to ignore all my usual defenses I'd grown accustomed to using daily for years.

One of the exercises I was instructed to do was to embrace a seven-year-old boy—the same age I was when I was molested. I was told to get down on my knees so I was on his level, give him a chaste hug, and then talk to him—not about my sexual attacks but about the types of things a seven-year-old boy likes to talk about, such as sports, TV, school, and his friends. The purpose of the exercise was to help me understand what I would have been like at that age of innocence and trust. It's hard for someone in his fifties really to recapture how you were and how you thought of yourself as a child. I could remember the abuse I'd suffered but nothing much more than those terrifying moments—I couldn't remember the little things, the *nuances* that made me a young, naïve boy.

When I did this exercise with one of my nephew's sons (who was also my godson), I saw the innocence in his eyes and realized this was how I was at seven. Without even trying I found myself looking into his soul and seeing how pure it was. That's what childhood is about. In that moment I realized all that had been ripped from my life.

The next step in the exercise was to take a few steps away from the child and look into his eyes and envision the vile, despicable, unmentionable acts that were done to me being done to him.

Believe it or not, at that point I almost felt a strange sense of peace because I realized I had survived. When I bonded with my godson, even for those few minutes, and then looked at him and envisioned my sexual abuse being done to him, I asked, *God, how could anyone survive that? How could anyone not want to kill himself after having suffered through such horrific events?* The fact that I was still alive and fighting for my life was an amazing testimony to the resilience of the human spirit. Yes, I was disconnected. Yes, I'd acted out irresponsibly in my life, but people sometimes do terrible things in order to survive.

I never would have known about this type of exercise had I not entered recovery. Thankfully, there are professionals who know how to lead you through these steps. The trained therapists guide you and evaluate what you can and cannot handle based on where you are in your recovery.

Another illuminating moment in recovery was hearing other people's tales of their own childhood molestations. The similarities between their tales and mine were frightening, but what I did *not* expect were the parallels between my life and theirs *after* their abuse. That was the part where I'd felt, going in, that I was unique; I felt my story of surviving sexual abuse was different from anyone else's. In my mind, no one but me reacted to being raped as a child by becoming addicted to multiple vices. No one but me could look at sex as the primary release from the trauma created. No one but me could lack intimacy in the aftermath of those attacks I'd sustained.

I learned this was far from reality.

It was just as the psychologists and doctors had told me, but still I had to hear it for myself; the groups presented me with this opportunity. Most of us were suffering similar consequences. I was in a roomful of people who all had these symptoms, which all had the same root cause!

In an odd way it was a form of vindication. When I was first diagnosed, I know Jane dismissed what the doctors were saying. She thought, *Oh, yeah; now Pete has an excuse for being a cheater!* Here was a roomful of other Petes, males and females, all with the same individual nuances of behavior—not just the *need* to have sexual relations, that part was too simplistic, but the inability to connect, the lack of intimacy, the agitation, the need to go through life constantly driving forward as if something were gaining on them, the need to prove themselves and their value, and especially the inability to commit truly to a loving relationship. In the beginning there were times when even *I* doubted some of what the therapists were saying, but the groups and their members validated the diagnoses I had received from three different doctors.

The better I began to feel, the more I went to the meetings. I didn't dread them as I once had when I had begun. In the beginning the meetings seemed so strange and at times uncomfortable, but I grew to look forward to them. They made me feel a new sense of purpose and accomplishment.

I started to understand the diagnoses I had received almost a year previously when I had entered recovery. I had been told I was making great strides for a person who had been in therapy for only that length of time. I had abstained from acting out sexually in any form and was excited that I would soon receive my first-year chip to celebrate a full year of "sobriety." But I knew I still had other roads to travel on my journey.

I'd been told that full recovery is a point where you begin to live a life of trust. To help me overcome my fear of tender human contact, I began two new approaches to change. One was a mind-body treatment called Thought Field Therapy. I was seeing a trauma specialist, Dr. Meg Miller, who directed me to tap spots on my face and chest while thinking of how the attacks disturbed me. New understanding about the plasticity of the brain has opened a door to deeper levels of healing. She also directed me to start, very slowly, to experiment with nonsexual physical contact—to hold a hand, to cup a loved one's face in my hands, to get used to being touched and touching and to experience safety and tenderness. These exercises were designed to help release the physical trauma and fear inflicted on me during the attacks and to help me begin to engage in healthy contact. This was an extremely difficult task for me, but I was determined to go through it.

I came to learn that staying "sober" was not enough. For me simply to abstain from sex was not the end of the road; in fact, it was just the beginning. I needed to understand the process of rewiring my brain from the attacks, and I needed to learn how I could form a positive and loving relationship. What is the quality of life without love? Now in recovery, I believed a healthy sexual life was a significant part of a relationship and of life itself. The organization Sexaholics Anonymous (SA) writes that "any form of sex with someone outside of a marriage or with one's self is self-destructive."

The goal of sexual addiction programs is not to turn everyone into people who should refrain from sex but, more importantly, to teach them to learn how to live in *healthy* sexual relationships. I wonder if I can ever reach that level of feeling and understanding. I think sex, love, and intimacy are parts of life that should develop naturally. No one should have to give up these wonderful, loving, human emotions I've struggled to embrace.

I've actually never experienced these emotions in a relationship. The sexual relations I had were never healthy, loving, or truly intimate. I never wanted to take those clichéd long, slow, moonlit walks on the beach, holding hands with the one I loved. But I realized I *should* want to. That's what the rewiring of my brain and the emotional development that was crushed and stunted at the age of seven is all about.

Unfortunately, a surgeon can't simply open my skull and tweak a few things and make me better, so I have meetings and exercises, and I have my morning prayers and meditations. When I see lovers holding hands and kissing, I tell myself not to look away. I try to imagine it as a good thing—the best thing in the world—but it's difficult for me to do so because it only takes me back to those terrible feelings of manipulation, entrapment, betrayal, and victimization.

To engage in acts of tender affection and intimacy would require me to trust someone, and I had not been able to do that in nearly fifty years. At seven I had placed my faith and belief in two people I thought cared for me, and they had used that trust against me and brought total devastation to my entire life.

Research shows that many survivors of childhood sexual abuse who develop sexual addictions often avoid any tender, loving touch or affection. Some reports document that as high as seventy percent of children who are sexually molested develop sexual compulsive disorders and/or addiction by the time they reach early adulthood. Whereas an alcoholic must avoid alcohol, a person like me is encouraged to change personal perceptions—conscious and unconscious—about sex and love and not to avoid those acts but to learn how to embrace them.

Sexual addiction is a relatively new area of study. Alcoholics Anonymous (AA) has been able to accumulate significant information on alcoholism backed by decades of studies. Research data on sexual addiction has just begun to be collected within the last twenty-five years or so. Because the study of sexual addiction is relatively new, I imagine it will take society and the healthcare system years both to understand and to accept that sexual addiction is a malady. The unfortunate rise of sexual compulsive behavior during the last two decades by very public figures from politics, sports, and entertainment will hopefully spur new interest in and focus on identifying and treating cases of sexual addiction.

As I invested more time in my own various forms of therapy, I knew I was getting clearer and healthier, and so did Paul and Luke—they told me so. Despite this, what would bring me down time and time again were my interactions with Jane. My progress wasn't going fast enough for her.

Hope

Chapter 22

Divorce

I kept wondering how long the window of opportunity would be open for Jane and me to make a go of things again, an attempt at reconciliation that would hold forever.

Jane, by that time, had been to a couple of therapists herself but had attended just a handful of sessions in total. From my perspective, none of the ones she had attended coordinated properly with the treatment I was receiving or offered the support Jane would need for her own journey. She clearly wasn't ready to be introspective about her own life let alone take the difficult path of recovery with me.

I accept and recognize how my destructive behavior caused so much pain and damage to my family. However, beyond the sexual acting out that took place in secret, I had many dissociative habits and rules that were on display for Jane every day of our marriage, which she had accepted. Why was that? Something in Jane had allowed a dysfunctional relationship—one without intimacy—and I thought she would want to know why.

Jane and her family, as well as many of my own family members, found it easier to ignore problems and difficult issues in the hope that they would somehow go away or just solve themselves on their own.

After a year in recovery I knew that approach simply did not and could not work for me. I was trying to get well, going to emotional and psychological places that made me feel horrible, but facing them was necessary to my existence and to my desire so I could truly live life and not merely survive it. It became more and more apparent that, in order for Jane and me to be a happy and healthy married couple, she would also have to go places she'd spent her entire lifetime learning to avoid—places that would make her feel uncomfortable.

Jane had been a wonderful wife and mother. She had done nothing wrong. I was asking her to take a huge leap, and I was doing so from a horrible bargaining position.

The first stages of grief are denial and anger. Jane was still experiencing these emotions even after I'd been in recovery for a year and even after we'd been apart for over a year. If she were dying of some horrible disease, she might have gone through the five stages faster, but to her I was the one who was sick, so there was no impetus for her to get past her anger.

For as much as we still got along on some of the occasions when we met, she was just as apt to send me a text message along the lines of, "I still can't believe you broke my heart!"

I'd reply, "Jane, it wasn't because of you. How many times do I have to say that? How many therapists have to tell you I was so traumatized by the sexual abuse as a child that I could have been married to any woman and it wouldn't have mattered? No degree of love with any woman could have stopped my unconscious, sexually compulsive behavior. The compulsions, the effects of the abuse, were bigger than love, bigger than me…bigger than us."

Denial and anger never went away; during the entire year Jane hadn't progressed in her ability to understand the sexual abuse and comprehend how it affected my entire life.

Strangely enough, we never mentioned divorce in the early days of our separation, but reconciliation was not assumed either. To reach a conclusion, to come to a crossroads in our relationship would be to go to a bad place, and Jane wasn't prepared to go to bad places; she never had been.

Relationships don't stay still; they're always growing or dying. With our being apart and Jane's choosing not to be a part of my recovery process, our relationship was slowly dying. I did recognize a part of my therapy would potentially include Jane taking a hard look at herself, which I knew firsthand was the most difficult process for a human being to undertake and would be especially difficult for Jane based on the family dynamics and system in which she had been raised.

Granted, another woman not only might have asked me to leave the house but would have also immediately called a lawyer and seized our assets. Partly through anger, Jane was able to ask me to leave our home, but she didn't take any vindictive action against me. She viewed my departure as the end of the problem. She was in a relatively good place without having to deal with me each day and see the reminder of her pain. Jane was able simply to stay in this safety zone of sorts without a desire to divorce me or fully embrace the steps necessary for us to reconcile. She had no desire to understand what truly had caused my sexual acting out, nor did she have the need to learn why she had existed in a relationship devoid of true intimacy.

As time went on, I asked Jane if she wanted a divorce. I wasn't asking because *I* wanted one; I still held out hope she would be part of my recovery and eventually my life, but Jane seemed to have other ideas. Maybe it was because as a Catholic she didn't believe in divorce, I don't know. Jane explained she didn't want me back in the house but didn't want to divorce me either, which left…what? Eventually one or both of us would want something more.

"Well, we could still be married and live out our lives," she said.

"No," I told her. "I can't accept that. If we're to be together, the relationship will have to include all the aspects of a healthy marriage." When I was to begin my new, self-actualized life, it would be a life without deception.

At least Jane could see the progress I was making in my recovery. One time, when we were together, she commented, "I can't believe how bright your eyes are, how much you're smiling!" What a thing to say about such basic emotions most people express daily! But for me it was a rare occurrence. While Jane meant it as a compliment, it also spoke volumes about how obvious my condition had been. No one could put a finger on it; no one—not even Jane—could really tell I was living in such a dark world. But could anyone deny the long-term damage of what I'd been through as a child once they'd been able to see me before and then after my first year in therapy?

I answered her, "Thank you, but if my eyes are brighter, it's because I've had a metaphorical hood lifted from my head after nearly fifty years."

Jane struggled with accepting why my molestations had made me unable to be loving and sexually intimate with her. No matter how many times and how many ways it would be explained to her by me or by my doctors, she still didn't want to accept it. I needed her acceptance, for it would be a foundation upon which we could build a relationship—a real marriage. Although we were best friends, without Jane's understanding there was no way we were going to make it as a healthy couple, which we had really never been.

Despite Jane's difficulty in grasping the full extent of my sexual abuse, its crippling results, and her unwillingness to embrace the recovery process, she never gave up on me or us entirely. When we saw each other for an occasional dinner, visited our sons at college, or even took in a movie—Jane and I actually got along quite well. But I was still surprised when I received an e-mail one day from Jane telling me she wanted to give our marriage a second chance. The only problem was she still *wouldn't* come to therapy with me, and she hoped I wouldn't be upset about that. She said I was one of the kindest and most generous people she had ever met and she didn't think there was a man on earth who could be a more supportive, caring, and loving father.

While she agreed my actions before had been deplorable, there was no denying she could see a different human being now when she looked at me following a year of recovery. My outlook was much healthier. It was clear to her I was healing.

I was so excited! I forwarded that e-mail to my sons and told them the real hero was their mom.

So we started to give it a try, quite tentatively, and without my moving back home. We began to date. Things seemed to be going well. One night we went to a recently refurbished theater. I noticed all the wonderful accoutrements at each turn: the colors of the inlaid tile, the exquisite stain on the handcrafted walnut woodwork, the plush, new seating. These were all things I would never have commented on or, for that matter, even noticed before entering recovery. I was coming alive! I was starting to feel things other than pain, guilt, fear, and shame.

As we sat down to dinner later that evening, Jane started to cry. My excitement tumbled like a ton of bricks. I immediately thought I had done or said something wrong. She explained I hadn't said or done anything wrong; in fact, she thought I looked the healthiest she'd seen me in the nearly thirty years she had known me. She said she could see and feel how hard I was working at getting better. The problem was, she also said, it felt like *I wasn't the same Pete she had fallen in love with!*

Where did this come from? I was better, far better than I'd ever been. That very evening I even tried to hold hands with her. Jane was not used to this from me. I could tell she liked it when I did it, but then came this breakdown at dinner.

It was as if this were a new relationship, one we were put in together through some computer dating service. Jane knew she had to talk to Pete this way, walk with Pete that way, and ride in a car with Pete another way. We'd been together so long we had our routines. Every couple has routines. But I had rules—*old* Pete's rules—that had been compromises to my damage. Don't sit too close to me. Don't touch me. Don't hold my hand. Don't make me go out in large crowds. Those boundaries were parts of me, and without them, I believe, Jane thought I was someone else. This frightened her.

My calm took her off guard. I was mellower. Gone was the hair-trigger temper, the negative feelings. I had never had any trouble expressing *those* emotions! I was never abusive to her or the boys, but I could get agitated and aggressive when the waiter took too long to take our order or when the valet took too long to bring the car around. Now those actions didn't unsettle me; I had learned to manage them. My new learned behaviors to handle stressful situations were taking effect. I was no longer actively living in my head or letting the addiction rule my behaviors on a day-to-day basis, so I could enjoy the scenery around me. It felt great; it felt peaceful. But to Jane I was a new and different person she would have to learn to be with if we were to reunite.

Although she tried to reconcile, as we neared the end of our second week of dating, Jane came to the conclusion that she just couldn't do it. I could see by her tears of frustration that our life as a couple was over.

There was nothing I could do; it was my fault, not hers. I had to let her go and live her life and find someone who could make her happy. I took her home and told her I would forward a draft of a divorce settlement.

When we separated, I had already made Jane a relatively wealthy woman. What I now drafted for a divorce settlement would make her a *very* wealthy woman. She had been my wife for twenty-six years and the mother of Paul and Luke. I felt fully responsible for how we had gotten to that point of despair.

Both my attorney and my accountant advised me that what I was stipulating to was completely out of bounds. I'd operated under financial pressure my entire life, and this commitment to give money I didn't have at the time would keep me in that same position, but I saw no reason not to do this for Jane. Her well-being and that of our two sons were my sole concern. While I committed to a significant amount I had yet to earn, I always had belief in my abilities to earn a living, and I held more promise to deliver now, coupling my newfound healthy energy with a spirituality I had sought my entire life—and had finally gained.

My insistence on the divorce was part of my therapy and my own journey to living a healthier life. At that point in my recovery I just could not live an undefined life, as I had done for decades. Our separation was fine for a time, but it had dragged on and needed to be more defined. I felt I had done everything I knew how to do to fix our marriage, and I asked Jane repeatedly to take my hand and go on this journey of healing with me, but I finally had to conclude it wasn't going to happen, and so it was best that I stopped trying to tantalize either of us and simply end our marriage amicably. Jane could be free to do what she wanted and seek other male companionship if she desired without feeling she had to keep secrets from me, the boys, or anyone else.

Even as we were moving forward with the legalities of our divorce, Jane was in denial. Her family had rituals of large get-togethers for Thanksgiving, Christmas, etc. She asked if I would still be attending.

The question unsettled me, although to Jane it seemed completely natural. Again, it was the pattern of her desperate need not to enter the world of trauma where I had resided since age seven. People who are going through or have completed a divorce do not get together with the whole extended family as if nothing has happened. Jane thought since things between us were amicable, we could still put on this front in the honor of family tradition. For me it was an unhealthy encounter. I told her, "I would love to have holiday dinner with you, Paul, and Luke. We can do things like that any time. Getting together with all of your family or my extended family at this stage of my recovery, as if nothing has changed, is something I can't do."

I was starting to understand that there was dysfunction in what I had believed was the perfect family. I could not participate in a world in which nothing was wrong when I now saw it so completely different.

Jane did not have an addiction problem—*I* did. I'd been completely sober for over a year and had been experiencing healthy emotions, but Jane was still in denial about me and my molestation and how it had left me so scarred. Yes, she wanted to get back together; she did not want to divorce me. But she wanted everything to be the same as it had been before my recovery were we to get back together. Unfortunately, the problem wasn't just about my sexually acting out but everything else that had shown up and had prevented us from having true intimacy.

After fifteen months apart, Jane signed the divorce papers.

When I first entered recovery, I was taught and told I would have more losses to come. There would be times when I would wonder why I was going through this painful journey and this intense work and would desperately want to go back to how I had been before, no matter how awful that had been in its own way. This was one of those painful times.

Chapter 23

Marriage—The Whole Is Greater Than the Sum of Its Parts

I heard from friends outside my recovery groups that a few in our circle thought the only reason I had stopped sexually acting out was that I got caught. When I repeated this to Dr. O'Connor, he quickly replied, "I think you should tell your so-called friends… that you were actually *caught* at the age of seven and *awakened* at the age of fifty-five."

Dr. O'Connor's analysis made sense because after all those years of being mentally tormented, I realized there was no pleasure in my destructive sexual behaviors or my other addictive patterns. While I was still in therapy, some two years after Dr. O'Connor's counsel, unbelievably one of Jane's sisters actually said the same thing to me almost verbatim: "Pete, didn't you really stop only because Jane caught you?"

I actually think the sexual attacks drove me to a certain degree of personal, internalized insanity. Outwardly I may have appeared normal, but I felt like a machine programmed to work, eat, sleep, and exist. Inside, my wires were disconnected, malfunctioning, and overloaded. I was ready to self-destruct at any minute.

As I continued in my groups, I began to learn more and more about what was going on inside me. One Saturday morning, after a prolonged overseas business trip, I went to one of my weekly SIA meetings and saw my friends Paul and Jeff waiting for me at the door. When I saw them, my heart started to race with excitement in a way it hadn't since before my abuse. Here were *my friends* waiting for me. Men who knew who I *really* was, men who understood what my violation had caused and had cost me, how it made me fearful to have friends, to trust anyone. They understood why I couldn't let my defenses down and be emotional with a woman or a man, for that matter. They knew all this, yet they were still my friends!

This moment sent me back to a time before the abusive sexual attacks, a time when I had trusted everyone in my life. As the doctors had promised, my wires were being reconnected. It was like being a little, innocent boy again. I suddenly remembered how I couldn't wait to get home from school, drop my book bag in my room, put on my play clothes, and go out to have fun with my friends.

I hadn't experienced that kind of heartfelt emotion or friendship in almost fifty years. It was a stark reminder of what my perpetrators had taken from me. Before I was even eight, John and Jimmy had robbed me of my trust and destroyed my ability to develop any real friends or any true friendships. The feeling I experienced from seeing Paul and Jeff that day gave me hope that if I could let my defenses down in order to have friends, then maybe, just maybe, I could learn what intimacy was and how it would feel to fall in love.

Had I not been so sexually violated, I believe I would have naturally developed the understanding of basic, human friendship and trust. It wasn't until decades later that I became aware of what I'd lost. I simply can't explain how happy I am that God didn't take my life those many times I had prayed for him to do so, before I was able to remember how it felt to trust and have true friendship.

While I had scoffed at the first AA meeting Gail had dragged me to, I now viewed all addictions through a different prism. I was shocked to find that many addicts, not just sex addicts, had been violated or traumatized as children, so that alcoholic, drug, or food addict getting help for his or her addiction might still not be touching upon the true root cause of his or her problem. Yes, it is natural to look at a person with sexual addiction like myself and say, "Maybe it was caused by something sexual in his past," but from what I've heard in my groups and learned in my individual therapy sessions, the cause of an alcoholic or narcotic addiction is not as easily traced to child sexual abuse. The focus of the struggle is on the resulting addiction, not the root cause of it.

The purpose of this book is not merely for me to divulge to the world my personal tale but to reach out to and draw into recovery as many men and women as possible. My sincere hope is that by sharing my story of—and hopefully my recovery from—childhood sexual abuse, I can give others the hope and courage to heal from their own sexual trauma experienced as a child. My message to those of you who have suffered is that you may have been too young or isolated to fend off your attackers when they stole your innocence, but you are not alone today.

While my lost years are unfortunate, I wouldn't want anyone who reads this book to pity me. First, I'm thriving and working to become a survivor; I am a functioning human being, and I won't leave this world as an emotionally disconnected man. By the grace of God I am slowly turning my life around from being a victim without value to a person worthy of love, friendship, and self-esteem. Even with all the lost years, the dissolving of my family unit, and the struggle of recovery, I've been blessed.

Second, as you will read in the epilogue, my sexual violations are far from unique. There are literally hundreds of millions of men and women who've experienced the same sorts of betrayal and sexual abuse I did—some experienced even worse. I am determined to become one of the fortunate survivors, with time, from here on out, to understand the words at the ending of the serenity prayer in my recovery groups; we join hands and say together, "Keep coming back—it works when you work it. So work it. You're worth it because God doesn't make junk!"

What was done to me as a child will always be a part of my life, but now I'm learning to let it go a little more each day and striving to live a life of clarity, stability, and happiness one day at a time.

Will I ever learn that sex is a loving, emotional activity? Will these two emotions always be mutually exclusive for me, or will I learn to love Jane—or anyone—and also be able to express that love to her through intimacy? I have yet to experience that sort of breakthrough, but I am told to be hopeful, and so I place myself in the hands of the experts and pray they are right.

The process of full recovery can take up to seven years. My doctors are amazed that, with the exception of one slip, I've not resorted to my old behaviors in the nearly three and half years since the start of my recovery—especially considering how horrifically I was sexually abused and how abominably I had acted out.

My slip came after seventeen months of complete sobriety and a couple of months following my divorce from Jane. I had avoided all social contact with women outside of my recovery groups, but I wasn't prepared for a woman to initiate contact with me. I was feeling lonely and despondent over the divorce when a woman approached me at a restaurant. She had struck up conversations with me during my many previous visits for dinner, and I felt our time spent talking was completely platonic. However, that night she offered to make me dinner, and that evening I lost my sobriety—but not the harsh reality of the damage inflicted on me by John and Jimmy that I still carried and acted out on once again, fifty-one years later.

I think what this woman thought was an intimate connection served only as a trigger for me—a link to the brutal sexual attacks at age seven and a dark reminder of my resulting disconnected behaviors and sexual acting out as an adult. Was I doomed to repeat my self-destructive behavior all over again?

I called my friend Paul in a state of panic the next morning. I felt I was sinking once again into a state of despair. Paul spoke to me for about an hour and finally calmed me down. Two hours later Jeff called me and was just as comforting; he suggested I share my experience with the group at our next session.

I'd been told early in recovery that the next time I slipped it could push me into a downward spiral from which I might not recover. This thought frightened me beyond words. I took Jeff's advice and shared my slip and my unnerving fear the next night at group. While everyone was supportive, Bill sensed a real panic in my voice and state of mind. After the meeting he pulled me aside in the parking lot and gave me his twenty-four-hour chip of sobriety, which he had held for over five years. Bill had been so sexually violated as a child that he had turned to drug and alcohol addictions so powerful most of us in the group wondered how he had survived. He had carried this chip because after seventeen years of sobriety he had relapsed, and it resulted in a four-year return to the nightmare of drug and alcohol addiction, which left him in the hospital, near death. Bill knew if I didn't recover and get back on course from my momentary relapse I could be headed back to years of insanity as well. It wasn't the value of the dollar chip he placed in my hand—it was the feeling of Bill's five years of *strength*, *courage*, and *work* and the *peace* he had regained and that he now wanted to give to me.

I never saw the woman again, and I've been completely celibate for over three years. The chip is a stark reminder that at all costs I can't go back—I must go only forward. I will carry Bill's chip with me for the rest of my life.

Going back to read the pages in this book about the beginning of my recovery—when I wrote about being in a fetal position all weekend long, wishing for death—I believe that was the most difficult period of my journey. But those first steps were critical, and while I can choose to look at the years wasted in chaos, I can also choose to look at the life I have ahead of me.

Had I not made changes in my life through my recovery process, I might not have been alive to write this book. My quality of life has improved and will continue to get even better. My life will also be lengthened, much to my delight as well as to the joy of those I hold most dear. While there have been difficult days and nights—and there are others, I am sure, to come—I've experienced days of calm and peace I had previously never thought possible.

On so many levels I'm happier today than I've ever been. My eyes are clear, and my brain and physical body are so much more stable. I talk to men and women in my groups in their late seventies who had finally woken up when they were in their sixties. These people finally admitted they were miserable, going blindly and thoughtlessly through life, toiling away at lives that were full of pain and suffering, all because they had never grappled with their root problems: the childhood sexual abuse they had experienced. They chose late in life to face their demons, to get help, and to address their inner needs, and are now working finally to be happy.

Meeting and hearing these living success stories is something that inspires me to keep my focus on my own healing journey. When I listen to a man or woman in one of my groups talk about how they've been clear, sober, and at peace for a period of ten years now, and about how they have addressed the core issue of their life, it gives me the feeling of not being alone. I can see a sparkle in their eyes that was never in mine for almost fifty years—a sparkle I never thought possible.

I found my first miracle in my healing process to be the incredible support I received. If this were a film, my list of credits would be long indeed, with God and Jesus Christ in the boldest, largest letters. My sons Paul and Luke, my godmother, my mother-in-law, my biggest supporters and friends Annie, Jeff, and Paul, my doctors, and my brothers and sisters in recovery, all of them were angels sent to me from heaven.

Closing in on my third year of recovery, Jane and I had been divorced for almost eighteen months. Struggling with the loss and emptiness was excruciating, but I was about to receive a second miracle. Jane called me; she wanted to try to reconcile again. A flood of conflicting emotions washed over me—the possibility we could reunite balanced by the reality of where the first tries had left us and where it had left me: alone and hurt.

If this attempt were to succeed, Jane would have to go someplace she had not been willing to go. I had always held out hope that Jane and I could somehow start anew. Despite her difficulties in dealing with the results of my sexual abuse, my sexual acting out, my dissociative behavior, and my struggle in recovery, I always felt Jane wanted us to be together.

My first response to Jane's attempt to reunite this time was to *refuse*. In my opinion it was pointless to attempt reconciliation if she weren't willing to enter the recovery process with me and to seek help for herself as well. But this attempt at reconciliation would prove to be different. I was surprised and excited to learn that this time Jane was indeed ready to embrace the recovery process—for both of us.

It's now been seven months since Jane and I began our new journey together. There is more work for us to do, but we're growing as a couple in a way I believe neither of us had ever thought possible.

We remarried almost three and a half years from the day our lives imploded.

I'm more at peace than I've ever been—or at least since before my nightmare began at age seven. The sexual abuse I suffered created *The Beast* of sexual compulsion and addiction that controlled my life for forty-eight years. Thanks to intensive therapy and support—and God's grace—I've come to understand *The Beast* that lives within me. While I will never fully control it, I can work one day at a time to manage it, to coexist with it, to be at peace with it.

I want to share what I believe was a spiritual intervention that touched me just when I needed it the most. The decision to cut off ties with my extended family was an extremely difficult but a necessary step for me. When I told my mother I had to leave our family, I was agitated and distressed. While I knew it was best for me to leave, I worried she would feel deserted—particularly since my father had been gone for nearly three years at that point, and I felt she looked to me then more than ever.

I'd never before had a dream about my father, nor have I had one since. The night I told my mother I couldn't stay within the family I tossed and turned for a few hours before falling asleep. To have a dream of my dad that night of all nights, a dream that would give me significant calmness, clarity, and insight, was truly a blessing and a message from God.

In the dream I met my dad in London, at the same quaint, English hotel where I had sent him and my mom for their fiftieth wedding anniversary. We were sitting in the lounge, having a cup of coffee, when I said, "Dad, I think Mom's really upset with me. I told her I had to leave the family because I need time and space to heal and recover from my childhood wounds. And I have to do it on my own…away from the family."

He answered me, "No, no, Pete. I've already talked to Mom. We know what happened to you as a child, and she and I want you to do this. We know you need to do this, and we both agree you should."

Then I woke up.

Epilogue
The Let Go...Let Peace Come In Foundation

The English author Albert Pine once wrote, "What we do for ourselves dies with us. What we do for others and the world remains and is immortal."

During the middle of my second year of recovery I was attending one of my Saturday survivor group meetings. They usually consisted of a core group of men and women, but at times a newcomer would join us. This particular day "Samantha" came to the meeting in a completely frantic state of mind. As she started to share her story she broke down into uncontrollable sobs.

Samantha was in the area only because the court had mandated she receive sessions at a psych ward close to our facility because she had attempted suicide twice in the previous six months. She was in crisis when she blurted out, "I debated this morning whether I should kill myself or come to this meeting." She told the story of how she had been sexually molested by a family member when she was nine or ten. In her teens Samantha sought help and told her parents about the sordid events, only to be told she must have imagined the sexual abuse. As I listened to her story I thought to myself that there was yet another person who was not only devastated by her childhood sexual abuse trauma, like me, but then had been completely violated once again when her parents wouldn't help or believe her.

Samantha had been suffering for twenty-five years without any support, and she didn't have the money to receive the one-on-one therapy she so desperately needed. Additionally, her health-care plan didn't provide adequate coverage for treatment from a qualified trauma therapist. Samantha's story reminded me of when I had asked God to take me in my sleep so I wouldn't have to live with the thoughts of the abuse or what it had made me become.

That day, at the end of the session, I decided that service to adult survivors suffering from childhood sexual abuse throughout the world would become a significant facet of my life. I am thankful I had the financial resources to begin my journey to heal and to learn how to live a peaceful existence. Now I'm striving to help others find that place of peace as well. There are sixty million adult survivors of childhood sexual abuse in the United States today (http://www.suebrownauthor.com). With the reported statistics of one out of three girls (Freyd, J., *Violations of Power, Adaptive Blindness and Betrayal Trauma Theory*) and one out of four boys (Fradkin, H.; http://www.businesswire.com/news/home/20101103006938/en/malesurvivor's-Dr.-Howard-Fradkin-200-Male-Sexual) being sexually violated before age eighteen, it could mean the *actual* estimated number of adult survivors in the United States could be even higher than sixty million (Forward, 1993).

If we were to expand these reported numbers to include the rest of the world population, the number of adult survivors sexually abused before age eighteen could be as high as 1.6 billion—possibly the worst affliction of the human race, greater than world hunger, which is what most societies believe to be the most pervasive affliction.

Children have been sexually molested and raped since the beginning of time. Unfortunately, the attention to this rampant problem—and more specifically the *support and recovery* for adult survivors and their families—is not as well known or addressed.

There are many splintered organizations throughout the globe addressing this pandemic. However, I believe the foundation

I created is the first organization to focus on raising capital to subsidize recovery and therapy for adult survivors by funding a minimum of thirty sessions with a trauma therapist. I believe these sessions to be integral in starting a survivor on his or her journey of healing from this life-altering devastation, just as it was for me.

There are no ribbons to wear, no telethons with celebrities performing and asking for money and awareness, because most people find it unnerving to speak about a child being sexually molested, and they can't comprehend or empathize with the recovery the child needs as he or she grew into adulthood. I think the vast majority of people around the world can't fathom an event that occurred in early childhood (even one as horrific as a child being sexually abused) as having such a lasting and debilitating effect on someone's life as an adult.

While most people are sympathetic about the violation of a child, they are far less understanding about the long-term impact it has on the adult or the behaviors the violation creates. The attitude seems to be, "Well, you're an adult now…just get over it." The survivors and the qualified psychologists and therapists who are reading this passage know that's just not possible.

I named my nonprofit Let Go…Let Peace Come In because the hardest action for a survivor to do is to let go…let go of the denial, let go of the shame, let go of the fear, guilt, emotional pain, havoc, frustration, anger, and, most of all, the addictions that manifest from the sexual abuse. Since beginning my recovery I have seen survivors—including myself—let go of afflictions and at times even let a sense of peace and calm they had never thought possible come into their lives.

Within a couple of months after starting Let Go…Let Peace Come In, five very gifted and caring men and women joined me as the foundation's initial board of directors. The six original board members—Paul Flanagan, Jeff DeHart, Natalie Berosh, Larry Miller, Mike Skinner (Michael later moved on to form his own nonprofit), and me—were later joined by Margie McKinnon, Alonni Pedneault, and Dr. Loren Due. These extraordinary people donated their time, completed research, helped construct the Web site, and enabled me to get the foundation off the ground; they also contributed greatly to its early outreach efforts.

Two members of the board of advisors, Alon Goldreich and Andy Pearl, have been extremely supportive and innovative. Alon, who lives in Lugano, Switzerland, structured and built a Web site for the foundation, the vehicle for visits from more than 100 countries and significant postings from around the world. Andy's constant support, participation, and ideas concerning the foundation's fundraising have been in-depth and consistent.

Gretchen Paules, the foundation's executive administrator, supports me, the board of directors, and the board of advisors. She is the human *connection* to the countless survivors around the world who contact us and seek the foundation's help and support. Gretchen has had interactions with survivors from Iceland, Pakistan, Africa, and quite a few European countries, not to mention *all* fifty states in the United States.

We are hopeful the foundation will be able to enlighten, help, and support survivors on the road to recovery and give them the ability to let go of their pain and learn how to live again. Once survivors are able to understand how their sexual violations as children caused so many of the difficult life issues and disconnected behaviors they have developed, we are hopeful they will be able to let go and let peace and civility come into their hearts and lives.

The foundation will work to complete ten mandates:

1. To educate societies throughout the world about the effects childhood sexual abuse has on adults and to impart to those who have suffered from sexual violation as children the

importance of understanding and connecting the havoc in their lives today to the sexual abuse they suffered as children.
2. To raise the necessary capital to assist one survivor at a time and to subsidize the trauma therapy sessions needed for a survivor to start the journey on the road to a healthy and peaceful recovery.
3. To revolutionize a standard of care worldwide that includes the much-needed insurance coverage for the therapy sessions mentioned above for adult survivors.
4. To ask survivors to post pictures of themselves (from their childhood or any other time they feel comfortable with) on the foundation's Web site, along with their first names, last initials, and the countries from which they hail.

We need to show the world that adults suffering from childhood sexual abuse are not just statistics or numbers but *souls* who have been damaged and have the right to live normal lives. On the following pages you will see thumbnails of courageous men and women who've already posted to the foundation's site.

In order to achieve the first three mandates, we have to show the world the magnitude of this affliction and the devastating effects it has on a human being and the entire human race. Most societies and people around the world take the position, "Don't tell me there's a problem—*show* me." A picture speaks a thousand words. So although you will see only a sliver of the foundation's first 100+ photos and captions in this chapter, one could say that through the foundation's Web site we have spoken our first *hundred thousand* words with millions still unspoken.

5. To galvanize the world to have *one day* set aside each year to recognize and honor, via radio, TV, print, and the Internet, the adult survivors trying to heal and learning how to live again.
6. To help and support future generations of children who unfortunately will also be sexually violated and abused.

It is our sincere hope that the foundation will take hold and find its place in the world so others will go to the site and see the thousands of men and women before them who spoke up. They found their voices not only to help themselves and other survivors but also to let the children of tomorrow know there is hope, there is help, there is recovery, and they're not alone.

While the foundation is focused on the recovery and the healing process for adults eighteen and older, it is a well-known fact that children model the systems of the families they come from and the adults they observe throughout their lives. By seeing the pictures and reading the captions of so many adults before them, we hope the children of the future will speak up and tell someone about the abuse they have suffered. Their voices will be heard and they will follow the lead of the courageous adults who have come forward—like those who have posted their stories on our site—and seek the path to recovery and healing even sooner than we did, long before their lives spiral out of control.

7. To provide guidance to survivors who are willing to reach out and develop kinships with others in their areas, through the use of a support book written and developed with the input of specialists for adult survivors

of childhood sexual abuse. The foundation believes this book will provide hope, guidance for recovery, and a new and healthier way of life.
8. To involve young adults in our educational intern program throughout the world. The thoughtful and caring young men and women who've donated their time to Let Go…Let Peace Come In may be receiving college credit for their efforts, but the passion and support they've brought to the foundation is immeasurable. Some of those involved in the early stages of the foundation have offered to share their experiences here:

Margaret, *Summer 2011*
I was drawn to the Let Go…Let Peace Come In Foundation after mentoring a group of girls in Mexico, some of whom had been sexually abused. Helping adult survivors heal from trauma that may have happened many years ago is a worthy cause that receives too little attention. My days at LGLPCI were spent commenting on news articles dealing with CSA, updating Facebook and Twitter, finding inspiring quotations to post on the website, and researching, then contacting organizations that help survivors around the world. The people who work here are very friendly and welcoming. I've learned a lot about the issue of childhood sexual abuse as well as how a small non-profit works, specifically how they get the word out about their organization. I am happy to have helped them in any way I could and hope this organization continues to grow and help survivors heal.

Leah, *Spring 2011*

The role of quotidian internships often involves mindless filing and getting coffee. My role at Let Go…Let Peace Come In Foundation was about reaching out to people who are survivors and making a positive, impactful change in their lives.

Getting coffee and helping out with miniscule tasks was never my role within the foundation. Helping others realize that they are not alone and that their voices can be stronger and more powerful than they ever imagined is something that is more rewarding personally than I could have thought. Making a positive change in the world is a cause that is immensely important to me. One of the major feelings that survivors feel before getting help is isolation, extreme guilt, and feeling "dirty." The isolation is so enormous that it can devour one whole. Uniting survivors can be efficacious in dissolving those symptoms.

There is something very potent in the fact that the organization tries to take people from the darkest, grimmest time of their life to an empowered, educated place. By empowering others I personally felt empowered; I left the office every day with a smile on my face, knowing that I helped survivors find their voice. I'm sad to leave the office at the end of the semester, but I know that I will remain in contact with the people I worked with who were some of the warmest, nicest people I've ever met. This internship was not just a job for me, it was a cause that I poured my heart and soul into, and that personally resonates with me.

Chelsea, *Fall 2010*

The reason I decided to intern at the Let Go…Let Peace Come In Foundation is because a relative of mine was sexually abused and never received the help they deserved. I see the struggles the person goes through, and my heart goes out. After interning and reaching out to other survivors who have been sexually abused and having them e-mail me back explaining how just by hearing my kind worlds has lifted their spirits has made everything I do completely worth it. There are so many facilities for addictions but barely any for sexual abuse, and the world needs to start realizing, sexual abuse is just as horrible as any other abuse. It is imperative for survivors to get the help they deserve so they can live a happy and healthy life! My daily tasks at this foundation have been to reach out to survivors, update the Web site, research about sexual abuse, find uplifting quotes for the survivors, and other tasks. I enjoyed everything I have done at this internship, and I love everyone that I work with. They are all friendly and very helpful. I loved interning here, and know that the people who intern here after me will think the same exact way.

Lonni, *Summer 2010*
My experience working with the Let Go…Let Peace Come In Foundation has impacted my life. I have learned firsthand how a nonprofit works. Also, it has been rewarding for me to reach out and help people who are childhood sexual abuse survivors. In my personal experiences some of my closest friends have told me their stories of childhood sexual abuse, and I knew that I wanted to help change things for the future. I appreciate the opportunity that I have to work with the Let Go…Let Peace Come In Foundation. While there is still more outreach to be done, it has been great to see the foundation grow as we are now at 99 countries that have viewed our Web site. I look forward to supporting survivors in the future and helping with their recovery.

Pooja, *Summer 2010*
The internship at Let Go…Let Peace Come In Foundation has opened up my eyes to the issue of childhood sexual abuse. I joined the internship in the hopes of being able to witness and understand the negatively influential effects childhood sexual abuse can have on an individual. Through the internship I have been able to

talk to, chat with, and reach out to survivors all over the world, including Pakistan, Australia, and Africa, to name a few. My main task was to find ways of reaching out to survivors and supportive organizations to join the foundation's mission and help expand our voice through the Web site. While researching, it came as a shock to me to uncover just how prevalent childhood sexual abuse is worldwide. There are and have been so many people affected by CSA; presidents, actors, musicians, authors, and so many more. All these people and many more need the proper counseling and healing services to allow them to accept their trauma and be able to move past it. I am very proud to have worked with an organization as LGLPCI where survivors can begin their healing process by telling their story, and find the appropriate support needed to let go of their tragedy and let the peace finally come into their lives.

Erica, *Spring 2010*
Childhood sexual abuse is something that I feel strongly about because someone I am very close to is a victim. She was lucky and able to get counseling and is now doing well. I saw how much telling her story helped her to heal, and when I found out about the Let Go…Let Peace Come In Foundation, I thought about how this would be a great opportunity to be able to help others who are suffering.

Through this internship experience I learned a great deal about Web site development and what it is like to work for a small nonprofit organization. This internship was beneficial because I was encouraged to come up with new ideas to help the foundation and was then able to implement those ideas.

This past semester working here has been a great learning experience for me. I am happy to have found the LGLPCI Foundation and for the chance to help others through the work that we do.

9. To release the foundation's song, "Let Go... Let Peace Come In," throughout the world. Our song can be viewed on YouTube at http://www.youtube.com/watch?v=b4PDC03Gl2k and purchased on iTunes and many other music sites. While the Internet has significant penetration throughout the globe, radio still reaches more people, especially those in Third World countries.
10. To cultivate an expansive organization deeply rooted in global societies where new and talented board members are attracted as the tenure of existing members concludes. Through the implementation of fresh ideas from new individuals, the LGLPCI Foundation can continue to grow and develop its outreach and philanthropic efforts.

It's time to take action against unspeakable, perverse sexual abuse and the damage it wreaks on adults for the majority of their lives. It is time reach out and assist those adult survivors eighteen and older who desperately need help. Childhood sexual abuse is a widespread crime perpetrated upon children of both sexes. It is inflicted by men and women of all races and creeds. Childhood sexual abuse happens in the poorest neighborhoods and in the most affluent towns throughout the world. Survivors of childhood sexual abuse universally have one thing in common—they have been controlled and manipulated by their abusers and unwillingly driven to a point of shame and fear, and left to a life of havoc, devastation, and usually some form of addiction.

Being passionate for a cause gives strength and significance to its success. But in reality, like every other cause, there is a significant amount of capital needed to build a grassroots effort and to enlighten the world. To date I have personally committed the capital to get the foundation off the ground, but there is still much more needed. The foundation has initiated its outreach for contributions, and the planning of its first major fundraising event is underway.

I have written to the top 100 CEOs in the United States, asking them to contribute to our nonprofit foundation—twenty-eight of them answered "not at this point in time," and seventy-two did not respond. The foundation intends to write to these 100 CEOs again—as well as the next 400 highest-ranking CEOs in the United States—with the same request. I plan to reach out to Bill and Melinda Gates, Warren Buffett, and the top forty billionaires who have recently come forward and pledged half their fortunes to charity.

Statistics tell us a certain percentage of these CEOs and billionaires—or someone they love—have been touched by childhood sexual abuse. We need only *one* of these caring and generous men or women to come forward courageously to help us break the silence and raise awareness and the capital needed to do so. I know part of their mandate is to help people in need, and I'm hopeful once they see the sobering research they will realize how many millions of people are in desperate need of help due to this life-changing perpetration.

Research indicates that adult survivors of childhood sexual abuse belabor the health-care system with *billions* of dollars of claims for both physical and mental health treatments because the root cause of their ailments is not being uncovered. The effects of childhood sexual abuse widely contribute to family dysfunction and broken families throughout the world.

There have been times during my endeavor with the foundation when I thought maybe this was just too big of a task, but at each crossroads I came to, there was always a sign or an occurrence that propelled me to move forward and stay the course.

The two most recent such events happened in the last few

months of finishing this book. During my separation from Jane, her cousin, Jamie DiDio, married Marla Green. Marla, who has been a philanthropist for many years, is one of the most passionate and caring individuals I have ever met. A tireless champion of worthy causes, she seeks to bring about change and support to foundations and endeavors that are dear to her heart.

A few weeks after hearing my story, Marla shared with me that a close friend of hers of some thirty years had suffered sexual abuse as a child. Marla was so moved and taken aback that she offered to do a fundraiser for the foundation and my efforts. Quite frankly, I didn't know how to approach the first fundraiser, but that answer came just a few months later.

I was on one of my many trans-Atlantic business flights. As I was settling into my seat, preparing for the nine-hour flight, I struck up a conversation with the passenger next to me. Prior to my recovery I usually avoided chatting on flights, but now that I have gained emotional strength, I actually enjoy making new friends.

On this flight I had the most fascinating and informative conversation with Dr. Jeffrey Melin, who had a PhD and an MD and was working in pharmaceuticals. Inevitably, because of his medical background, our conversation led to my telling him about the foundation as well as my own story. After listening intently, he paused for a moment and said, "You are the second person who has told me about sexual abuse trauma as a child. Like the person I spoke with twelve years ago, I really don't know what to say."

But what he said in the next fifteen minutes put me on a direct path hopefully to coordinate the work I started with the foundation with the largest and most-respected public health school in the world—the Johns Hopkins University Bloomberg School of Public Health. The school is unique for many reasons, among them is that it is the only one that has a Department of Mental Health.

Dr. Melin said, "I believe what you're doing through your

foundation is a valiant effort to help survivors and to educate the world, but from my perspective, if you want to create real change and inform the world of the effects of childhood sexual abuse on a human being's life, the answer is in the data. Data is power."

He continued,. "If you could show the statistics on how a sexually abused child burdens the health-care system as he or she grows into adulthood, I would think you could raise funds through your foundation for survivors to receive the therapy they need and to raise the much-needed capital for research on the topic."

With that he took out one of his business cards and wrote down contact information for Dr. Michael Klag at John Hopkins University. He told me to tell Dr. Klag that he had recommended I contact him about our conversation. Below is my e-mail to Dr. Klag and his response.

> From: Peter S. Pelullo
> Sent: Friday, March 11, 2011 10:30 AM
> To: Klag, Michael
> Subject: Introduction (Dr. Jeffery Melin, MD)
>
> Dear Dr Klag,
>
> Allow me to introduce myself. My name is Peter Pelullo and I reside in the city of Lower Gwynedd right outside of Philadelphia.
> I'm a 59 year old corporate executive that has been self-employed for 35 years.
> While what I›m writing to you about might sound a bit foreign, Dr. Jeffrey Melin, MD suggested I contact you. I met Jeff on a trans-Atlantic flight and had the opportunity to inform him of a foundation (www.letgoletpeacecomein.org) I

started that addresses the effects of childhood sexual abuse throughout an adult›s life.

As a survivor myself, I shared my personal story with Jeff which included being sexually violated as a 7 year old in 1959. While I knew something was dramatically wrong with me my entire, life it was not until 2007 when a life altering event caused me to start the process of recovery.

In speaking to Jeff and telling him how the foundation›s website has had thousands of visits originating in more than 3,500 cities from 114 countries (out of 260 on Earth), has been read in 33 languages, and is financially assisting adult survivors to start the journey of learning how to live, he felt the public health issues would be the «data of power» to bring this worldwide affliction to the forefront of public awareness.

From that perspective he thought I should contact you and you could possibly assist or direct me on how to start assembling the data regarding how the debilitating sexual violations to a child cause an adult to labor the health care systems throughout the world. I believe the research will show that the cost of treating the residual effects as well as mental health treatment costs expand into the billions.

If you have a moment to look at the website, we have constructed a unique procedure for survivors to post a childhood photo and caption. As you will see, they are from all over the world.

While Jeff thought the Foundation was a valiant effort, he believed that if society understood the billions of dollars that are extended to help the survivors the issue would be addressed and given much more attention.

In closing there have been many new disclosures in the news recently from different walks of life; Queen Latifah in the music sector, Senator Scott Brown in Massachusetts, and the daughters from the classical musical group "The 5 Browns" just to name a few. This affliction knows no geographical boundaries, race, creed or social status.

Thank you in advance for your thoughts and direction.

Peter S. Pelullo

Subject: Re: Introduction (Dr. Jeffery Melin, MD)
From: "Klag, Michael"
Date: Mon, 14 Mar 2011 00:52:46 -0400
To: «Peter Pelullo»

Dear Peter,

Thank you for your email. I am originally from Norristown and lived in Lower Gwynedd for a short time while I was in medical school, so I know it well.

Your email could not have come at a more fortuitous time as our School is engaged in thinking about how to apply the public health paradigm to the issue of childhood sexual abuse, I.e., quantifying the societal burden, identifying risk factors, determining the long-term effects, and developing preventive interventions. Using funds from a donor, we have just recruited a new faculty member to take this issue on.

> I am traveling in Asia presently and don't have reliable internet access but will look at your website as soon as I can. I don't return to the US until April but I have copied Dr. Bill Eaton who is the chair of our Department of Mental Health. He is leading our effort in this regard. In addition, I am copying Ricky Fine. She is from our department of external affairs and is working with Bill to help coordinate our efforts. They can start the conversation but I look forward to communicating personally when I return.
>
> Thank you again for reaching out.

The odds against meeting Dr. Jeffery Melin and, through him, Dr. Michael Klag were astronomical, but on Thursday, April 28, 2011, that chance encounter on an airplane led to Marla Green DiDio's, Gretchen Paules', and my meeting with quite an esteemed group of people to discuss the foundation and our goals—Dr. Michael Klag, Dr. William Eaton, Dr. Fred Berlin, and Ms. Ricky Fine. I hope and firmly believe the result of this initial meeting will be the next chapter in my journey and will expand our efforts to awaken the world to the effects of childhood sexual abuse on survivors, their families, their friends, the health-care system, and society as a whole. While at this moment I'm not sure how our collaboration will work, what I am sure of is that I will be working with the foundation's board of directors to allocate a percentage of the funds we raise to further the research that is being pioneered by this elite institution.

I have learned through my own recovery process that it takes a certain amount of time, acceptance, and work before one gains the strength to begin the journey to learn how to live again. It is our goal to show those who have been exploited—and those who care for them—that there is a path to recovery that begins with telling their stories. The pictures the adult survivors have posted on the foundation's Web site to date represent a fraction of the simply unbelievable number of those who have been affected by childhood sexual abuse. They symbolize a worldwide community of men and women who are dedicated to supporting themselves and other survivors as well as to breaking the silence of this horrible pandemic.

If you're a survivor, know, when you're ready, that the foundation is here and waiting to help and support you as you begin your journey. To the survivors who are reading this book and say, "I've handled that and I have it under control," know there are hundreds of millions who haven't—and we need your voice to tell the world what happened to you. To those of you who have lost hope, I say you deserve and have the right to live in peace, and that's why you shouldn't give up. Please don't be afraid to share your pain and trauma, because you are not alone.

To the survivors who have responded anonymously to the foundation's poll and have said they don't want to be recognized, please remember you were just a child; it wasn't your fault, and it's not your shame. If you're fearful because you think it will upset or break up your family, please know your family is already fractured. If you're fearful because you think people will feel differently about you, that is even more reason you need to stand with us—together we can show the world what was taken from us as children and remove the stigma associated with childhood sexual abuse. Our voices can speak to the hundreds of millions of sexual abuse victims out there today—and most unfortunately the millions of tomorrow's children—who will need help and courage to come forward and let go of the pain, and let peace come into their lives.

On the following pages you will see just a few of the survivors throughout the world who have posted on the foundation's Web site and have shared their photos and captions. Please visit the Web site to see the countless other courageous survivors who have lent their voices to help raise awareness.

As seen on the foundation's web site: www.letgoletpeacecomein.org.
Men and women of strength and courage to recover, heal, and educate the world about the effects of childhood sexual abuse on an adult's life.

Mike S. *(United States)*
"Why" I have asked this question all my life. Why did no one lend a hand to this sad little boy. And why do so many in society still ignore child sexual abuse? Why?

Annie B. *(United States)*
I was nine years old when this picture was taken. By that time, I had been involved in years of sexual activity with adults and older children, and while I knew how to please someone sexually, I hadn't yet learned long division at school. I silently hoped someone would see in my eyes what I could not say, what I didn't have words for. No one ever did, so I carried it alone.

Paul F. *(United States)*
I was 12 when I took this picture. I wanted to see if the feelings of shame were visible on the outside. The abuse happened over the course of a few years. I don't remember how many times. I have never trusted anyone or had a close friend since. I was sexually abused again at the age of 16 by a Sunday school teacher. I have kept silent until I reached my 50s where depression and addiction filled my life.

Tricia *(United States)*
I am a survivor of childhood sexual abuse, not a victim. My father is the victim because he took his

life in 1987. He couldn't live with himself. There have been many times over the years where I wish that I had taken my life as well. Instead of running from my past, I have been trying to embrace it, because it is definitely a part of who I am. I tried for many years to "escape" from what happened to me, but realized that no matter where I go, my past will always be with me. I grew up in a home where incest was an everyday occurrence, along with physical and emotional abuse. Between my father and my three brothers I could not escape the never ending abuse, so much so, that I simply gave in to it. It defined me once, but it no longer defines who I am today.

Philip *(United Kingdom)*
Each new day I take loving action to my wounded child of Philip. Just for today, I honor Philip with loving actions to myself. I do not let my inner wounded child take over my life, so that I start to ACT OUT or use MY arrested addictions or Behavior to STOP any inner pain from MY childhood. I MUST live in the NOW, one day at a time. I honor the Spirit in you which is also in me.

Anonymous *(United States)*
It happened in 1981, and it began when I consulted a lawyer about sexual abuse I had experienced at the hands of my 33-year-old uncle. I had been 8 years old at the time. The lawyer made a suggestion: "Write this man a letter and, in a nice way, suggest he pay for counseling for the trauma which you now recall. We'll see what happens." It wasn't long before we found out what would happen. My uncle drove to our house. At first he acted as sweet as sugar to my family, hugging

them and visiting with them. Then he came to where I was by myself, and the threats literally glued me to my chair. I felt like I was being abused all over again. He was saying, "You can take me to court—you see, we have a Big Court—but you will LOSE!"

Portia *(United Kingdom)*
I was determined to break this cycle of abuse. At 11 I was sexually abused by a neighbour. This went on for 2 years. I told my mother but she did nothing, except order me to wash my mouth out with soap and water. At 14, on becoming a woman, I realized the seriousness of the sexual abuse and wanted to commit suicide, blaming myself, as I was brainwashed to do in the Catholic cult. To them all females are Satan. My brother made 2 attempts on my life, once with an axe and second by smothering. So, from that time on, I never slept deeply and always with one leg out of the bed, in case I needed to escape. The smothering almost worked and I have no idea where the strength came from to survive. My brother was not reprimanded in any way. My father brought me with him everywhere, lest my mother bring the priests in again.

Grace *(Germany)*
Age 3. "Nursery School Graduation"… Why is the diploma so large? Why don't I look happy? A mother would have straightened the dress out.

Ed P. *(United States)*
Unfortunately, the Devil touched me. My Sunday School teacher was a pedophile, and I was his next victim. He was my football coach, the neighborhood Citizen of the Year, Mister all around nice guy—Ted

Lane. For some reason he picked me out on the football field and then baited me with attention (what adolescent boy wouldn't want to get a football autographed by the Washington Redskins in person at their practice facility?—He made it happen). Over a period of eighteen to twenty-four months he sexually molested me. On Sundays we would go to church early in the morning and travel into DC to clean a trailer lunch stand that he operated on the construction site where the Library of Congress was being built. During that day while we cleaned he would put the big gray industrial trash cans up on the counter to block the windows and then he would proceed to molest me. Other times he would molest me at his house -- once in the attic at his house where I could hear his unsuspecting wife cooking dinner downstairs. Mr. Lane was arrested some years later and is now a registered sex offender in Northern Virginia. I don't know how many victims he has left in his wake.

Norwood Y. *(United States)*
Norwood Y. in the 6th grade. A victim of sexual abuse. Now a victor!

Tom S. *(United States)*
Until 2 years ago I was a survivor of child sexual abuse. This means that I was reasonably successful at hiding the self-destructive behaviors, the depression and confused boundaries from others. It was not until I joined a support group that I learned that I could do better than just survive, that I could have victory. As a result, I have true joy in my life, I have honest and sincere friendships without anxiety and live life

looking forward, not backward. I have been able to use the experiences of my youth to write a book (Terrible Things Happened to Me) and serve as Executive Director of VOICE Today, Inc. which is dedicated to breaking the silence and the cycle of child sexual abuse.

Susannah *(United Kingdom)*
I feel strongly that through all our individual courage we can unite to bring about global change.

Martha W. *(United States)*
I grew up as a child actress. I excelled at taking directions—I was paid well for being a submissive, cooperative, obedient, little girl. Not only did this pave the way for a successful childhood acting career, but it also led me into the talons of a church leader/Sunday school teacher with insidious intentions. He molested me for over five years. However, along my journey of healing, I have chosen to no longer be a victim of my circumstances. I am a victor over them. I am no longer shackled to my perpetrator. I am free, because the truth has set me free. I chose not to say, "Why me?" I am a more mature and complete woman, because I have walked the path of brokenness and am confident that this path is the road to wholeness and true beauty. Out of brokenness comes the most radiant beauty. I believe I was allowed to walk this journey so that I can be part of the process of stopping childhood sexual abuse and empower survivors to begin the process of healing by telling my story. I am growing up as a victorious survivor. I am Martha W., founder of A Quarter Blue—Stopping Childhood Sexual Abuse.

(For more information about the work of A Quarter Blue—Stopping Childhood Sexual Abuse go towww.aquarterblue.org)

Jeff D. *(United States)*
An older, stronger, neighborhood boy. One solitary memory. Is it real? Was it abuse? Was there more? Why I may never know...But it was real. I wanted to be accepted and loved at any cost...my being, my soul...The shame, the sadness, the desperation, the silence...no child should ever know.

Beautifuldreamer *(United States)*
SURVIVOR. What I want to be when I grow up.

Loren D. *(United States)*
Loren D. = Survivor of Rape, Incest, Sexual Abuse, and Molestation

My name is Loren D. and I am a survivor over comer of childhood sexual abuse, incest, rape, and molestation. I was 4 or 5 years-old when I was raped and molested by my teenage brother and my father over a period of time. My father was an ordained Pentecostal Elder. You may ask where my mother was; she worked 2 and sometimes 3 jobs to keep food on the table and a roof over our heads. My father worked odd jobs; mostly as a janitor. Other times he was off running revivals and trying to build a church which he never completed.

When I was 36 and my son was 12, I sat him down and shared with him the facts of life as the Holy Spirit instructed me to teach him and not touch him as I had been touched. The Lord blessed me with a 12 year-old daughter when I married my wife and I was 44. Through all this transition the Lord made it clear that I was not to touch my children; which includes my grandsons and granddaughters.

The Lord has brought healing and deliverance in my life by blessing me to forgive and love my dad who is deceased and my brother who is a pastor. In 2006, 60 years after I was born I got a breakthrough that Jesus loves me and that I can love him, my wife and others—I am learning to really love.

My mission is to spread the good news about Jesus Christ love and expose, confront and reveal the truth about child sexual abuse by bringing healing and deliverance to perpetrators and victims.

Loren C. Due, Ph.D.
Award Winning Author, Speaker, Consultant
P.O. Box 273048, Fort Collins, CO 80527
Office: 970 204 1559, Fax 970 267 9925
Toll Free: 877 373 8399
Email: loren@drdue.com
Website: www.blogtalkradio.com/dr-due
Website: www.drdue.com

Linda F. *(United States)*
My name is Linda F. and I have finally broken my silence after decades of suffering in shame. My preacher father sexually abused me for ten years when I was a child. Naturally, this completely polluted my concept of God, love, father and trust. I have written my story in a book entitled, "Out of the Miry Clay: Freedom from Childhood Sexual Abuse." It is a story about the carnage that sexual abuse leaves in the heart of every child. It is my story of being a preacher's

daughter in search of a loving Heavenly Father who would give me the courage to forgive and trust again. A Heavenly Father so unlike my earthly father that the difference would literally baffle me for years. "Out of the Miry Clay" was published in June of 2008 and has gone to over 31 different countries in the first year of publication. To learn more, please visit my website at www.LindaFossen.com.

Nathan *(United States)*
Healing really is possible, it will take you to dark places but with consistency and persistence you to can over come. Let the healing begin!!

Dennis D. *(United States)*
I was a very scared and needy boy. My mother would joke about giving me a bottle every time I cried as a baby. She said she was so overwhelmed. It is no wonder that I was obese (32 lbs.) at one year old. There were 5 of us all together. I was number 2. Being obese haunted my childhood until I was 14 and lost some weight. In the meantime, my mother never allowed us to fight or be aggressive like the other boys in a pretty rough neighborhood. She was manipulative and my 3 brothers and myself used to fight over who was going to sleep with her when my Father went away on business. There was no overt incest but plenty of the covert.

Coupled with a strict Catholic upbringing, I first needed a psychiatrist at age 11 for an " overly scrupulous conscience". There have been 4 other periods in my life for treatment of OCD.I grew up afraid that a god of their making was going to punish me for being disobedient. I tried to be perfect and all that brought was more pain because no one can be perfect. Physical spanking at home being slapped at hit at school were considered normal and routine.

At age 56, I am finally dealing with my addiction caused by this perfect storm of neglectful alcoholic parents, abusive clergy(nuns and priests), and typical youthful torture for being fat. I am working hard to finally get over my fears and get to a place of peace. The last 6 months of my life since entering Recovery have been the most difficult of my life. I am hopeful for a better tomorrow. I am coming to see that they were all reacting from their own trauma but I need to own all of the rage and anger and then let it go.

Barb *(United States)*
Best Forever Friends

Karen R. *(United States)*
Molested at four years old by my father, I grew up fearful and depressed. I'm eight in the photo. My fear shows in my face.

In my early twenties I landed in the hospital twice, after two psychotic breakdowns. Jesus had taken my hand when I was 19, but I had lots of forgiving and grieving work to do, including much wrestling with God himself, before I could enjoy the abundant life Jesus promises.

After many years of working through trust issues, depression, and anxiety, I've now been a psychotherapist (M.S.W.) since 1986, married to my best friend since 1972, and have recently released a memoir, Trading Fathers, Forgiving Dad, Embracing God. Life is good.

Healing is possible, if we don't give up. That sense of deficiency and shame that survivors feel is a feeling, not a truth. Read chapter 1 of my story from the link on the bottom of the "Books" page: http://www.letgo-letpeacecomein.org/books.html

Courtney R. *(United States)*
My name is Courtney and this is my first grade picture. This is about the time my stepfather came into my mother's life, and forever changed mine. From the time he arrived till I was 13 he sexually abused me. I can still feel the metal rails of my youth bed in my hands as I tried to keep him from turning me over. I had to "confess" twice before one of the parish priests took me aside for counseling and told me I had to tell him to stop. I didn't know I was allowed. My stepfather has been dead for several years now and at the end I confronted him to ask him why he did it. From within his withered, grey face, bald from the chemo, he fixed his horrible eyes on me and said "It takes two, sister." His alcoholism and pot addiction wrecked not only his own life, but mine, my 4 siblings and my mother's. At 42, I cannot sustain a healthy relationship and have finally realized that I need serious help to rebuild my shattered self esteem. I am getting this help, and posting my story here is just one step towards healing.

Tracy
Hi my name is Tracy and I am an adult survivor of child abuse.

By the time I was 16 I had had at least three near death experiences thru abuse:

I was held outside of a four story building window by my hair at 2 1/2 as a threat to my mother. He was my step father who did everything he could to hurt me. Beatings verbal abuse, etc. I survived thru my imagination. I had a white winged Unicorn come and I sat on him so as not to fall.

At 8 I was raped and knife point on the roof of my Bronx, NY apartment building. I had so many emotional fragments around me and an Angel who held me in her wings to redirect my attention. I could hear my inner voice soothing my assailant with her words. I asked for some sign of survival and I received it.

At 16 I was drugged, raped and left for dead. As my stomach was being pumped My creator told me that I had had a choice of severing my ties with this lifetime or go in and complete my agreement to help other abuse survivors.

As a result I became a certified Imagery guide and clinicle Hypnotherapist helping others thru natural healing via Imagery.

I wrote a book about my experiences and how Imagery and internal spiritual and animal guides have helped me to release all of that dark stuff so my body and mind could heal. The book "This Too Shall Pass" is FREE to all. I am interested in helping others. If you are interested you can download it at WWW.chat4healing.com under the Bio tab.

Saved *(United States)*
I was sexually abused at 10 by my father, 12 by my grandfather, raped at age 19 and raped two times by my ex husband. I have a gentle kind man now and have had extensive counseling.

Diane *(United States)*
I was so dehumanized by incest I developed multiple personalities. I have now recovered and am helping other survivors.

Penny *(United States)*
I was hurt by both my mom and dad. You dont know the damage it brings being raped over and over and no one there to help you. I'm a fighter 'cuz of the way I was raised.

Billy S. *(United States)*
I was abused my whole life by people who were supposed to love and care for me. My stepfather tied me to a tree and put a dress on me. I never fit in with children or my peers. I was sexually abused at 13 by a group of older teenagers. I had no trust for anyone. I brought the sexual abuse home to my brother and sister. I have found it hard to get on with life and have lived in a drug, alcohol and sex addicted existence for the majority of my life. I am now on my way to recovery from the sexual, drug and alcohol addictions…Thank God.

Davinia P. *(United States)*
Davinia P.—Survivor

Angela *(United States)*
I was sexually abused by my Step-Father for many years. He theatened to kill my mother and little sister if I told. He told me I was ugly and he was doing me a favor. He sexually abused many children in the family. I went to the police to tell the about the abuse. That is the day I would never forget. Being in that room with

two male officers and my mother. After a scared little girl told her story the one officer said there is nothing I can do. As my mother drug me out of the room I turned and saw the officer toss the cassette tape and the paper he wrote on in the trash. He never spent one day in jail for the abuse he inflicted on the children. He died later in life of cancer. I also found myself with others who would rape me. I finally was told by others I am not ugly but beautiful and sometimes I wish I was ugly then no one would look at me sexually. Anyone who does this to a child are the ugly ones.

Jeannie *(United States)*
God grant me the serenity to accept the things I cannot change; courage to change the things I can; and wisdom to know the difference.

Kristen K. *(United States)*
From the age of 18 months or so, to 15 years, my grandfather and others abused me.

Dave S. *(United States)*
I am in Kindergarten here and this is the only picture of myself where I do not feel shame, fear or horror. It is the last time I can remember feeling truly safe, secure and cared for, the time before I lost my trust, my faith, my spirit and my true love of the world. Having been in recovery for about a year now I have grown stronger and no longer fear the demons the way I once did, now I need to learn to not fear my own image. For those of you still searching know that there is love and kindness in the world and it can begin here at this site. Thanks for taking a step forward I welcome you.

Karen *(United States)*
So here's me, the year that my sexual assault began. I was picked off the path home from school by a socially & developmentally delayed young adult male. My abuse was ongoing for several years until we relocated. I had no memory of my childhood prior to 13yo (after we'd relocated) and then it all caved in on me with the birth of our daughter (when I was 21yo); I began to remember and it nearly destroyed me. That was some 27 years ago and I finally got up the courage 6 years ago, to take my life back. It's been hell, but what keeps me going is knowing that there's a whole world full of hurting adults and children that are suffering from abuses as I type this. I want to get better so that I can be of hope and help to a hurting world. Child abuse is a mess that one person alone can't clean up, but with all our hands, we can make our world a better and safer place for the children's sake.

Barbara R. *(United States)*
Went on for years from 5ish till I spoke at age 12, Went to court but he fled country. Now age 22 they caught him and I must face him again in court. I'm a strong and beautiful mother to be and it's a girl. I already fear for her safety since my molester was a man my family trusted, my brother's father-we had separate ones. He never hurt me or struck fear in me but what he did was wrong and I deserve to not have to relive this again but the courts won't let me be and I figure if I can't avoid it I'll set the best example I can and do this with my head held high. I pray for strength. But for those put there know that my support system was

my mom and my now fiancé...that's it just two people, though I had counseling it didn't work for me. My two person support group was more than enough.

Teal *(United States)*
I was raised in the Wasatch-Cache National Forest of Utah, a location with an intensely religious climate (over 90% Mormon). In the first year of my life, it became immediately apparent that I had been born with unusual talents that set me apart from other children. My parents did not understand them. But in time, they came to find out that they were extrasensory abilities which did not go away with age. Because of the size of the town and the predominate local religion, word of my unusual abilities got out very quickly and they were not only frowned upon but also feared by many in the community. My parents did not recognize the "red flags" for what they were. It did not occur to them that this thing went on in the world much less with someone whom they ended up trusting completely. They mistook my "issues" for mental illness. It ripped our family apart. After having gone through five years of specialized psychotherapy for acute PTSD specifically tailored to ritual abuse victims, I decided to use my experience and extrasensory abilities for the greater good of mankind. I have assumed the title of "The Spiritual Catalyst" and am now developing a growing following as I embark on a mission as a contemporary spiritual guide to remind people of the united, energetic nature of this universe and to teach people how to find health, freedom and bliss in the midst of even the most extreme circumstances.

Jeanne M. *(United States)*
One by one we survived. Together we can thrive.

Andy *(United States)*
When I was about age 6 my parents separated. My Mom was lonely, probably felt scared and began to use me as a substitute for my Dad. Though there was no overt incest, mine could best be described as covert incest. I slept in my Mom's bed until I was seventeen years old. My Dad was not around and when he was he was angry and abusive. I had no idea the confusion and suffering this would cause as I became an adult. Through a lot of hard work and therapy I have learned to re-parent myself. It's taken 35 years of effort and desire. I really believe in the work and purpose of this foundation, being so fully aware of the devastating problems and suffering childhood sexual abuse causes. I know that with intention and desire it is possible to grow and change, and lead a happy fulfilling life. I have seen what seems like a miracle transformation in many of the people I've met in recovery.

Olga *(United States)*
I was sexually assaulted as a child, around the age of 4. While my mother had gone to the authorities, the professionals had told her that I was too young to remember the attacks and that the trauma would dissipate itself. They had said that the trial would be more damaging to me than the sexual assault. As I entered adolescence I had always felt that there was a dark pool within myself. As nighttime would approach I would feel this intense depression, isolation, repulsive feelings within myself. I had no idea why. I struggled

with depression as a teenager enormously; I used to play a game with myself. If could find nothing to live for, for one week, then I would end my life. Fortunately, I never went an entire week without finding one thing to be happy about. As a teenager, I acted out enormously and had conduct disorder symptoms. While I always had straight A's in school, my life in every other aspect was dysfunctional. I sought out environmental situations that were destructive to my mental health and wellbeing. After an intense altercation with an ex-boyfriend my mother decided I needed to go to therapy to find out why I was placing myself into such horrible situations. In therapy, I realized that the sexual abuse was the reason I had always felt so dirty and shameful. It was the reason I was so depressed and numb inside. The connection is obvious, but I needed to talk about my ordeal and work through it with a professional. Through therapy I learned to love myself, to value myself, and accept the sexual abuse. My self worth skyrocketed. I used to feel as if I was in a pool filled with darkness and that I would never reach the surface, never really breathing, drowning and overcome with dark depression. The depression and the shame would overwhelm me. Through therapy, I was able to get out of that pool, to reach the surface and not only breathe but also enthusiastically swim.

Doug *(United States)*
My name is Doug. When I was 14 I was raped by a "family friend." I was young, weak and frightened. I didn't want anyone to know what had happened. I tried to tell my parents that I didn't want to go back to the place this happened, but I wouldn't say why. I think

I finally told my older brother or sister that this man had tried something but I wouldn't give any details. My parents found out and told me I wouldn't have to go back there... but I still never told anyone the extent of what had happened. It is now 24 years later and this secret, this demon, has finally come out. I was forced to face what happened to me or I may have become like the monster that raped me. Luckily it didn't come to that. I am now getting help and learning to deal with what happened to me and my own issues in the present. I think not talking about it, not dealing with it at the time it happened made things so much worse. I had all of this fear, hatred and pain bottled up inside of me... but I pretended my life was fine. It is finally out and I'm no longer ashamed. I can heal and be the man I want to be.

Rachel N. *(United States)*
When I look at this picture, I can see how young I was. It is so clear now that he was a man and I was a young girl. I was 14, and just got my braces off. He was almost 25, and in Graduate School. When he told me that I was "special," that was his entrance into his Magic Kingdom. His Magic Kingdom which nurtured his desire, fed by his need to overpower, manipulate, con and corrupt a young innocent girl. I was incredibly needy for attention and affection and I frighteningly and blindly trusted him-----just because he told me that I was "special." How many other girls my age had an older "boyfriend" who was a model? I MUST have been something special!

Erin *(United States) aka Kylee Jones or btrflywngs*
For 28 years, I hid my face in the shadows for fear of the consequences that could come from openly sharing the ugly truth that I was sexually abused. I did not want to speak those words in the presence of people who knew me because I feared they would see me as less, that I would have to deal with accusations and questions from my family, or even worse, someone would find some type of sick pleasure from my pain.

Yet, in recent months I have realized one truth that is greater than any of my fears: To hide in the shadows is to help my abusers hide their shame, which in turn puts others in danger as well. Hiding also allows the people to go on believing that sexual abuse doesn't happen to people they know, and therefore, lulls them into thinking the subject can be swept under the rug. I have spent the last 13 years advocating for and encouraging survivors from the comfort of my own anonymity. However, I will no longer hide my face because I want the world to know that we are not just statistics on a page.

I am Erin, I am a survivor, and I am silent no more.

Notable Child Sexual Abuse Survivors

To help you understand the devastation of childhood sexual abuse and how it reaches all walks of life, here is a list of highly recognizable courageous men and women from the entertainment, sports, corporate, and political worlds who have disclosed the sexual violations they suffered as children.

A few of these brave people are also trying to bring public awareness and change to the world's perspective on the effects of childhood sexual abuse on an adult's life. I think it speaks volumes to note just how pervasive the effects of childhood sexual abuse have been by pointing out that this list of notable figures includes a United States Senator and a former queen of England. (http://www.aest.org.uk/survivors/famous.htm.)

Currently Living

Oprah Winfrey (talk-show host)

Queen Latifah (musician, television and film actress, label president, Flavor Unit Entertainment, author, entrepreneur)

Tyler Perry (actor, author, screenwriter, film director, theater producer, theater director, television director, playwright, film producer, television producer)

Tom Arnold (actor, comedian, television host)

Roseanne Barr (actress, comedienne, writer, producer, director)

Marilyn Van der Bur (Miss America 1958—HAS POSTED TO OUR SITE)

Martha Wade (actress, *The Waltons*—HAS POSTED TO OUR SITE)

Terri Hatcher (actress, *Desperate Housewives*, presenter, writer)

Rose McGowan (actress, *Scream*)

Lorraine Chase (British actress, *Emmerdale* soap star)

Angela Shelton (American screenwriter, actress, documentary film producer, *Tumbleweeds*)

Carlos Santana (musician, Columbia Records)

Eve Ensler (playwright, *The Vagina Monologues*)

Marilyn Manson (singer-songwriter, musician, Interscope, artist, poet, film director)

Mary J. Blige (singer-songwriter, actress, record producer, rapper, Geffen)

Pamela Anderson (actress, *Baywatch*, model, producer, activist, author, former showgirl)

Sinead O'Connor (singer-songwriter, musician, priest, Irish Orthodox Catholic and Apostolic Church)

Mackenzie Phillips (actress, *One Day at a Time*)

Corey Feldman (film and television actor, *The Goonies*, *The Lost Boys*)

Mo'Nique (actress, *Precious*, *The Parkers*, comedienne, talk-show host, author)

Gabriel Byrne (actor, *The Usual Suspects*, *Stigmata*, film director, film producer, screenwriter, author)

Catherine Oxenberg (actress, *Dynasty*)

Julie Andrews (Academy Award-winning actress, *The Sound of Music*, singer, author)

Angelina Jolie (Academy Award-winning actress, *Girl Interrupted*, humanitarian)

Theo Fleury (retired professional hockey player)

Marlee Matlin (deaf Academy Award-winning actress, *Children of a Lesser God*)

Anne Heche (actress, *Six Days, Seven Nights*, director, screenwriter)

Anne Sexton (Pulitzer Prize-winning poet, *Live or Die*)

Antwone Fisher (director, screenwriter, *New York Times* best-selling author, *Finding Fish*, film producer)

Axl Rose (musician, lead vocalist of hard-rock band Guns N' Roses)

Baby Lyssa Chapman (famous bounty hunter, daughter of Dog the bounty hunter)

Billy Connolly (actor/comedian, *The X-Files: I Want to Believe*)

Chester Bennington (lead vocalist and songwriter, Linkin Park)

Derek Luke (actor, *Friday Night Lights*)

Drew Barrymore (award-winning actress, film producer, film director)

Elizabeth Loftus (UCLA-graduate psychologist specializing in human memories)

Erin Gray (actress, *Silver Spoons*)

Fantasia (musician, Grammy-nominated Broadway/TV actress, *The Color Purple*)

Fiona Apple (Grammy Award-winning musician)

Gabrielle Union (actress, *Bring It On, Bad Boys II*, model)

Henry Rollins (singer-songwriter, Black Flag, raconteur, stand-up comedian, spoken-word artist, writer, publisher, actor, radio DJ, activist)

Janice Mirikitani (poet, president of the Glide Foundation)

Jonathan Davis (lead vocalist, front man, Korn)

Joyce Meyer (author, speaker, televangelist)

Kirk Hammett (lead guitarist, songwriter, Metallica)

Laveranues Coles (professional football player, New York Jets)

Lynn Tolson (author—HAS POSTED TO OUR SITE)

Marie Waldrep (*Editor's Choice* award-winning poet, *Still I Cry*, activist—HAS POSTED TO OUR SITE)

Maya Angelou (*New York Times* best-selling author/poet, *I Know Why the Caged Bird Sings*)

Maynard James Keenan (rock singer, songwriter, musician, record producer, winemaker, actor, Tool)

Mike Patton (singer-songwriter, composer, producer, lyricist, multi-instrumentalist, film actor, voice actor, Faith No More)

Missy Elliot (recording artist, producer, actress, former member of R&B band Sista and Swing Mob collective, the only female rapper to have six albums certified platinum by the RIAA)

Paula White (Christian preacher, life coach, author, motivational speaker, senior pastor of Without Walls International Church in Tampa, Florida)

Rain Pryor (actress, comedienne, jazz/blues vocalist)

Rosie Perez (actress, *White Men Can't Jump*, dancer, choreographer, director, community activist)

Viva (actress, Warhol superstar)

Alison Arngrim (actress, Nellie, *Little House on the Prairie*)

Toni Childs (musician, Berlin)

Patty Duke (Academy Award-winning stage, film, and TV actress, *The Patty Duke Show*)

Ozzy Osbourne (musician, Black Sabbath, known as the godfather of heavy metal)

Anurag Kashyap (Academy Award-nominated Indian actor/director, *Water*)

Todd Bridges (actor, *Diff'rent Strokes*)

Ricki Lake (actress, television host)

Noelia (Puerto Rican pop singer)

Gloria Trevi (Mexican pop/rock singer)

Charlotte Lewis (British actress assaulted by Roman Polanski)

Shivani Saxena (Indian entrepreneur)

Timothy Redline (actor, *Punks*)
Ashley Judd (musician, actress)
Sugar Ray Leonard (Olympic and professional boxer)
Scott Brown (US senator)
Don Lemon (CNN Anchor)

Notable, But Disclosed Before Passing

Billie Holiday (musician)
Clara Bow (actress)
Elizabeth I (queen of England)
Johannes Brahms (musician)
Marilyn Monroe (actress)
Rita Hayworth (actress)
Sandra Dee (actress)
Virginia Woolf (author)
Dorothy Marie Marsh, aka Dottie West (musician)
Robert Blake (actor, *Baretta, In Cold Blood*)

I ask you to please go to www.letgoletpeacecomein.org, where you will see and read the stories of other survivors and where you will learn that the foundation has received visits from *all* fifty states in the United States and from over 3,500 cities throughout the country. To help readers visualize the impact and sheer volume, we have listed every state and city that has visited the foundation's Web site to date in Appendix III.

In addition, at the time of the completion of this book, the foundation has received visits from 136 countries worldwide (which represents over *half* of the 260 nations in the world)—with over 100,000 pages viewed—and the information on the site has been read in thirty-six of the fifty-three available languages.

All of the visits, stories, photos, and contacts came from six of the seven continents in the world, with only Antarctica not represented. There are no permanent inhabitants of Antarctica, but through New Zealand we are attempting to reach the approximately 250 part-time inhabitants who reside in twenty or so camps there.

The foundation has released a YouTube video, "Let Go…Let Peace Come In," which we believe depicts the thoughts and feelings of what a human being suffers due to childhood sexual abuse. The video has now been viewed over 13,000 times and I believe the below comment posted on our YouTube channel from Ruth in the United Kingdom speaks to all survivors throughout the globe.

> *This is absolutely fabulous! I shall forward it to everyone I know, who knows me—especially my 5 broken sisters who have but buried it. This serves as the first tangible way I can 'speak' to them about beginning the process of healing.*
>
> *May this video touch and begin change in many, many lives. As someone who lived in fear, isolation, and incessant nightmares, I can only hope God uses me in some way to spread the word and break the silence—like you are doing.*
>
> *You are my heroes!!*

Please take ten minutes out of your life and experience the impact of what sixty survivors have said regarding their feelings at the time of the abuse or about the trauma suffered from the abuse. Tell your friends, family, and coworkers about the foundation's efforts and worldwide presence. Tell the people on the softball team and the people you jog with or the people you meet for a cup of coffee or a few beers. It's a statistical impossibility that there isn't someone in your circle who is either a survivor or knows a survivor—it might even be you.

The overwhelming response to the foundation's site from around the world has strengthened my resolve to reach even more survivors and made me realize there's a nerve the foundation has touched and an invisible community we've summoned, which is growing in leaps and bounds every day.

As the writing of my manuscript was drawing to a close, I noticed the foundation's Web site was receiving a significant amount of traffic and visits from a foundation in London named the National Association for People Abused in Childhood (NAPAC). Just on a lark I picked up the phone and asked to speak to the foundation's founder, Mr. Peter Saunders. After Peter and I shared our own stories with each other, it was clear to both of us what the world needed now was to speak with one unified voice about the problems of adult survivors of sexual abuse and how the lasting effects of that abuse were tearing away the fabric and breaking down the systems in every society throughout the globe.

Peter said, "We obviously don't know each other, but I can't believe you have called me today, because in our morning meeting just two hours ago we discussed if it could be possible that we could speak to other nations in a unified forum." With that comment, I invited Peter to Philadelphia to participate in our foundation's next board meeting.

Following that board meeting, I spoke to Ms. Anuja Gupta in New Delhi, India, who formed the Recovering and Healing from Incest (RAHI) Foundation; and Ms. Nikki Wells in Sydney, Australia, who founded Survivors Australia. Both Anuja and Nikki had similar visions of a unified voice, and shortly after my conversations with them, all four of us had a conference call that concluded with a resolution that we were going to join forces and formulate a global alliance, starting with a representative from each continent.

On December 15, 2010, Anuja and her cofounder, Ashwini Ailwadi, traveled from India, Nikki from Australia, and Peter from England, all to Philadelphia to participate in what we termed the first global alliance meeting with representation from four of the seven continents. By the end of our meeting we had agreed that as a group we would identify South American and African-based foundations that would complete the global representation from six of the seven continents to formulate our alliance. With approximately only 250 people in Antarctica at different times of the year, we concluded the footprint of the global alliance would just be the six continents. Four weeks later, we named this alliance World Alliance for People Sexually Abused as Children (WAPSAC). WAPSAC's Web site is up and running at www.wapsac.org, but we're only in the beginning, with much more content and partnerships to come. Following our meeting in Philadelphia I met with Ms. Joseline Fugar of Juniper Tree Foundation from Kumasi, Ghana who has become the fifth member of our alliance, representing the continent of Africa.

There's not much more I can say about this undertaking at present other than I'm hopeful I'll have *many* things to say in the coming years.

Although the four of us had thousands of miles of distance between us, our stories as survivors were eerily similar. We left this meeting with a feeling of stability and excitement about the reality we all thought we could achieve in this mammoth quest to help the billion-plus adult men and women from our combined nations who have survived childhood sexual abuse.

The foundation has already financed two survivors on their journeys to healing. Please read their testimonials below about how they feel the trauma therapy sessions provided by the foundation have helped them take their first steps on their journeys to recovery and how these sessions have changed the courses of their lives:

Gary L. *(New Jersey, United States)*
I was a child raised in over 23 foster homes and 16 institutions before the age of 16. In those years, I suffered sexual, physical, mental and emotional abuse from countless individuals. I knew it was wrong and I knew that was not the way it should be, but after some time, I began to accept abuse from everyone that knew me.

Instead of telling anyone about how I felt or what was going on, I turned to heavy drug and alcohol use and then ran at the age of 16; and have been running ever since.

At the age of 17 I discovered prostitution. This role seem to fit well with what I expected from everyone because the only reason they wanted to love me was because they would get something in return. That was the way it would be until I was 24. I was in a very abusive relationship with a woman and we had a child. The inevitable happened, she left me and took the baby. I was crushed and went on a drinking and drug binge. I found myself at one point wanting to kill myself, so in a desperate move, I went to the Emergency room of Jefferson Hospital. I was not able or willing to understand most of what they were saying but they did make me go to AA meetings. Hence the start of a very long recovery process in and out of the rooms of AA.

25 years later, and after 3 more lost, long term relationships ruined, I found myself back to square one again; wanting to kill myself, nowhere to go, my wife taking the children and nowhere to turn. This time, with much of a fight in me still, I was willing to try the recovery process once again, though the results I have seen and the pain I have been willing to endure have been profound. I owe everything to the the Let Go Let Peace Come in Foundation and thank them for helping me receive trauma therapy sessions that put me on my road to recovery and for helping me become the man I was put on this earth to be. Those sessions made me realize I was previously treating the "symptoms" of alcohol and

drug addiction and not the core issue of my sexual abuse. I am now more willing to listen and learn than in any other time in my life. I was introduced to the Let Go Let Peace Come in Foundation by Vince DiPasquale, the founder of The Starting Point. Through that contact with Vince, I received 30 subsidized trauma therapy counseling sessions from the LGLPCI Foundation. I did not know how much it would change my life.

Thanks to the financial subsidy from the LGLPCI Foundation I have been in counseling sessions and I have been able to see the traumas in my life and how they impacted everything I do; the people I pick for relationships, how distorted my view on life is, and most of all, how bankrupt my heart and soul had become. I am just starting out but the results have been, like I said, very dramatic. I am very blessed to have the counseling I need to grow and live like a human maybe for the first time in my life. I thank whole heartedly the Let Go Let Peace Come in Foundation for everything they have done for me and for helping me connect how the sexual, physical, mental, and emotional abuse affected every facet of my life. I look forward to continuing my journey through the process of recovery.

Maureen *(Pennsylvania, United States)*
My sexual abuse was a suppressed memory. It wasn't until high school when I became sexually active that the memory of my attack resurfaced. My attacker was my uncle. I was around 4 or 5 years old. Although I have always remembered the sexual encounter I experienced with my cousin (my attacker's son) as a 7 year old. This I always knew was wrong, but didn't understand why I was even curious to try. We both decided to try when we were playing house. I was the "mom" and he was the "dad." Neither one of us till this day ever mention it to each other.

Once the memory of my attack resurfaced, I have always felt

betrayed, sad, scared, weak, angry all the time, DIRTY AND WORTHLESS. Along with these feelings deep inside I always felt like I needed a man in my life or their attention. I felt as though I always had to please them. I never had the strength to say NO. I would want to, but couldn't. Mostly because I feared what would happen to me if I had said no. I even felt this way with men I was in long-term relationships with. I have always picked a man who was emotionally unavailable. I felt I had to HELP THEM. I became a very co-dependent person. Whenever my relationships failed I would always become promiscuous with the help of alcohol. I didn't care about the consequences, I just needed to fill the pain and void inside. I would turn to alcohol so I would feel more comfortable. I was having unprotected sex. Sometimes with complete strangers, I would drink so much that the next morning I wouldn't even remember the sexual encounter ever occurring.

I have kept my sexual abuse a complete secret. No one knew my darkest secret till the Fall of 2009. I started to feel it was okay to tell somebody about my abuse when I read a manuscript that was sitting on John's (my ex) table. The manuscript was about a man's childhood sexual abuse trauma (CSA) and his road to recovery. The manuscript's author was my friend Peter, the founder of Let Go, Let Peace Come In foundation. Peter's story touched my soul so deep and I admired him for finding the strength to even tell someone his story. As I have mentioned before, I have never told anyone about my abuse. I felt like it was my fault, alone, and dirty.

Peter told me about the LGLPCI foundation and gave me the contact number to a counselor/therapist, Annie, of The Starting Point. The LGLPCI foundation subsidized 30 sessions for me to begin my road to recovery of CSA. Together Annie and Allie (therapist of EMDR) have changed my life tremendously. I am still the same person I have always been, just a better, stronger version of myself. By my last session with Allie, I felt that pain and void deep inside disappear. Allie left me with the affirmation:

I embrace my sexuality, it is an expression of my health, wholeness, and worthiness. I say this to myself everyday!!!! I know now I am not at fault for what has happened to me or for the impact my attack has had on me. My perpetrator is at fault and the cause. My sessions at the Starting Point has taught me and reminded me I am WORTHWHILE!

A few days before this book went to print the foundation has subsidized 30 therapeutic trauma sessions for one of the young men associated with the Penn State childhood sexual abuse case involving Jerry Sandusky. The foundation is hopeful that these sessions will start this young man on his arduous journey to recovery and is prepared to help others from this tragedy as well.

Appendices

Appendix I

It helps survivors to know they are not alone. On these pages are the names of other Web sites that offer support and encouragement to survivors through blogs, message boards, and chat rooms.

1 in 6: Provides support for male survivors of childhood sexual abuse and their families.
A Life Restored: A blog offering encouragement and information to survivors.
A Quiet Shame: A Web site dedicated to sharing survivor stories. Also provides links for survivors who wish for legal assistance regarding their situations.
A Voice Within: One survivor's blog about her personal story. Contains links and hotlines.
Abuse Consultants: Offers online counseling and information to survivors.
Admit to Child Abuse: A forum to tell other people how the author felt about being abused.
Adult Survivors of Child Abuse: Provides information, materials, and online e-meetings for individual and group-support programs for adult survivors of physical, sexual, or emotional child abuse or neglect.
After Silence: A nonprofit organization, message board, and chat room for rape, sexual abuse, and sexual assault survivors.

After Silence: Rape and My Journey Back: Exploring attitudes toward rape and its survivors and the process of recovery from trauma.

Angelic's Abuse Survivors: For survivors of all types of abuse. Includes forums, poetry, and resources.

Angels in the Night: Support site for children of sexual abuse. Offering scheduled and moderated chats, tips, and other resources.

Art of Healing: Artist Linda Ness shares her many paintings about her journey of recovery.

Askios: Self-help group for women survivors of incest providing online information and support via Web site, message board, and e-mail.

Aurora Health Foundation: A registered charity in the UK specializing in holistic therapy services.

Beautiful Warrior: Works to inspire and convey the message of the human spirit to overcome obstacles, the beauty of nature, and God's healing love.

Becoming Gold: Virtual support network for survivors of childhood sexual abuse that encourages balance in the healing process through creativity, education, and support.

The BirdSong Organization: A NYC-based nonprofit self-help group for female incest survivors offering a variety of support services including regular weekly meetings.

The Black Sheep Chronicles: Adult incest survivor's experiences with the aftermath of incest and how and why it affected her relationships with her entire family.

Blatt Afram: A survivor resource based in Iceland that provides education and outreach to prevent childhood sexual abuse.

Breaking the Silence: Blog site of author/counselor Terri White, where survivors can follow Terri through her journey and utilize her tips for healing.

Broken Wings Shattered Dreams: A site built by a survivor of child abuse to show that life can go on, to bring awareness of what the mother of an abused child feels, and to remember the children who died from the abuse they suffered.

Bryn Alyn: A Web site created for people who were at Bryn Alyn to connect and talk about their trauma.

Butterfly Gardens: A site dedicated to victims/survivors of sexual abuse and incest.

Catharsis Foundation: A site created to help survivors of all forms of child abuse.

Chasing the Wind: Poetry about sexual and physical abuse by a proud survivor.

Chat4Healing: Offers self-healing through breath, awareness, imagery, and gratitude.

Child Abuse Survivors Support: A peer-support forum for survivors of child abuse.

Colchester Rape Crisis Line: Provides counseling and support for rape victims, families, and survivors of childhood sexual abuse.

Dancing in the Darkness: Help and support for survivors of rape and sexual abuse. A safe place to share stories, hope, and courage.

Do EFT: Emotional Freedom Techniques (EFT) are used to reduce stress associated with trauma and PTSD. Dr. Kim Eisen provides services.

Echoes: Created for survivors of rape and sexual abuse. Includes a personal story, articles, poems, and links.

EeyoreGirl's Page: A Christian's experience with childhood sexual abuse, her healing, and her faith.

Encouragement for Childhood Sexual Abuse Survivors: A site for those who have been sexually abused.

Erin Merryn: Live for Today is a blog about one woman's healing journey and her work to break the silence.

Fort Refuge: Supportive community for survivors of all types of abuse including child abuse, incest, rape, ritual abuse, and psychological and verbal abuse.

From Surviving to Thriving: Support for rape and sexual assault survivors from a survivor. Includes forum, chat, and survivor stories.

Gary: A Personal Essay: Memorial for a child abuse victim who didn't survive.

Generation Five: A movement to end child sexual abuse in five generations through survivor leadership, community organization, and public action.

Gift From Within: A nonprofit organization dedicated to those who suffer from PTSD.

Healing Angels: A forum Web site where survivors can safely express themselves.

Healing Broken Angels: Information and help for survivors of sexual assault and rape.

Healing Broken Men: A Web site offering resources and workshops for men healing from the effects of sexual abuse.

Healing From Abuse: This site addresses the unique issues of the emotionally, physically, and sexually abused. Chat room, helpful links, book recommendations, support groups, healing steps, and more are included in the healing journey.

Healing Minds: A site dedicated to survivors of abuse and sexual assault.

Healing Through Creativity: A site that provides survivor links and information. They host an annual art event for survivors of trauma.

The Hope of Survivors: Provides support, hope, and encouragement for victims of clergy sexual abuse and misconduct.

I Am a Survivor Not a Victim: A survivor shares her story of sexual abuse.

I Forgive You, Daddy: A blog where survivors can share their stories with other survivors.

Appendix I

Inscriptions of Hope: Newsletter of writings from survivors of childhood abuse.

Isurvive.org: A nonprofit online community center for abuse survivors providing anonymous discussions boards, chat rooms, and other resources.

It Happened to Alexa Foundation: A resource for victims of sexual assault to receive money to ease the burden of attending criminal trials.

Jane Rowan: Jane shares her experience of healing from childhood sexual abuse.

Jenny's Child Abuse Survivor Support: Jenny shares her story and poetry and offers support to fellow survivors.

The Journey Home: Victim of childhood sexual abuse until the age of fifteen, Pat Swinger tells the story of her healing journey.

Journey to Freedom: Hope and healing for victims and survivors of child sexual abuse and sexual assault.

Journey to Healing: Offers help and healing for victims of sexual abuse, incest, and rape.

Kingdom Abuse Survivors Project: A resource for survivors of childhood sexual abuse in the form of forums, chat rooms, help, and advice.

Ksenia Oustiougova: A blog about one woman's journey of recovery from incest.

The Lamplighters: A movement for victims of incest and child sexual abuse. Offers a recovery program for children and adults.

Linda Fossen: A help site created and maintained by a female survivor.

Losing the Way: Author Kristen Skedgell tells her story about surviving abuse in a religious cult.

The Lost Sparrow Movie: Documentary about the effects of CSA and how it shattered one man's family.

Lynne Finney: Web site of author Lynne Finney, JD, MSW, of the classic guide *Reach for the Rainbow: Advanced Healing for Survivors of Sexual Abuse* (and incest and ritual abuse), with extensive free information, articles, research, and resources.

Male Survivor: A community established to help male survivors of sexual victimization. Provides information, chat, and message boards.

Midnight Secrets: Provides information and support for sexual abuse and incest survivors.

The Mighty Phoenix: Offers survivors of sexual abuse information to help the healing process.

Miss Kitty's Place: A site that offers useful information for victims, abusers, and survivors.

Mollykat's Resources for Survivors: Information about depression, PTSD, dissociative identity disorder, and borderline personality disorders.

My Family Secrets: a blog where users can anonymously type any secret they wish to divulge.

My Painful Smiles: A site to help the healing of childhood sexual abuse. A place for families to learn what the victims are going through.

My Twisted Sukha: This site deals with the effects of sexual abuse by a female perpetrator.

National Association for People Abused in Childhood (NAPAC): NAPAC is a registered charity set up as a result of a key recommendation by the National Commission of Inquiry Into the Prevention of Child Abuse.

Netter's Place: Abuse Survivor Links: Offers links to different sites for abuse survivors seeking support and self-help.

New Jersey Coalition Against Sexual Assault: Provides links and information for support groups throughout the state of New Jersey.

Nubia Nations: A social networking site with links and information about the Karama Sadaka Foundation (KSY2). We all have voices!

Off My Knees: A blog to help promote supportive conversation between victims and their families.

Optimystic: This site is about living with optimism and faith to overcome childhood abuse.

Our Writes: A forum where survivors can gather to find support and understanding amongst other survivors.

Pagan Survivors of Sexual Assault: A Yahoo! group for pagans, witches, and wiccan wanderers who are survivors of sexual assault or are friends and family members of pagan survivors of sexual assault.

Pandora's Aquarium: A nonprofit charitable organization that provides a message board, information, and chat room for survivors and their supporters.

Peaceful Haven: A personal experience of emotional, mental, and sexual abuse.

Pressing On…: A site dedicated to the survivors of sexual abuse and incest. Provides practical info about sexual abuse, self-injury, eating disorders, quotes, and fun links to nurture the child within.

Prysmstar: A survivor's story, message board, poetry, and links to other resources.

R.A.D. Online: A Web site designed to bring the Reactive Attachment Disorder Community together.

Rainbow Hope: A Web site dedicated to providing support and information for lesbian survivors of abuse.

Recovery: Short, original essays about all aspects of recovery from childhood abuse.

Recovery: A woman's continuing fight to overcome the trauma of sexual abuse.

Restored by Him: One woman's inspirational words about her journey toward restoration.

Ritual Abuse, Ritual Crime and Healing: Provides information and resources for survivors and therapists about ritual abuse.

Safe Haven: A site for survivors of sexual abuse and rape. Includes personal stories, poetry, tips, advice on coping day to day, and an interactive message forum.
Safeline: This UK site provides information and help for adults who were sexually abused as children.
Sexual Abuse Centre: Provides support, counseling, and information to survivors of sexual abuse and rape through a variety of services.
Sexual Violence Research Initiative (SVRI): An organization that promotes research to identify sexual violence as a global public-health problem.
Share Your Survival Story: A Web site where people can share their personal stories of survival. Includes helpful links and other resources.
S.H.E.: Survivors Helping Each Other: Self-help charity for women survivors of childhood sexual abuse. Encourages a creative approach to healing and promotes public education and awareness.
The Silver Braid Survivors of Sexual Exploitation: Providing helpful information to those who have been victims of sexual exploitation.
Speaking Truth in Love: A religious site offering support and prayers for survivors.
Stop It Now: Offers an online resource for survivors of childhood sexual abuse that helps to answer common questions related to recovery. Also offers a help hotline: 1-888-PREVENT (1-888-773-8368).
Stop the Silence: A page dedicated to helping fellow survivors of sexual abuse. Includes support forums, useful links, and personal experiences.
Survive: Survive is a registered voluntary organization that provides support and help to survivors of child sexual abuse.
Surviving by Grace: A survivor blog that provides inspiration and resources.

Survivor Matters: Information and support forum for survivors of any type of abuse, created by survivors for survivors.
Survivors Can Thrive: Meditations, resources, and tips for sexual abuse survivors.
Survivors Chat: A support site, chat rooms, and resources for survivors of rape, incest, sexual abuse, or SRA.
Survivors and Friends: Offers articles, books, and forum resources for survivors and their families.
The Survivors Forum: A site that offers chat rooms, forums, and other resources for survivors of sexual abuse.
Survivors Healing: Information to help survivors of sexual abuse in healing and the opportunity to share stories, experiences, triumphs, and challenges.
Survivors of Abuse in Religion (SOAR): An online support group for survivors of sexual abuse in any religion.
Survivors of Green: Dedicated to the survivors of Dr. Green, guilty of multiple counts of indecent assault against male patients in Loughborough, Leicestershire.
Survivor's Personal Healing Journey:- A survivor and publisher shares her stories of surviving sexual abuse.
Safe House: A safe and secure site for survivors and victims of sexual abuse regardless of age or gender.
Survivors Sanctuary: A safe place of support and resources for survivors of abuse, sexual, mental, or physical. Everyone is welcome regardless of gender.
Survivors UK: Provides information, support and counseling for men who have been raped or sexually abused.
Survivorship: Provides resources for survivors of ritualistic abuse.
Taalk: A Web site designed to bring resources and educational materials to survivors of childhood sexual abuse.
Taking Back Control: A resource and message board for sexual assault survivors.

Tamar's House: Provides programs to aid in alleviating the long-term effects of childhood sexual abuse and assist survivors in healing from this devastating experience.

Tamar's Voice: A nonprofit offering help and support for victims of sexual abuse by clergy.

True Perspective of Sexual Trauma: Information on blame, therapy, dissociation, and anger. Includes resources, predator types, and behavior patterns.

Victorious Heart: Raising public awareness of ritual and sexual abuse.

Voice the Silence: A personal blog about one man's journey from statistic to survivor and advocate.

WCSAP: A site that provides information and tools to get help after sexual assault.

We Are Survivors: A Web site that provides a platform for information about how adult survivors can cope with the effects of their trauma.

Wind Traveler: An online resource for survivors and their partners. Offers a self-test and links for counseling (in English and Dutch).

Whitedoves Nest: A site dedicated to sexual abuse survivors and their supporters. Share your story, poetry, art, and tips on recovery.

Appendix II

Recommended Books for Female Survivors:
- *Lonely All the Time* by Ralph Erle and Dr. Gregory Crow
- *Little Girl Fly Away: A Shattering True Story of Psychological Terror* by Gene Stone
- *Thou Shalt Not Be Aware: Society's Betrayal of the Child* by Alice Miller

Recommended Books Written by Female Survivors:
- *Finding Angela Shelton* by Angela Shelton
- *A Child's Heart Speaks: Surviving Sexual Abuse* by Claire Silva
- *The Third Floor Window, A True Story of Secrets, Survival and Hope* by Colleen Spiro
- *The Enemy Between My Legs* by Stephanie L. Jones
- *As If It Didn't Happen* by Maggie Claire
- *The Doghouse Angel: From the Darkness of Abuse to the Light of Healing* by Kimberly Steward
- *Warming the Stone Children* [addressing mother-daughter incest] by Christine Sandor

Appendix II

- *When the Piano Stops: A Memoir of Healing From Sexual Abuse* by Catherine McCall
- *Stolen Innocence* by Erin Merryn
- *Living for Today: From Incest and Molestation to Fearlessness and Forgiveness* by Erin Merryn
- *My Name Is Kendra* by Kamichi Jackson
- *Silver Platter Girl* by Trish Kinney
- *Trading Fathers: Forgiving Dad, Embracing God* by Karen Rabbitt
- *Listen to the Cry of the Child: The Deafening Silence of Sexual Abuse* by Barbara Hansen
- *Memory Slips: A Memoir of Music and Healing* by Linda Catherine Cutting
- *Beyond the Tears: A True Survivor's Story* by Lynn C. Tolson
- *From Sorrows to Sapphires* by Angela Williams
- *Sexual Abuse Defined: Bondage It Is Time to Tell* by Vera Milestone
- *Beyond Survival: A Writing Journey for Healing Childhood Sexual Abuse* by Maureen Brady
- *Cry the Darkness: One Woman's Triumph Over the Tragedy of Incest* by Donna L. Friess, PhD
- *Reflections in the Night: A Survivor's Story of Total Mind Controlled Slavery and Torture* by Mauri
- *Go Ask Alice: A Real Diary* by Anonymous
- *I Forgive You Daddy* by Lizzie McGlynn
- *A House Full of Whispers* by Sharon Wallace
- *Surviving a House Full of Whispers* by Sharon Wallace

Appendix II

- *Out of the Miry Clay: Freedom From Childhood Sexual Abuse* by Linda Fossen
- *The Thursday Group: A Story and Information for Girls Healing From Sexual Abuse* by PeggyEllen Kleinleder and Kimber Evensen
- *Rising Above the Beauty of Life* by Dolores M. Miller
- *Losing the Way* by Kristen Skedgell
- *Breaking the Silence* by Terri White
- *REPAIR Your Life: A Program for Recovery from Incest & Childhood Sexual Abuse* by Marjorie McKinnon and Marcie Taylor
- *REPAIR for Kids: A Children's Program for Recovery from Incest & Childhood Sexual Abuse* by Marjorie McKinnon and Tom McKinnon
- *It's Your Choice! Decisions That Will Change Your Life* by Marjorie McKinnon
- *Thin Places* by Mary DeMuth
- *Stolen Innocence: The True Life Terror I Experienced As a Child* by Elaine Carole
- *Beautiful Warrior Poetry & Prose* by Dolores M. Miller

Recommended Books for Male Survivors:
- *Abused Boys* by Mic Hunter
- *Victims No Longer* by Mike Lew
- *Leaping Upon the Mountains: Men Proclaiming Victory Over Sexual Child Abuse* by Mike Lew
- *Beyond Betrayal* by Dr. Richard Gartner
- *Betrayed as Boys* by Dr. Richard Gartner
- *Wounded Boys, Heroic Men* by Daniel Jay Sonkin

Appendix II

Recommended Books Written by Male Survivors:
- *Secret Life* by Mike Ryan
- *The Tricky Part* by Martin Moran
- *Half the House* by Richard Hoffman
- *Shhhh…Don't Say a Word About This: Exposing and Confronting Sexual Perversion* by Dr. Loren Due
- *Am I Bad? Recovering From Abuse (New Horizons in Therapy)* by Heyward Bruce Ewart III
- *Silence of Men* by Richard Newman and Yusef Komunyakaa
- *Nigel: A Damaged Boy* by Nigel King
- *Recovery For Male Victims of Child Sexual Abuse* by Hank Estrada

Recommended Books for Couples:
- *Trust After Trauma: A Guide to Relationships for Survivors and Those Who Love Them* by Aphrodite Matsakis
- *Easy Does It Relationship Guide for People in Recovery: Drama-free, Step-friendly Advice on Attaining, Maintaining, and Sustaining a Committed Relationship* by Mary Faulkner

Recommended Books for Spouses:
- *Allies in Healing: When the Person You Love Was Sexually Abused As a Child* by Laura Davis
- *If the Man You Love Was Abused* by Marie H. Browne, PhD and Marlene M. Browne

Books for Family Members of Survivors:
- *Families in Recovery* by Beverly Engel
- *As You and the Abused Person Journey Together* by Sharon Cheston
- *Family Fallout: A Handbook for Families of Adult Sexual Abuse Survivors* by D. Landry

Recommended Books for Children and Teens:
- *Please Tell* by Jesse Ottenweller
- *A Terrible Thing Happened* by Margaret M Holmes, Cary Pillo, and Sasha Mudlaff
- *Helping Your Child Recover From Sexual Abuse* by Caren Adams, Jennifer Fay, and A.G. Fawkes
- *Repair for Kids: A Children's Program for Recovery* by Marjorie McKinnon and Tom W. McKinnon
- *The Me Nobody Knows: A Guide for Teen Survivors* by Barbara Bean and Shari Bennett

Recommended Books From Helping Professionals:
- *EMDR [Eye Movement Desensitization and Reprocessing]: Therapy for Overcoming Anxiety, Stress, and Trauma* by Francine Shapiro, PhD and Margot Silk Forrest
- *The Wounded Heart: Hope for Adult Victims of Childhood Sexual Abuse* by Dr. Dan B. Allender
- *Trauma and Recovery* by Judith Lewis Herman, MD
- *Beyond the Darkness: Healing for Victims of Sexual Abuse* by Cynthis A. Kubetin and James Mallory, MD

- *Child Sexual Abuse: A Hope for Healing* by Maxine Hancock and Karen Burton
- *Healing Your Sexual Self* by Dr. Janet G. Woititz
- *The Sexual Healing Journey: A Guide for Survivors of Sexual Abuse* by Wendy Maltz LCSW, DST

Recommended Books for Helping Professionals:
- *Treating Child Sex Offenders and Victims: A Practical Guide* by Anna C. Salter
- *Transforming Trauma: A Guide to Understanding and Treating Adult Survivors of Child Sexual Abuse* by Anna C. Salter
- *Treating the Adult Survivor of Childhood Sexual Abuse: A Psychoanalytic Perspective* by Jody Messler Davies, PhD and Mary Gail Frawley
- *Child Sexual Abuse: A Handbook for Health Care and Legal Professionals* by Diane H. Schetky, MD and Arthur H Green, MD

Books About Healing From Trauma:
- *Dark Water: Stress After Trauma* by Opal Rose
- *Toxic Parents* by Dr. Susan Forward
- *Getting Through the Day: Strategies for Adults Hurt As Children* by Nancy Napier
- *Healing the Shame That Binds You* by John Bradshaw
- *Post Traumatic Stress Disorder: The Victim's Guide to Healing and Recovery* by Raymond Flannery, Jr., PhD

Appendix II

Books About Healing From Depression:
- *Overcoming Depression* by Demitri Papolos, MD and Janice Papolos
- *When Someone You Love Is Depressed: How to Help Your Loved One Without Losing Yourself* by Laura Epstein Rosen, PhD and Xavier Francisco Amador, PhD
- *Depression: Finding Hope and Meaning In Life's Darkest Shadow* by Don Baker and Emery Nester
- *Care of the Soul* by Thomas Moore

Journals:
- *Many Voices Press*: www.manyvoicespress.com
- *Sidran: PTSD and Dissociation Resources for Survivors, Supporters, and Professionals*: www.sidran.org
- *Safer Society: Safer Society Foundation, Inc. Resources and Referrals for the Treatment of Sexual Abuse*: www.safersociety.org
- *Sage Publications*: online.sagepub.com
- *Hazelden*: www.hazelden.org

Excerpts and Previews:
- *Trading Fathers: Forgiving Dad, Embracing God* by Karen Rabbitt: Chapter 1 preview
- *Mothers Surviving Sexual Abuse* by Carol-Ann Hooper
- *This Too Shall Pass* by Tracy Childers

Appendix III

Google Analytics Page

The Google analytics page is a statistics page that allows the Foundation to view how a user visits our site, how long a user views the site, and where that user is located throughout the world.

We have been tracking user habits and hits to our site and here are those results:

The Let Go...Let Peace Come In Foundation has reached 6 out of the 7 continents of the world. The only continent the Foundation has not received visits from is Antarctica. Antarctica has no permanent inhabitants.

www.letgoletpeacecomein.org has had **25,099** visits from **136** countries worldwide, **4,752** cities.

AFGHANISTAN
Kabul

ALBANIA
Tirana

ALGERIA
Algiers

Appendix III

ARGENTINA
Buenos Aires   Cordoba   Curuzu Cuatia
Lomas de Zamora   Neuquen   Puerto Madero
Rosario   Salta   San Miguel de Tucuman

ARMENIA
Yerevan

ARUBA
Oranjestad

AUSTRALIA
Adelaide   Bathurst   Brisbane   Canberra
Cranbourne   Dubbo   Geelong   Hobart
Melbourne   Morwell   New Castle   Perth
Redcliffe   Richmond   Sydney   Traralgon
Victoria Point

AUSTRIA
Salzburg   Tribuswinkel   Vienna

AZERBAIJAN
Baku   Stepanakert

BAHAMAS
Nassau

BANGLADESH
Dhaka

BARBADOS
Bridgetown

BELARUS
Minsk

BELGIUM
Antwerp	Berchem	Beveren	Borgerhout
Brussels	Ixelles	Leuven	Liege
Schiede	Sint-Andries	Zoersel	

BELIZE
unidentified

BENIN
unidentified

BERMUDA
Hamilton

BOSNIA AND HERZEGOVNIA
Sarajevo

BRAZIL
Barueri	Bauru	Belo Horizonte	Brasilia
Campo Grande	Criciuma	Curitiba	Fortaleza
Ibaiti	Maceio	Passo Fundo	Pelotas
Petropolis	Porto Alegre	Recife	Ribeirao Preto
Rio de Janeiro	Rio Grande	Santo Andre	Santos
Sao Paulo			

BULGARIA
Blagoevgrad	Dobrich	Pernik	Sofia
Stara Zagora			

Appendix III

CAMBODIA
Phnum Penh

CANADA
unidentified	Abbotsford	Barrie	Belleville
Bramalea	Brampton	Brandon	Brantford
Bridgewater	Burlington	Burnaby	Calgary
Cambridge	Campbell River	Canmore	Charlottetown
Chilliwack	Clearbrook	Clinton	Cloverdale
Cochrane	Cold Lake	Cooksville	Coquitlam
Cornwall	Courtenay	Cranbrook	Dartmouth
Delta	Dollard-des-Ormeaux		Don Mills
Dorval	Duncan	Dundas	Duvernay
Edmonton	Etobicoke	Fredericton	Ft. Saint John
Ft. McMurray	Gatineau	Granby	Grande Prairie
Gravenhurst	Grimsby	Guelph	Halifax
Hamilton	Hull	Islington	Joliette
Jonquiere	Kamloops	Kanata	Kelowna
Kingston	Kitchener	Lachine	Ladner
Langley	Larochelle	Laval	Lethbridge
London	Markham	Masset	Mississauga
Moncton	Montreal	Mont-Royal	Mount Pearl
Nanaimo	Nelson	Nepean	New Liskeard
New Westminster	Niagara Falls	North Battleford	
North Bay	North Vancouver		Oakville
Oliver	Orangeville	Orillia	Oshawa
Ottawa	Outremont	Penticton	Peterborough
Pickering	Point Edward	Pointe-Claire	Powell River
Prescott	Prince George	Provost	Red Deer
Regina	Rexdale	Richmond	Sardis
Sarnia	Saskatoon	Sault Sainte Marie	
Scarborough	Shawnigan Lake		Sherbrooke
Sparwood	Spruce Grove	St. Catharines	St. John
St. John's	St-Laurent	St-Leonard	Stratford
Streetsville	Sudbury	Summerside	Surrey
Swift Current	Sydney	Thunder Bay	Timmins
Toronto	Tottenham	Truro	Unionville

Appendix III

Vancouver	Victoria	Waterloo	West Vancouver
Westmount	Weston	Whitby	White Rock
Whitehorse	Windsor	Winkler	Winnipeg
Woodstock			

CAYMAN ISLANDS
Georgetown

CHILE
Providencia	San Miguel	Valdivia

CHINA
Aksu	Ankang	Anqing	Anshun
Anyang	Baicheng	Baiyin	Baoding
Baoji	Baotou	Bayannur	Beihai
Beijing	Bengbu	Bozhou	Bijie
Binzhou	Cangzhou	Changchun	Changde
Changsha	Changzhi	Changzhou	Chaohu
Chaoyang	Chaozhou	Chengde	Chengdu
Chenzhou	Chifeng	Chongqing	Chongzuo
Chuzhou	Dali	Dalian	Daqing
Datong	Dazhou	Deyang	Dezhou
Dongguan	Dongying	Enshi	Ezhou
Fengchenggang	Foshan	Fushun	Fuxin
Fuyang	Fuzhou	Ganzhou	Guang'an
Guangyuan	Guangzhou	Guilin	Guiyang
Haikou	Handan	Hangzhou	Hanzhong
Harbin	Hebi	Hechi	Hefei
Hengshui	Hengyang	Heyuan	Hezhou
Heze	Hinggan	Hohot	Hotan
Huaian	Huaibei	Huaihua	Huainan
Huanggang	Huangshan	Huangshi	Huizhou
Huludao	Hulun Buir	Huzhou	Ili
Ji'an	Jiamusi	Jiangmen	Jiaozuo
Jiaxing	Jieyang	Jilin	Jinan
Jincheng	Jingdezhen	Jingzhou	Jinhua

Jining	Jinzhong	Jinzhou	Jiujiang
Jixi	Jiuquan	Kaifeng	Kaxgar
Kunming	Laiwu	Lanzhou	Leshan
Lhasa	Liangshan	Lianyungang	Liaocheng
Liaoyang	Liaoyuan	Lijiang	Linfen
Linyi	Lishui	Liupanshui	Liuzhou
Longnan	Longyan	Loudi	Luan
Luohe	Luoyang	Luzhou	Lvliang
Maanshan	Maoming	Meishan	Meizhou
Mianyang	Mudanjiang	Nanchang	Nanjing
Nanning	Nanping	Nantong	Nanyang
Neijang	Ningbo	Ningde	Ordos
Panzhihua	Pingdingshan	Pingxiang	Pu'er
Putian	Puyang	Qiandongnan	Qianxinan
Qingdao	Qingyang	Qinhuangdao	Quinzhou
Qiqihar	Qoqek	Quanzhou	Qujing
Quzhou	Rizhao	Sanmenxia	Sanming
Shanghai	Shangluo	Shangqiu	Shantou
Shanwei	Shaoguan	Shaoxing	Shaoyang
Shenyang	Shenzhen	Shijiazhuang	Shiyan
Shizuishan	Shunde	Siping	Suihua
Suining	Suizhou	Suqian	Suzhou
Tai'an	Taiyuan	Taizhou	Tangshan
Tianjin	Tianshui	Tieling	Tonghua
Tongliao	Tongling	Tongren	Ulanqab
Urumqi	Weifang	Weihai	Weinan
Wenshan	Wenzhou	Wuhan	Wuhu
Wuxi	Wuzhong	Wuzhou	Xian
Xiamen	Xiangfan	Xiangtan	Xiangxi
Xianning	Xianyang	Xiaogan	Xingtai
Xinxiang	Xinyang	Xuancheng	Xuchang
Xuzhou	Ya'an	Yan'an	Yanbian
Yancheng	Yangjiang	Yangzhou	Yantai
Yibin	Yichang	Yichun	Yichun
Yinchuan	Yingtan	Yiyang	Yongzhou
Yueyang	Yulin	Yuncheng	Yunfu
Yuxi	Zaozhuang	Zhangjiakou	Zhangzhou
Zhaoqing	Zhengzhou	Zhenjiang	Zhongshan

Zhokou   Zhoushan   Zhuhai   Zhumadian
Zhuzhou   Zibo   Zigong   Ziyang
Zunyi

COLUMBIA
Barranquilla   Bogota

COOK ISLANDS
unidentified

COSTA RICA
Cartago   San Jose

CROATIA
Osijek   Split   Zagreb

CYPRUS
Nicosia

CZECH REPUBLIC
Prague   Strakonice

COTE D'IVORIE
Abidjan

DENMARK
Aabyhoej   Arhus   Copenhagen   Fredericia
Frederiksberg   Haderslev   Kolding   Maribo
Odense   Silkeborg   Soborg   Svendborg

DOMINICA
unidentified

DOMINICAN REPUBLIC
Santo Domingo

ECUADOR
Guayaquil   Quito

EGYPT
Cairo   Shibin Elkom

ELSALVADOR
Santa Ana   San Salvadore

ESTONIA
Tallinn

ETHOPIA
Adis Abeba

FALKLAND ISLANDS [ISLAS MALVINAS]
unidentified

FIJI
Suva

FINLAND
Helsinki   Kerava   Tampere

FRANCE
Amiens	Annely	Chatou	Colmar
Lille	Lyon	Marseille	Medan
Montlhery	Montrouge	Nantes	Nice
Niort	Paris	Perpignan	Rennes
Roubaix	Savigny-sur-Orge		St –Ouen
Strasbourg	Talence	Villeneuve- Loubet	

FRENCH GUIANA
Cayenne

GERMANY
unidentified	Baumholder	Berlin	Bochum
Bonn	Buhl	Chemnitz	Cologne
Dresden	Duisburg	Dusseldorf	Eschborn
Flensburg	Frankfurt am Main		Frakenberg
Freiburg	Freiburg Im Breisgau		Gottingen
Halle	Herne	Karlsruhe	Kempten
Krefeld	Magdeburg	Monchengladbach	
Mulheim	Munich	Munster	Neu-Anspach
Neumunster	Schweinfurt	Schwetzingen	Stuttgart
Ulm	Unterhaching	Vilshofen	Waldorf
Weinsberg	Wetzlar	Wurzburg	

GHANA
Accra   Kumasi

GREECE
Athens	Iraklion	Kavala	Patrai
Thessaloniki			

GUAM
Dededo

GUATEMALA
Guatemala

GUERNSY
unidentified

GUAYANA
Georgetown

HAITI
Port Au Prince

HONDURAS
San Pedro Sula   Tegucigalpa

HONG KONG
Hong Kong

HUNGARY
Budapest

ICELAND
Keflank   Kopavogur   Reykjavik

INDIA
unidentified	Ahmedabad	Allahabad	Amritsar
Bangalore	Belgaum	Bhopal	Calcutta
Chandigarh	Chennai	Cochin	Coimbatore
Delhi	Ghaziabad	Gurgaon	Guwahati
Haldwani	Hubli-Dharwad	Hyderabad	Indore
Jaipur	Kandivli	Kanpur	Kharagpur
Ludhiana	Mangalore	Mumbai	Nagpur
New Delhi	Noida	Ponidcherry	Pune
Surat	Vijayawada	Vishakhapatnam	

INDONESIA
Bandung   Banjarmasin   Jakarta   Malang
Semarang   Surabaya

IRAN
Esfahan   Tehran

IRAQ
unidentified

IRELAND
An Uaimah	Cork	Dublin	Galway
Kilkenny	Limerick	Sligo	

ISRAEL
Givatayim	Jerusalem	Ramat Gan	Tel Aviv

ITALY
Ancona	Bergamo	Caldiero	
Casalecchio Di Reno		Cinisello	Eboli
Florence	Guanzate	Lecce	Lodi
Milan	Naples	Palermo	Perugia
Ponsacco	Rome	Torino	Treviso
Verona	Vicenza		

JAMACIA
unidentified	Kingston	Ocho Rios

JAPAN
Ayase	Fukuoka	Ichikawa	Kawasaki
Kyoto	Minato	Mito	Naha
Oita	Shibuya	Shinjuku	Tokyo
Urasoe	Urawa	Yamatokoriyama	Yokohama

JERSEY
unidentified

JORDAN
unidentified	Amman

KENYA
unidentified   Nairobi

KUWAIT
unidentified   Kuwait

LATVIA
Riga

LEBANON
unidentified   Beirut

LITHUANIA
Kaunas   Vilnius

LUXEMBOURG
Luxembourg

MACEDONIA
Bitola   Gevgelija   Skopje

MADAGASCAR
Antananarivo

MALAWI
Blantyre

MALAYSIA
unidentified   George Town   Johor Bahru   Kuala Lumpur
Marang   Petaling Jaya   Seri Kembangan
Shah Alam

MALDIVES
Male

MALI
Bamako

MALTA
Msida San Gwann

MAURITIUS
Port Louis

MEXICO
Acapulco	Cabo San Lucas	Cancun	Chihauhua
Colima	Cozumel	Guadalajara	Hermosillo
Jiutepec	Leon	Leon de los Aldama	Merida
Mexico City	Monterrey	Pachuca	
Playa del Carmen	Puebla	Tehuacan	Tijuana
Toluca de Lerdo	Villahermosa	Xalapa	

MOROCCO
Ifrane

MYANMAR (BURMA)
Rangoon

NEPAL
Kathmandu

NETHERLANDS
unidentified	Amstelveen	Amsterdam	Arnhem
DeBilt	Delft	Eindhoven	Elburg
Geleen	Groningen	Hoorn	Leider
Mierlo	Rotterdam	s Gravenhage	

NEW CALEDONIA
Noumea

NEW ZEALAND
Auckland	Christchurch	Dunedin	Hamilton
Lower Hutt	Nelson	Palmerston North	Pukekohe
Waitakere	Wellington	Whangarei	

NICARAGUA
Managua

NIGERIA
unidentified	Abuja	Ikeja	Lagos

NORWAY
Drammen	Lysaker	Oslo	Tromso
Trondheim			

OMAN
Masqat

PAKISTAN
unidentified	Islamabad	Lahore	Peshawar
Quetta	Rawalpindi		

PANAMA
undefined	LaChorrera

PARAGUAY
Asuncion

PERU
LaVictoria   Trujillo

PHILIPPINES
unidentified   Angeles   Bacolod   Baguio
Cagayan de Oro   Cebu   Davo City   Legazpi
Makati   Mandaluyong   Manila   Ozamiz
Pasay   Quezon City   San Fernando   Tuguegarao

POLAND
Biala Podlaska   Gorzow Wlkp   Warsaw

PORTUGAL
Almada   Lisbon   Oeiras   Ponta Delgada
Porto   Santarem

PUERTO RICO
Aguadilla   Bayamon   Rio Piedras

QATAR
Doha

ROMANIA
Arad   Brasov   Bucharest   Cluj Napoca
Oradea   Sibiu   Suceava   Timisoara

RUSSIA
Ivanovo   Moscow   Nizhny Novgorod
St. Petersburg   Ukhta   Volgograd

SAINT KITTS & NEVIS
unidentified

Appendix III

SAINT VINCENT AND THE GRENADINES
Kingstown

SAUDI ARABIA
unidentified	Jiddah	Riyadh

SENEGAL
Dakar

SERBIA
Belgrade	Jagodina	New Belgrade	Pristina

SINGAPORE
unidentified	Singapore

SLOVAKIA
Bratislava	Lucenec	Piestany

SLOVENIA
Koper	Ljubljana

SOUTH AFRICA
unidentified	Bellville	Benoni	Berea
Bertshan	Bramley	Bryanston	Cape Town
Centurion	Cramerview	Durban	Garden View
Glenstantia	Hatfield	Hennopsmeer	Hyde Park
Isando	Johannesburg	Ndabeni	Paarden Eiland
Parow	Pinetown	Potchefstroom	Pretoria
Randsburg	Sandton	Sanlamhof	

SOUTH KOREA
Ansan	Anseong-si	Anyang	Ansan-si
Boryeong-si	Bucheon	Busan	Changwon

Appendix III

Cheonan	Cheongju	Cheongwon-gun	
Chuncheon	Chungju	Daegu	Daejeon
Damyang-gun	Dangjin-gun	Gincheon-si	Ginje-si
Ginpo-si	Goyang	Gumi	Gwachon
Gwangju	Gwangmyeong	Iksan	Incheon
Jecheon-si	Jeju	Jeonju	Masan
Mokpo	Muju-gun	Namyangju-si	Okcheon-gu
Pohang	Pusan	Pyeongtaek	Seongnam
Seosan-si	Seoul	Siheung	Suncheon-si
Suwon	Uijeongbu	Ulsan	Wonju
Yangsan	Yeosu-si	Yongin	

SPAIN
Alicante, Barcelona, Bilbao, Cadiz, Getafe, Granada, La Coruna, Las Palmas de Gran Canaria, Leon, Madrid, Malaga, Palma de Mallorca, Ripollet, San Cristobal de la Laguna, Sevilla, Tarragona, Tarrasa, Valencia, Villanueva i la Geltru, Zaragoza

SRI LANKA
Columbo

SUDAN
Khartoum

SWEDEN
Bromma, Goteborg, Lund, Orebro, Skelleftea, Solina, Stockholm, Uddevalla, Uppsala

SWITZERLAND
Ballwil, Basle, Bellinzona, Bremgarten, Geneva, Hedingen, Herrenschwanden, Hitzkirch

Liebfeld   Lugano   Massagno   Ostermundigen
Otelfingen   Renens   Rudolfstetten   Friedlisberg
Winterthur   Wohlen   Zofingen   Zufikon
Zurich

SYRIA
Damascus

TAIWAN
Chiayi   Chilung   Chu-Nan   Chu Tang
Chungli   Hsin-Chu   Hua-Lein   Nei Hu
San-Ch'Ung   Taipei   Taoyuan

TANZANIA
unidentified

THAILAND
Bangkok   Chiang Rai   Pattani   Phitsanulok
Samut Sakhon

TRINIDAD AND TOBAGO
Port of Spain

TUNISIA
Tunis

TURKEY
Adapazari   Ankara   Antalya   Bolu
Corlu   Erzurum   Icel   Istanbul
Izmir   Samsun   Trabzon

U.S. VIRGIN ISLANDS
Christiansted

Appendix III

UKRAINE
Donetsk	Horlivka	l'Viv	Kharkov
Lutsk	Odessa	Simferopol	

UNITED ARAB EMIRATES
Abu Dhabi Dubayy

UNITED KINGDOM
unidentified	Aberdeen	Aberystyth	Aldershot
Andover	Ashford	Atherton	Aveley
Aylesbury	Ayr	Bagshot	Barhead
Barnsley	Basildon	Baskingstoke	Bath
Bedford	Beeston	Belfast	Belmont
Biggleswade	Billericay	Billingham	Billingshurst
Birmingham	Blackburn	Blackpool	Bolton
Bootle	Bournemouth	Bracknell	Bradford
Bredbury	Brentford	Brentwood	Bridgend
Brierley Hill	Brighton	Bristol	Burford
Bushey	Byfleet	Camberley	Cambridge
Cannock	Cappenhurst	Cardiff	Charing
Chatham	Cheadle Hulme		Chelmsford
Cheltenham	Cheshunt	Chester	Clevedon
Colchester	Congleton	Coventry	Cranfield
Crawley	Crewe	Croydon	Crumlin
Cumbernauld	Darlington	Dartford	Daventry
Derby	Doncaster	Dorkin	Dumbarton
Dunstable	Dundee	Durham	Eastbourne
Eastleigh	Edgbaston	Edinburgh	Egham
Epsom	Esher	Evesham	Ewell
Exeter	Falkirk	Fareham	Farnborough
Ferndown	Fordingbridge	Frome	Gateshead
Glasgow	Gloucester	Great Missenden	
Grimsby	Guilford	Halifax	Harlow
Haydock	Hemel Hempstead		Henfield
Heywood	Hitchin	Horsham	Hove
Howden	Huddersfield	Hull	
Huyton-with-Roby	Ilkesten	Ipswich	Irlam

Appendix III

Iver	Johnstone	Kearsley	Kenilworth
Kensington	Kettering	Kings Langley	Kirkintilloch
Kirklees	Knutsford	Lambeth	Lancaster
Leatherhead	Leeds	Leicester	Lincoln
Little Chesterford	Liverpool	Livingston	London
Londonderry	Loughborough	Luton	Lutterwoth
Maidenhead	Maidstone	Manchester	Matlock
Melton Mowbray	Meriden	Middlesbrough	Milton Keynes
Mirfield	Mossley	Mountain Ash	
Newark-on-Trent	Newcastle upon Tyne		Newport
Newton Abbot	Newry	Northampton	Northhampton
Northowram	Norwich	Nottingham	Nuneaton
Oldham	Olney	Oundle	Oxford
Paisley	Pangbourne	Peashaw	Perth
Peterborough	Peterlee	Plymouth	Pontefract
Poole	Poplar	Portsmouth	Prenton
Preston	Pudsey	Rayleigh	Reading
Redditch	Redhill	Redruth	Rochester
Rock Ferry	Romsey	Rotherham	Rowley Regis
Royal Leamington Spa		Royal Tunbridge Wells	
Rushden	Rutherglen	Sale	Salford
Salisbury	Saltaire	Sandbach	Sandwell
Scole	Scunthorpe	Sheffield	Shepreth
Shipley	Sittingbourne	Slough	Smethwick
Solihull	Somecotes	South Tyneside	Southampton
St. Andrews	St. Albans	St. Helens	Stevenage
Stock	Stockport	Stockton-on-Tees	
Stoke Gifford	Stoke on Trent	Stowmarket	Sunbury
Sunderland	Sutton	Sutton Coldfield	
Sutton in Ashfield	Swansea	Swindon	Tadworth
Taunton	Teddington	Telford	Tewkesbury
Tipton	Thames	Thames Ditton	Thatcham
Uddingston	Wakefield	Wallington	Walsall
Waltham Cross	Walton-le-Dale	Warrington	Watford
Welwyn Garden City		Wembley	West Bromwich
Westcliff-on-Sea	West Malling	West Moors	Westhoughton
Wigan	Willenhall	Windsor	Winnersh
Witham	Woking	Workingham	Wollaston

Appendix III

Wolverhampton Woodley Woodside Worcester
Wrexham Yeovil York

UNITED STATES
Alabama
Alabaster Anniston Auburn University
Birmingham Chelsea Cullman Daleville
Dothan Eight Mile Enterprise Florence
Ft. Rucker Fultondale Guin Gulf Shores
Huntsville Jasper Madison Marion
Mobile Montgomery Orange Beach Ozark
Rainbow City Shannon Toney Trussville
Wetumpka

Alaska
Anchorage Bethel Fairbanks Haines
Homer Kenai Sitka Soldotna
Wasilla

Arizona
Benson Buckeye Camp Verde Casa Grande
Chandler Cortano Cottonwood Fayetteville
Flagstaff Florence Ft. Defiance Gilbert
Glendale Greenwood Green Valley Kingman
Marana Maricopa Mesa Morristown
New River Peoria Phoenix Prescott
Prescott Valley Queen Creek Scottsdale Show Low
Sierra Vista Sun City Sun City West Surprise
Tempe Tolleson Tucson Yellville

Arkansas
Alma Bentonville Cabot Cherokee Village
Conway Eureka Springs Fayetteville Harrison
Hot Springs National Park Jasper Jonesboro
Little Rock Maynard Mountain Home
North Little Rock Pine Bluff Russelville Siloam Springs
Warren

Appendix III

California

Agorra Hills	Alameda	Albany	Aliso Viejo
Alviso	American Canyon		Anaheim
Antelope	Antioch	Apple Valley	Arcadia
Atwater	Bakersfield	Baldwin Park	Bellflower
Belmont	Berkeley	Beverly Hills	Brisbane
Buena Park	Burbank	Burlingame	Calabasas
Calexico	Camarillo	Canyon County	Capistrano Beach
Cerritos	Carlsbad	Carmichael	Castro Valley
Citrus Heights	Chico	Chino Hills	Chula Vista
Corona	City of Industry	Claremont	Clovis
Covina	Corona del Mar	Corte Madera	Costa Mesa
Davis	Culver City	Cypress	Dana Point
Durham	Del March	Downey	Dublin
Elk Grove	East Irvine	El Cajon	Elmonte
Encinitas	Elmira	Elverta	Emeryville
Fremont	Escondido	Eureka	Fountain Valley
Garden Grove	Fresno	Ft. Irwin	Fullerton
Hayward	Glendale	Half Moon Bay	Hawthorne
Inglewood	Huntington Beach		Huntington Park
Lakewood	Irvine	Laguna Hills	Laguna Niguel
La Jolla	Lake Elsinore	Lake Forest	La Hobra
Lawndale	La Mesa	La Mirada	LaVerne
Los Alamitos	Livermore	Loma Linda	Long Beach
Lynwood	Los Altos	Los Angeles	Los Gatos
Menlo Park	Malibu	March Afb	Mc Clellan
Modesto	Merced	Mission Hills	Mission Viejo
Moreno Valley	Montclair	Montebello	Monterey
Newbury Park	Mountain View	Murrieta	Newark
North Highlands	Newhall	Newport Beach	Norco
Ontario	Norwalk	Oakland	Oceanside
Oxnard	Orange	Orange County	Oroville
Palo Alto	Pacoima	Palmdale	Palm Springs
Piedmont	Parlier	Pasadena	Pico Rivera
Pleasanton	Pittsburg	Placentia	Pleasant Hill
	Point Reyes Station		Porterville

Appendix III

Poway
Rancho SantaFe
Redding Redlands
Reseda
Rohnert Park
San Bernardino
San Dimas
San Luis Obispo
San Martin
Santa Ana
Santa Cruz
Santa Monica
Sebastopol
South Gate
Tahoe
Stockton
Sunol
Thousand Oaks
Turlock
Universal City
Valencia
Ventura
Walnut
Westminster
Yorba Linda

Rancho Cordova
Rancho Santa Margarita
Redwood City
Ridgecrest
Rosemeade
San Carlos
San Francisco
San Luis Rey
San Ramon
Santa Barbara
Santa Fe Springs
Santa Rosa
Simi Valley
South San Francisco
Stanford
Studio City
Tarzana
Topanga
Tustin
University City
Valley Village
Victorville
Walnut Creek
Whittier

Rancho Cucamonga

Redwood Estates
Riverside
Roseville
San Clemente
San Jose
San Marcos
San Rafael
Santa Clara
Santa Maria (offset)
Santee
Sonoma
Stanton
Sun Valley
Tehachapi
Torrance
Twenty Nine Palms
Upland
Van Nuys
Villa Park
West Hollywood
Wildomar

Rocklin
Sacramento
San Diego
San Leandro
San Marino
Sanger
Santa Clarita
Santa Maria
Seaside
South El Monte
South Lake
Stevenson Ranch
Sunnyvale
Temecula
Tracy
Vacaville
Venice
Vista

Windsor

Colorado

Arapahoe
Boulder
Del Norte
Englewood
Greeley
Louisville
Parker
Westminster

Arvada
Broomfield
Denver
Ft. Collins
Lafayette
Louviers
Pueblo
Wheat Ridge

Aurora
Colorado Springs
Durango
Ft. Morgan
Littleton
Montrose
Silverthorne
Windsor

Black Hawk

East Lake
Grand Junction
Longmont
Monument
Strasburg

Appendix III

Connecticut

Avon	Bolton	Branford	Cheshire
Danbury	Darien	East Berlin	East Haddam
Enfield	Fairfield	Glastonbury	Granby
Greenwich	Groton	Guilford	Haddam
Hamden	Hartford	Ivoryton	Killingworth
Manchester	Meriden	Middletown	Milford
Avon	Mystic	New Britain	New Canaan
New Haven	New London	New Milford	Newington
Newtown	Norwalk	Norwich	North Haven
Redding	Ridgefield	Simsbury	Stamford
Storrs Mansfield	Southbury	Southington	Torrington
Trumball	Wallingford	Waterbury	Weatogue
Westbrook	West Hartford	West Haven	Weston
Willimantic	Wilton	Woodbridge	

Delaware

Bear	Claymont	Dover	Hockessin
Houston	Lewes	Newark	New Castle
Rehoboth Beach	Rockland	Townsend	Viola
Wilmington			

District of Columbia

Washington

Florida

Alachua	Apopka	Arcadia	Belleview
Boca Raton	Boynton Beach	Bradenton	Brandon
Broward County	Callahan	Cape Coral	Clarcona
Clearwater	Clermont	Crestview	Crystal Springs
Dania	Darby	Daytona Beach	Deerfield Beach
Delray Beach	Destin	Eglin Afb	Elfers
Estero	Ft. Lauderdale	Ft. Myers	Ft. Pierce
Gainesville	Goldenrod	Haines City	Hallandale
Hernando	Hialeah	Hollywood	Jacksonville
Jacksonville Beach	Jupiter	Key Biscayne	Key West
Kissimmee	Lakeland	Lake Worth	Land-o-Lakes
Largo	Leesburg	Loxahatchee	Lutz
Maitland	Marathon	Melbourne	Miami

Appendix III

Miami Beach	Middleburg	Naples	Neptune Beach
New Port Richey	North Miami	North Miami Beach	
North Palm Beach	Ocala	Ocoee	Odessa
Okeechobee	Oldsmar	Opa Locka	Orange City
Orange Park	Orlando	Oviedo	Palm City
Palm Coast	Palm Beach	Palm Harbor	Panama City
Pembroke Pines	Pensacola	Pinellas Park	Pompano Beach
Ponte Vedra Beach	Port Charlotte	Port Orange	Port Saint Lucie
Punta Gorda	Riverview	Rockledge	Safety Harbor
Sarasota	Satellite Beach	Sebastian	Seffner
Spring Hill	St. Augustine	St. Cloud	St. Petersburg
Stuart	Tampa	Tallahassee	Tavares
Thonotosassa	Venice	Vero Beach	
West Palm Beach	Windermere	Winter Garden	Winter Park

Georgia

Albany	Alpharetta	Athens	Atlanta
Augusta	Brunswick	Buford	Calhoun
Canton	Clarkston	Columbus	Commerce
Conyers	Cumming	Dahlonega	Dallas
Dalton	Darien	Decatur	Douglasville
Dublin	Duluth	Evans	Experiment
Fayetteville	Gainesville	Griffin	Jeffereson
Kingsland	Lagrange	Lawrenceville	Lilburn
Lithonia	Marietta	McDonough	Morrow
Newnan	North Metro	Oakwood	Oxford
Ringgold	Rossville	Roswell	Sarasota
Savannah	Smyrna	Snellvile	Statesboro
Stone Mountain	Suwanee	Swainsboro	Toccoa
Tifton	Trenton	Tucker	Valdosta
Warner Robins			

Hawaii

Hickam Afb	Hilo	Honolulu	Kapaa
Kihei	Lahaina	Lihue	Wailuku
Waipahu			

Appendix III

Idaho

Boise	Coeur d Alene	Driggs	Garden City
Hayden	Idaho Falls	Ketchum	Mccall
Meridian	Pocatello	Post Falls	Rexburg
Sandpoint	Twin Falls		

Illinois

Addison	Aurora	Arlington Heights	
Bartlett	Batavia	Bloomington	Carbondale
Carol Stream	Champaign	Cherry Valley	Chicago
Collinsville	Crystal Lake	Dale	Darien
Decatur	Deerfield	Des Plaines	Downers Grove
Edwardsville	Elgin	Elk Grove Village	
Elmhurst	Elmwood Park	Energy	Fairview
Heights	Franklin Park	Freeport	Galesburg
Geneva	Glen Carbon	Glendale Heights	
Glen Ellyn	Greenville	Gurnee	Hamel
Harvard	Harwood Heights		Highland Park
Hines	Hinsdale	Hoffman Estates	
Homewood	Ingleside	Itasca	Joliet
La Grange	Lake Forest	Lake Zurich	Lemont Woods
Libertyville	Lincolnwood	Lisle	Lombard
Loves Park	Mattoon	McHenry	Miledgeville
Minonk	Mokena	Montgomery	Morrison
Morton Grove	Mount Prospect	Mundelein	Naperville
New Lenox	Niles	Normal	Oak Brook
Oak Forest	Oak Lawn	Oak Park	Orland Park
Palatine	Park Ridge	Peoria	Peru
Plainfield	Plato Center	Pontiac	Rock Island
Rockford	Rolling Meadows		Round Lake
Schaumburg	Skokie	Sparta	Spring Grove
Springfield	St. Charles	St. Clair County	
Staunton	Stonefort	Stone Park	Sycamore
Tinley Park	Urbana	Villa Park	Waukegan
Westchester	Westmont	Wheaton	Milmette
Wood Dale	Woodridge	Woodstock	

Appendix III

Indiana

Anderson	Avon	Beech Grove	Bloomington
Brownsburg	Carmel	Clarksville	Columbia City
Columbus	Connersville	Dunkirk	Elkhart
Evansville	Fishers	Fowler	Ft. Wayne
Greenwood	Hanover	Hobart	Huntington
Indianapolis	Jeffersonville	Kentland	Lafayette
Laporte	Leo	Milford	Mooresville
Mount Summit	Muncie	New Albany	New Paris
Noblesville	Plymouth	Portage	Richmond
Southbend	St. John	Terre Haute	Valparaiso
Warsaw	Winona Lake	Zionsville	

Iowa

Albert City	Algona	Ames	Bettendorf
Carroll	Carson	Cedar Falls	Cedar Rapids
Clinton	Council Bluffs	Davenport	Des Moines
Dubuque	Dyersville	Emmetsburg	Estherville
Fairfield	Forest City	Ft. Dodge	Granger
Iowa City	Lake Mills	Newell	North Liberty
Oakdale	Onawa	Oskaloosa	Pella
Perry	Sioux City	Spencer	Urbandale
Waterloo	West des Moines		

Kansas

Carbondale	Franklin	Ft. Scott	Gardner
Hays	Hillsboro	Kansas City	Lawrence
Leavenworth	Leawood	Lenexa	Manhattan
Mission	Newton	North Newton	Olathe
Overland Park	Pittsburg	Sabetha	Shawnee
Spring Hill	Sylvan Grove	Topeka	Wellington
Wichita			

Kentucky

Ashland	Bellevue	Berea	Bowling Green
Burkesville	Dawson Springs	Dayton	Elizabethtown
Florence	Frankfort	Ft. Mitchell	Glasgow
Hyden	Jefferson County		Latonia
Lawrence	Leavenworth	Lexington	London

Appendix III

Louisville	Morehead	Mount Sterling	Murray
Owensboro	Princeton	Pee Wee Valley	Radcliff
Silver Grove	Versailles	Wickliffe	Winchester

Louisiana

Abbeville	Bastrop	Baton Rouge	Bossier City
Broussard	Covington	Hammond	Kaplan
Lafayette	Lake Charles	Mandeville	Metairie
Monroe	New Iberia	New Orleans	Oakdale
Pineville	Prairieville	Shreveport	Slidell
Ville Park			

Maine

Bangor	Bath	Brunswick	Damariscotta
East Waterboro	Edgecomb	Freeport	Gorham
Hartland	Houlton	Kennebunk	Lewiston
North Berwick	Orono	Pittsfield	Presque Isle
Portland	South Portland	Stetson	Waterville
Westbrook			

Maryland

Aberdeen	Abingdon	Annapolis	
Annapolis Junction	Baltimore	Bel Air	Beltsville
Bethesda	Bowie	California	Capitol Heights
Catonsville	Chester	Chevy Chase	Clarksville
Cockeysville	College Park	Columbia	Crofton
Damascus	Denton	Dundalk	Easton
Elkridge	Ellicot City	Essex	Finksburg
Frederick	Ft. George G. Meade		Gaithersburg
Garrett Park	Glen Echo	Glen Burnie	Grasonville
Greenbelt	Gwynn Oak	Hagerstown	Halethorpe
Huntington	Huntingtown	Hyattsville	Ijamsville
Jessup	Kensington	Lanham	Laurel
Linthicum Heights	Lusby	Lutherville/ Timonium	
Middletown	Mt. Rainier	Myersville	Oakland
Odenton	Olney	Owings Mills	Oxon Hill
Nottingham	Parkville	Pasadena	
Patuxent River	Pikesville	Potomac	Prince Frederick

Appendix III

Ridgely	Rockville	Salisbury	Silver Spring
Suitland	Sykesville	Takoma Park	Temple Hills
Towson	Waldorf	Washington Grove	
Westminster	White Marsh	White Plains	

Massachusetts

Acton	Agawam	Allston	Amherst
Andover	Arlington	Arlington Heights	
Attleboro	Babson Park	Barnstable	Bellingham
Belmont	Berlin	Beverly	Braintree
Brighton	Brockton	Brookline	
Brookline Village	Boston	Burlington	Cambridge
Chelmsford	Chicopee	Concord	Dalton
Danver	Duxbury	Fall River	Fitchburg
Florence	Framingham	Foxboro	Hamilton
Hanson	Hatfield	Haverhill	Hingham
Holliston	Holyoke	Hopkinton	Hudson
Jamaica Plain	Lancaster	Lawrence	Lexington
Littleton	Lowell	Lynn	Malden
Manchaug	Marion	Marlborough	Mashpee
Medford	Milbury	Milford	Milton
Needham	New Bedford	Newburyport	Newton
Newton Center	Newtonville	North Scituate	Northampton
North Attleboro	Oxford	Palmer	Peabody
Pepperell	Pittsfield	Randolf	Roslindale
Sandwich	Somerville	Southbridge	South Easton
South Hadley	Springfield	Stoneham	Swansea
Taunton	Turners Falls	Wareham	Waltham
Watertown	Wellesley	Westfield	West Newbury
West Roxbury	Weymouth	Wilbraham	Woburn
Worcester			

Michigan

Adrian	Alma	Ann Arbor	Auburn
Battle Creek	Berkley	Big Rapids	
Bloomfield Hills	Brimley	Caledonia	Canton
Carleton	Caro	Center Line	Clawson
Clinton Township	Commerce Township		Dearborn
Dearborn Heights	Detroit	Douglas	East China

Appendix III

East Lansing, Edwardsburg, Elk Rapids, Escanaba, Farmington, Fenton, Ferndale, Flint, Flushing, Franklin, Grand Blanc, Grand Rapids, Greenville, Harper Woods, Henderson, Highland Park, Houghton, Huntington Woods, Holland, Interlochen, Jenison, Kalamazoo, Keego Harbor, Kent County, Lambertville, Lansing, Livonia, Ludington, Marquette, Midland, Mount Pleasant, New Lothrop, Northville, Novi, Oak Park, Owosso, Peck, Plymouth, Pontiac, Port Huron, Redford, Rochester, Roseville, Royal Oak, Saginaw, Southfield, Springlake, Springport, St. Joseph, Sterling Heights, Swartz Creek, Taylor, Traverse City, Trenton, Troy, University Center, Utica, Walled Lake, Warren, Washtenaw County, West Bloomfield, Westland, Willis, Wyandotte, Ypsilanti

Minnesota

Alexandria, Anoka, Aitkin, Backus, Bell Plaine, Bemidji, Blue Earth, Buffalo, Burnsville, Champlin, Chaska, Circle Pines, Duluth, Eden Prairie, Elk River, Excelsior, Farmington, Forrest Lake, Grand Rapids, Hennepin County, Hopkins, Hugo, International Falls, Inver Grove Heights, Mankato, Minneapolis, Minnetonka, Monticello, Newport, Northfield, Osseo, Pipestone, Rochester, Rosemont, Savage, South St. Paul, St. Cloud, St. Paul, Virginia, Waite Park, Walker, Willmar, Winona

Mississippi

Amory, Cleveland, Clinton, Fayette, Gulfport, Hattiesburg, Jackson, Kiln, Laurel, Louisville, Meridian, Picayune, Southaven, Starkville, Tupelo, Vicksburg, West Point

Appendix III

Missouri
Arnold	Ballwin	Branson	Cape Girardeau
Columbia	Crystal City	Fenton	Florissant
Grand View	Greenwood	Gower	Hazelwood
Herculaneum	Huntsville	Independence	Jefferson City
Kansas City	Lees Summit	Liberty	
Maryland Heights	Mt. Vernon	Nixa	o Fallon
Oak Grove	Perryville	Plattsburg	Riverside
Sedalia	Sikeston	Smithville	Springfield
St. Ann	St. Joseph	St. Louis	St. Peters
Troy	Wentzville	Wright City	

Montana
Billings	Bozeman	Corvallis	East Helena
Great Falls	Hamilton	Helena	Kalispell
Missoula	Plentywood		

Nebraska
Allen	Beatrice	Bellevue	Cozad
Creighton	Hartington	Kearney	La Vista
Lincoln	Nebraska City	Norfolk	Omaha
Petersburg	Scottsbluff	Wayne	

Nevada
Elko	Henderson	Las Vegas	Mesquite
North Las Vegas	Reno		

New Hampshire
Bedford	Concord	Contoocook	Derry
Dover	Durham	East Derry	Hampstead
Hanover	Hudson	Keene	Lyme
Manchester	Merrimack	Nashua	New Fields
North Salem	Plymouth	Portsmouth	Rochester
Salem	Swanzey	Weare	

New Jersey
Absecon	Albany	Allendale	Allenwood
Andover	Annandale	Asbury Park	Audubon
Avalon	Barnegat	Barrington	Beach Haven
Bellemeade	Belleville	Belmar	Bergenfield

Appendix III

Berkeley Heights	Beverly	Birmingham	Bloomfield
Bogata	Bound Brook	Bradley Beach	Brick
Bridgewater	Brielle	Browns Mills	Budd Lake
Caldwell	Camden	Cape May	Carteret
Cedar Grove	Cherry Hill	Chester	Clark
Clarksboro	Clayton	Clementon	Cliffside Park
Clifton	Cliffwood	Collingswood	Colts Neck
Cranford	Crosswicks	Dayton	Denville
Dover	East Brunswick		East Orange
Eatontown	Edgewater	Edison	Egg Harbor Twp
Elizabeth	Elmwood Park	Farmingville	Flanders
Franklin	Freehold	Gibbsboro	Great Neck
Hackensack	Hackettstown	Haddonfield	Haddon Heights
Hainesport	Hammonton	Harrington Park	
Harrison	Haworth	Highland Park	Hightstown
Hillsborough	Hoboken	Hopewell	
Hunterdon County	Iselin	Jersey City	Johnsonburg
Johnstown	Keansburg	Kearney	Kingston
Lakehurst	Lakewood	Landing	Lawnside
Ledgewood	Lincroft	Linden	Little Falls
Livingston	Lodi	Long Valley	Mahwah
Manahawkin	Marlboro	Margate City	Maple Shade
Marlton	Marmora	Matawan	Martinsville
Medford	Mendham	Merchantville	Metuchen
Middletown	Milltown	Millville	Mays Landing
Maywood	Moorestown	Monmouth Junction	
Montague	Montclair	Morganville	Morristown
Morris Plains	Mount Holly	Mount Laurel	
Mullica Hill	Newark	New Brunswick	
New Milford	North Brunswick		Northfield
Nutley	Oaklyn	Ocean City	Old Bridge
Oradell	Orange	Palisades Park	Palmyra
Paramus	Parlin	Parsippany	Passaic
Paterson	Pennington	Pennsauken	Pennsville
Penns Grove	Pequannock	Perth Amboy	Piscataway
Pitman	Plainfield	Plainsboro	Pleasantville
Port Murray	Potsdam	Princeton	Raritan
Red Bank	Ridgewood	Rio Grande	River Edge

Appendix III

Riverside	Riverton	Rochelle Park	Roselle
Rutherford	Saddle Brook	Saddle River	Sayreville
Schenectady	Sea Isle City	Sewell	Short Hills
Shrewsbury	Sicklerville	Somerset	South Amboy
South Orange	South Plainfield	Springfield	Spotswood
Stanhope	Stirling	Stratford	Stillwater
Succasunna	Summit	Swedesboro	Teaneck
Tenafly	Thorofare	Trenton	Tuckerton
Union	Union City	Ventnor City	Verona
Vineland	Voorhees	Waretown	Warren
Washington	Wayne	Westfield	West Orange
Westville	Wharton	Wildwood	Williamstown
Willingboro	Windsor	Woodbridge	Woodbury
Woodcliff Lake	Wrightstown	Wyckoff	

New Mexico

Albuquerque	Clovis	Corrales	Farmington
Gallup	Hobbs	Las Cruces	Rio Rancho
Santa Fe			

New York

Addison	Albany	Albertson	Alexander
Altamont	Amsterdam	Auburn	Babylon
Bainbridge	Baldwinsville	Bayshore	Bayside
Bethpage	Binghamton	Bohemia	Bowmansville
Briarcliff Manor	Brentwood	Brockport	Bronx
Bronxville	Brooklyn	Buffalo	Carmel
Chappaqua	Cicero	Clifton Park	Cortland
Copiague	Cross River	Delmar	Depew
Eastchester	East Elmhurst	East Northport	East Syracuse
Elba	Elmira	Elmont	Elmsford
Endwell	Farmington	Farmingville	Floral Park
Flushing	Fresh Meadows	Getzville	Glens Falls
Gloversville	Granville	Great Neck	Greenwich
Hamburg	Heckimer	Hicksville	Highland Mills
Hilton	Holbrook	Honeoye Falls	Hoosick Falls
Hopewell Junction	Hudson	Huntington Station	
Hyde Park	Islip Terrace	Ithaca	Jackson Heights
Jamaica	Jamestown	Jefferson Valley	Johnson City

Appendix III

Johnstown	Kew Gardens	Kingston	Lake Grove
Lansing	Latham	Little Valley	Liverpool
Macedon	Malone	Mamaroneck	Manhasset
Marlboro	Mayville	Medford	Melville
Merrick	Middle Village	Middleton	Mineda
Monroe	Monsey	Monticello	Mount Kisco
Mount Vernon	Nesconset	New City	New Hyde Park
New Paltz	Newtonville	New Rochelle	New Windsor
New York	Niagara Falls	North Greece	Norwich
Nyack	Ogdensburg	Oneonta	
Onondaga County	Oswego	Ozone Park	Pelham
Plattsburgh	Port Chester	Port Washington	
Pottersville	Poughkeepsie	Purchase	Queensbury
Queens Village	Rensselaer	Rexford	Richmond Hill
Ridgewood	Rochester	Rockaway Park	Roosevelt
Roslyn Heights	Rye	Salamanca	Saratoga Springs
Schenectady	Selden	Smithtown	
South Glens Falls	Spencer	Spring Valley	Staten Island
Stony Brook	Syosset	Syracuse	Tarrytown
Tonawanda	Troy	Trumansburg	Uniondale
Valley Stream	Walden	Wappinger Falls	
Warwick	Washington	Watertown	Watervilet
Webster	West Babylon	West Point	Whitestone
Williamson	Williston Park	Woodmere	Woodside
Yonkers	Yorkville		

North Carolina

Asheboro	Asheville	Belmont	Boiling Springs
Boone	Brevard	Cary	Chapel Hill
Charlotte	Cherryville	Columbus	Concord
Cornelius	Creedmoor	Davidson	Dunn
Durham	Eden	Elizabeth City	Ft.Bragg
Forest City	Fuquay Varina	Garner	Greensboro
Greenville	Havelock	Henderson	Hendersonville
High Point	Holly Springs	Horse Shoe	Jacksonville
Kannapolis	Kernersville	Kill Devil Hills	Leland
Lexington	Lincolnton	Louisburg	Matthews
Mooresville	Morehead City	Morrisville	Mountain Home

Appendix III

Mt. Airy	Nags Head	New Bern	Newell
Newton	Oxford	Pinehurst	Pineville
Pittsboro	Raleigh	Reedsville	Roanoke Rapids
Rocky Point	Rutherfordton	Sanford	Skyland
Smithfield	Wake Forest	Waxhaw	West Jefferson
Wilkesboro	Wilmington	Winston Salem	

North Dakota

Bismark	Fargo	Grand Forks	Valley City

Ohio

Akron	Amelia	Amherst	Ashley
Ashtabula	Athens	Bath	Bay Village
Beachwood	Belbrook	Bowling Green	Bridgeport
Brookpark	Brunswick	Bryan	Canton
Centerburg	Cincinnati	Circleville	Cleveland
Columbus	Cuyahoga Falls	Dayton	Defiance
Delaware	Dover	Dublin	East Sparta
Elyria	Englewood	Ft. Jennings	Fairborn
Fairfield	Findlay	Galion	Hillard
Holland	Independence	Lancaster	Lima
Lorain	Madison	Mansfield	Maple Heights
Marion	Martins Ferry	Marysville	Mason
Maumee	Medina	Mentor	Middletown
Miamitown	Miamiville	New Albany	Newcomerstown
New Philadelphia	Niles	North Ridgeville	
Oregon	Orrville	Pataskala	Perrysburg
Reynoldsburg	Rome	Rossford	Sandusky
Sidney	Stow	Sycamore	Tallmadge
Toledo	Twinsburg	Vandalia	West Chester
Westlake	Westerville	Wilmington	Wooster
Xenia	Youngstown	Zanesville	

Oklahoma

Ada	Ardmore	Bartlesville	Broken Arrow
Claremore	Edmond	Enid	Jenks
Miami	Oklahoma City	Poteau	Tulsa

Appendix III

Oregon

Albany	Ashland	Aumsville	Beavertown
Bend	Canby	Cave Junction	Central Point
Coos Bay	Corvallis	Eugene	Grants
Gresham	Hillsboro	Independence	Lake Oswego
Mcminnville	Medford	Newberg	Ontario
Oregon City	Pass	Portland	Salem
Talent	Tualatin	Wheeler	Wilsonville

Pennsylvania

Abington	Adams County	Alison Park	Allentown
Altoona	Ambler	Ardmore	Baden
Bala Cynwyd	Bath	Beaver Falls	Bensalem
Bernville	Berwyn	Bethel Park	Bethlehem
Biglerville	Birdsboro	Blandon	Bloomsburg
Blue Bell	Braddock	Brookhaven	Broomall
Bryan Athyn	Bryn Mawr	Butler	Camp Hill
Carlisle	Carnegie	Catasauqua	Chadds Ford
Chalfont	Chambersburg	Cheltenham	Chester
Chester Heights	Clarks Summit	Clifton Heights	Coatesville
Conshohocken	Coplay	Corapolis	Cranberry Twp
Dallas	Dallastown	Danville	Darby
Dickson City	Dillsburg	Douglassville	Doylestown
Dover	Downingtown	Doylestown	Dresher
Drexel Hill	DuBois	Duncannon	Duryea
East Petersburg	Easton	Elverson	Emmaus
Enola	Ephrata	Erie	Essington
Exton	Fairless Hills	Feasterville	Fleetwood
Flourtown	Folcroft	Folsom	Forest City
Franklin	Ft. Washington	Gilbertsville	Gillet
Gladwyne	Glenolden	Glenshaw	Glen Mills
Glen Riddle Lima	Gwynedd	Harleysville	Harrisburg
Hatboro	Hatfield	Haverford	Havertown
Hazelton	Hershey	Holmes	Homestead
Horsham	Hummelstown	Huntington	Jamison
Johnstown	Jenkintown	Kennett Square	
King of Prussia	Kingston	Kintnersville	Kutztown
Lafayette Hill	Lancaster	Langhorne	Lansdale
Lansdowne	Lawrence	Lebanon	Levittown

Appendix III

Lewisburg	Lewistown	Leetsdale	Lititz
Lionville	Lock Haven	Macungie	Malvern
Manheim	Matamoras	Mc Kees Rocks	Mechanicsburg
Media	Meadville	Merion Station	Middletown
Milford	Millersburg	Millersville	Monroeville
Moosic	Morrisville	Mount Holly Springs	
Mount Joy	Murrysville	Narberth	New Brighton
New Castle	New Cumberland		New Hope
New Kingston	Newton	Newville	Norristown
North Wales	Oakmont	Perkasie	Philadelphia
Phoenixville	Pine Grove	Pittsburgh	
Plymouth Meeting	Pottstown	Pottsville	Quakertown
Quarryville	Reading	Red Lion	Richboro
Salford	Sayre	Scranton	Sellersville
Sewickley	Souderton	Sharon Hill	Southampton
Spring House	Springfield	State College	Stroudsburg
Swarthmore	Tamaqua	Trevose	Uniontown
Upper Darby	Uwchland	Villanova	Wallingford
Warfordsburg	Warminster	Warrington	Wayne
Waynesburg	West Chester	Wexford	Whitehall
Wilkes-Barre	Williamsport	Williamstown	Willow Grove
Wynnewood	Wyoming	York	

Rhode Island

Chepachet	Cranston	East Greenwich	
East Providence	Jamestown	Lincoln	Middletown
Narragansett	Newport	Pascoag	Pawtucket
Providence	Riverside	Smithfield	Warwick

South Carolina

Aiken	Arcadia	Beaufort	Campobello
Charleston	Clemson	Columbia	Florence
Gaffney	Goose Creek	Greenville	Greer
Hilton Head Island	Honea Path	Irmo	Ladson
Lake City	Liberty	Mauldin	Myrtle Beach
North Charleston	Pawleys Island	Pickens	Richland
Rock Hill	Round	Simpsonville	Spartanburg
St. Stephen	Summerville	Sumter	Taylors
Williamstown			

Appendix III

South Dakota

Brookings	Chancellor	Mitchell	Rapid City
Renner	Sioux Falls	Winner	

Tennessee

Athens	Autioch	Bristol	Chattanooga
Clarksville	Cleveland	Collierville	Columbia
Cordova	Dunlap	Dickson	Franklin
Gainesboro	Gallatin	Gatlinburg	Germantown
Hendersonville	Hermitage	Jackson	Jefferson City
Johnson City	Knoxville	Livingston	Loretto
Loudon	Louisville	Memphis	Millington
Murfreesboro	Nashville	Oakridge	Shelbyville
Smyrna	White House		

Texas

Abilene	Addison	Allen	Amarillo
Arlington	Austin	Ballinger	Barker
Bastrop	Baytown	Beaumont	Bedford
Carrollton	Cedarpark	Cleaveland	College Station
Columbus	Conroe	Coppell	Copperas Cove
Corpus Christi	Crosby	Cypress	Dallas
Dayton	Deer Park	Del Rio	Denton
Desoto	El Paso	Elgin	Ennis
Euless	Farmersville	Flower Mound	Friendswood
Frisco	Ft. Worth	Galena Park	Galveston
Garland	Georgetown	Grand Prairie	Hallsville
Haltom City	Hamilton	Helotes	Henderson
Hillsboro	Houston	Humble	Huntsville
Hurst	Irving	Jourdanton	Katy
Keen	Keller	Kennedale	Killeen
Lake Dallas	Lake Johnson	Laredo	League City
Lindale	Little Elm	Longview	Lubbock
Manchaca	Mcallen	McNeil	Midland
Mineral Wells	Mesquite	Mont Belvieu	Montgomery
Nacogdoches	New Braunfels	North Richland Hills	
Onalaska	Pampa	Parker County	
Pasadena	Pearland	Pinehurst	Plano
Pleasanton	Port Lavaca	Prosper	Quinlan

Appendix III

Richardson	Richmond	Roanoke	Round Rock
Sachse	San Angelo	San Antonio	San Benito
San Marcos	Schertz	Sherman	Silsbee
Spearman	Spicewood	South Houston	South Lake
Spring	Spring Branch	Sugar Land	Sulphur Springs
Texarkana	The Colony	Tomball	Tyler
Waco	Webster	Wichita Falls	Wylie

Utah

American Fork	Bountiful	Cedar City	Hill Afb
Kanab	Kaysville	Lehi	Logan
Midvale	Ogden	Orem	Pleasant Grove
Price	Provo	Richfield	St. George
Salt Lake City	Sandy	South Jordan	Spanish Fork
West Jordan	Woods Cross		

Vermont

Bennington	Bratttleboro	Burlington	East Hardwick
Hinesburg	Jericho	Manchester	Marlboro
Montpelier	Newport	South Burlington	
St. Johnsbury	Winooski		

Virginia

Abingdon	Albermarle County		Alexandria
Amelia Court House		Arcola	Arlington
Ashburn	Blacksburg	Bluefield	Bristow
Burke	Centreville	Chantilly	Charlottesville
Chesapeake	Chester	Christiansburg	Clifton Forge
Danville	Dayton	Dumfries	Dunn Coring
Dunn Loring	Fairfax	Fairfax Station	Falls Church
Farmville	Fincastle	Floyd	Fredericksburg
Ft. Belvoir	Ft. Eustis	Ft. Myer	Gainesville
Glen Allen	Great Falls	Hampton	Harrisonburg
Herndon	Jonesville	Leesburg	Lexington
Lorton	Low Moor	Luray	Lynchburg
Madison	Manassas	Merrifield	Middleburg
Midlothian	Newport News	Norfolk	Oakton
Occoquan	Petersburg	Portsmouth	Reston
Richmond	Roanoke	Saluda	Springfield

Appendix III

Stafford · Sterling · Vienna · Virginia Beach
Warrenton · Warsaw · West Mclean · Winchester
Wise · Woodbridge

Washington
Anacortes · Bainbridge Island · · Bellevue
Bellingham · Bremerton · Bothell · Burlington
Camas · Enumclaw · Everett · Federal Way
Friday Harbor · Gig Harbor · Granite Falls · Issaquah
Kennewick · Kingston · Kirkland · Lacey
Lakewood · Leavenworth · Long View · Lynnwood
Mercer Island · Maple Valley · Mountain Lake Terrace
Mountlake Terrace · Mukilteo · Naselle · Oak Harbor
Olympia · Pasco · Port Orchard · Port Townsend
Poulsbo · Pullman · Puyallup · Redmond
Renton · Sammamish · Seahurst · Seattle
Sequim · Snohomish · Spanaway · Spokane
Stanwood · Tacoma · Tracyton · University Place
Vancouver · Wenatchee · Woodinville · Yakima

West Virginia
Beckley · Bridgeport · Charleston · Harrisville
Lewisburg · Martinsburg · Morgantown · Nitro
Parkersburg · Princeton · Ranson · Romney
Snowshoe · Williamson

Wisconsin
Antigo · Barron · Burlington · Butler
Clear Lake · Cochrane · DeForest · Dresser
Eau Claire · Edgerton · Elm Grove · Endeavor
Ft. Atkinson · Fond du Lac · Green Bay · Greendale
Greenville · Hudson · Kenosha · Kimberly
LaCrosse · Madison · Mequon · Middleton
Milwaukee · Monroe · Monticello · New Richmond
Onalaska · Oshkosh · Palmyra · Platteville
Prairie du Sac · Racine · Random Lake · Rice Lake
Sauk City · St. Croix Falls · Stevens Point · Sun Prairie
Superior · Waukesha · Wausau

Wyoming

Afton	Casper	Cheyenne	Cody
Fe Warren Afb	Gillette	Laramie	Sheridan

URUGUAY
Montevideo

VENEZUELA

Caracas	Merida	Valencia

VIETNAM

Hanoi	Thanh Pho Ho Chi Minh	Vung Tau

YEMEN
Sana

ZIMBABWE
Bulawayo

Overall the foundation has had more than **102,217** individual page views on the site.

The site was viewed in 36 different languages. They were English, Italian, German, Spanish, Turkish, a dialect from Belgium, Greek, Portuguese, Thai, Dutch, Chinese (Hong Kong), Chinese (China), Chinese (Taiwan), French, Croatian, Hungarian, Catalan, Norwegian, Romanian, Filipino, Icelandic, Finnish, Czech, Japanese, Bulgarian, Polish, Latvian, Danish, Hebrew, Swedish, Arabic, Indonesian, Slovene, Korean, Armenian, and Russian.